SHAPING THE WORLD ECONOMY

Suggestions for an International Economic Policy

SHAPING THE WORLD ECONOMY

Suggestions for an

International Economic Policy

by *JAN TINBERGEN*

THE TWENTIETH CENTURY FUND

New York 1962

FOREWORD

The present work grew out of a desire on the part of the Fund to
further serious and objective thinking on the problems of the international economy. In particular, the Trustees wanted to see explored what the nations of the West could do to concert their economies and to work out new relationships with the economically
less developed parts of the world.

The Fund was fortunate in enlisting the interest of Professor Jan
Tinbergen, Director of the Netherlands Economic Institute. Apart
from Professor Tinbergen's international standing as an economist,
and the skill and competence of his staff, we have benefited from
having a European undertake the work — a European representing
one of the smaller countries. The present study, lucid, rational, optimistic in regard to the possibilities of constructive action, speaks
clearly for itself.

Not everyone will agree with Professor Tinbergen's specific recommendations, of which there are many in the following pages. It
will be seen that he has not stopped at action by the West, but has
gone on to lay the groundwork for a truly international policy
working through the United Nations. Some will doubt that progress along this line can be as substantial as he believes. But this
quality of patiently working at the roots, of keeping an open mind

and a basic confidence in the good sense of men of all countries, is needed now — is indeed greatly needed.

We thank Dr. Tinbergen and his associates for their work; its influence, we believe, will be widely felt.

AUGUST HECKSCHER

Director, The Twentieth Century Fund

41 East 70th Street, New York
July 1962

PREFACE

This study has been prepared by a team organized under the auspices of the Netherlands Economic Institute Division of Balanced International Growth. The team was headed by Jan Tinbergen, professor of development planning at the Netherlands School of Economics, and included the following members:

Deputy Research Director: Hans Linnemann, M.A., member of the teaching staff of the Netherlands School of Economics, Rotterdam, and senior member of the research staff of the Netherlands Economic Institute in charge of the current organization and supervision of the project;

Dr. Aleida van Oven, economist with N. V. Philips' Gloeilampenfabrieken, Eindhoven, temporarily attached to the Netherlands Economic Institute;

Hendrikus M. L. Oudendijk, M.A., economist, formerly with the Royal Dutch Shell Group of Companies, temporarily attached to the Netherlands Economic Institute;

Peter A. Cornelisse, junior economist;

Hendrik E. Chin, junior economist;

Hisao Massaki, visiting junior economist;

Chikao Tsukuda, visiting junior economist;

and, as Special Advisers:

Dr. Floor Hartog, professor of economics at the State University of Groningen;

Dr. Henri Rijken van Olst, professor of statistics and econometrics at the State University of Groningen.

Most of the main text was written by Dr. Tinbergen, while a number of specialized sections and the appendices were written by Dr. van Oven, Dr. Hartog, Dr. Rijken van Olst, Mr. Oudendijk, and Mr. Linnemann. Twenty-four developing countries were visited by various members of the group (reports on these trips are included in the appendices). Our sincere thanks are due to the many government officials and independent experts who were willing to inform us about their country's and region's economic problems. The active help received during these visits is greatly appreciated.

Our thanks are extended also to Mrs. Maud Fonteyn-Robinson of the Economic Information Service, the Hague, and to the staff of the GATT Secretariat, Geneva, for providing us with detailed information about tariffs and other trade restrictions; to the staff of the Dr. Neher Laboratory of the PTT, Leidschendam, for their cooperation in performing the computations for Appendix VI; and to Mrs. Suze van Willigenburg for typing the manuscript.

We are grateful to Mr. Philip M. Ginsberg for the preliminary editing job he was kind enough to undertake, to Professor Alfred H. Conrad of Harvard University, this year visiting professor at the Netherlands School of Economics, who supervised this first editing, and to Mrs. Katharine Beyer for her skillful editing of the final manuscript.

To the Trustees of the Twentieth Century Fund and to Messrs. August Heckscher and Ben T. Moore, Director and Associate Director, respectively, of the Fund, we wish to express our deep gratitude for their encouragement and help as well as for the Fund's generosity in financing this project.

JAN TINBERGEN

CONTENTS

LIST OF TABLES

LIST OF ABBREVIATIONS AND SYMBOLS

AID	Agency for International Development
ASA or ASAS	Association of South-East Asia
BLEU	Belgium–Luxembourg Economic Union
CAFEA	Commission on Asian and Far Eastern Affairs of the International Chamber of Commerce
CENTO	Central Treaty Organization
ECAFE	Economic Commission for Asia and the Far East (United Nations)
ECE	Economic Commission for Europe (United Nations)
ECLA	Economic Commission for Latin America (United Nations)
ECOSOC	Economic and Social Council of the United Nations
ECSC	European Coal and Steel Community
EDF	European Development Fund
EEC	European Economic Community
EFTA	European Free Trade Area
EPU	European Payments Union
FAO	Food and Agriculture Organization
GATT	General Agreement on Tariffs and Trade
IADB	Inter-American Development Bank
IAEA	International Atomic Energy Agency
IBRD	International Bank for Reconstruction and Development (World Bank)
ICA	International Cooperation Administration
ICAO	International Civil Aviation Organization
IDA	International Development Association
IFC	International Finance Corporation
ILO	International Labor Organization

List of Abbreviations and Symbols

IMF	International Monetary Fund
ITO	International Trade Organization
ITU	International Telecommunication Union
MIT	Massachusetts Institute of Technology
OECD	Organization for Economic Cooperation and Development
OEEC	Organization for European Economic Cooperation
OPEC	Organization of Petroleum Exporting Countries
OPEX	Operational and Executive Personnel
TAB	Technical Assistance Board
UAR	United Arab Republic
UK	United Kingdom
UN	United Nations
UNESCO	United Nations Educational, Scientific and Cultural Organization
UNSF	United Nations Special Fund
UNTA	United Nations Technical Assistance (all programs)
US, USA	United States of America
USSR	Union of Soviet Socialist Republics
WHO	World Health Organization
WMO	World Meteorological Association
$	United States dollar unless otherwise indicated
£	English pound unless otherwise indicated

PART I

THE WORLD AND THE WEST

A Survey of Today's Tensions

NEW COUNTRIES
AND
OLD PROBLEMS

1.1 INTRODUCING THE BOOK

The world is in the process of a great transformation. In a considerable part of it a new economic order, "communism," is being vigorously tried out. Elsewhere an old order is passing as one country after another throws off the yoke of colonialism. The wholesale introduction of Western techniques and ways of life is shaking the foundations of numerous beliefs and attitudes, for good or for evil. A spurt of population growth accompanies this development. All of these changes, with their multiple potentialities for conflict, are taking place in an era in which mankind has just discovered the possibilities of nuclear warfare.

The Western countries, not so long ago the masters of the world,

have been deposed by the very forces they liberated. This drastic change is not yet fully understood by the Western nations themselves.

The world, characterized by a vast gap between technical ability and moral power, is in desperate need of a policy — a policy which will give it shape, and create a framework for the solution of its urgent problems.

This book is an attempt to analyze that need and to make constructive suggestions for means to satisfy it. It is a book written by Westerners, possibly with many Western biases. Nevertheless the author and his associates have tried to free themselves as much as possible from bias and to apply in their analysis the objectivity of that scientific attitude to which the West, however much it may be open to criticism, has given rise. Thus they have tried their best to look at the world's problems from the standpoint of all concerned. In this they have had the advantage of consulting with many people representing other continents and other convictions than their own.

The book does not contain a great deal which is new. Apart from a few modest contributions to the quantitative analysis of some of the problems encountered, only the arrangement of the subject matter purports to be novel. The plan of the book is to discuss, in Part I, the tensions characteristic of our present world and, in Part II, policies which might ease the situation.

Part I consists of four chapters. The first begins with a brief description of the main tensions in international life, then concentrates on what is believed to be the most important economic problem — that of the development of economically backward countries. Chapter 2 describes the two competing economic systems — the Western and the Communist — which have succeeded in bringing about a measure of economic development in their own parts of the world, and discusses the essential features of each. At the same time, this chapter deals with some of the main instruments of development policy, especially those to be used by the developing countries themselves. The two remaining chapters deal with the international environment in which development has to take place and describe the setting with regard to trade and stabilization policies.

Part II represents an attempt to deal systematically with the problem of an optimum international policy, mainly but not wholly in the economic field. In Chapter 5, the basis of such a policy is discussed, i.e., the interests it must serve. Chapter 6 defines the aims, and discusses the most important means open to the policy-makers. Chapter 7 is devoted to the core of development policies — investment. Chapter 8 deals with the complicated matter of trade policy. Chapter 9 covers what is thought to be the clearest lacuna in our international economic order — the lack of an international financial authority. Finally, the last chapter summarizes the conclusions reached, and, going somewhat beyond the boundaries of economics, makes some suggestions regarding the wider problem of coexistence between Communist and non-Communist countries.

1.2 POLITICAL AND ECONOMIC STRUCTURE OF TODAY'S WORLD

This section tries to give a summary picture of the political units which comprise our world, indicating only their basic economic and political characteristics and their main groupings. No summary view could do justice to the complexities of the world's structure, but it is questionable whether a more detailed picture would serve our purpose better. Involved are over a hundred different countries, loosely arranged into various groups which are somewhat more homogenous than the world at large.

The first feature to be mentioned is the existence of a group of countries under the rule of Communist parties. The West usually speaks of them as the "Communist" countries or the "Communist bloc," whereas they prefer to speak of themselves as "socialist countries."[1] Western socialists feel that socialism should incorporate the element of political democracy in the Western sense, that is, that the population should exert an active influence on gov-

---

1. In the terminology of these countries, communism is a state in which the distribution of income is based on needs, whereas socialism is, in this respect, characterized by incomes based on productive contributions. Both systems are based on communal ownership of the most important means of production.

ernment. All countries outside the Communist group may be called non-Communist although they are very different, as will be set forth below. When using the breakdown just mentioned we will call Yugoslavia a Communist country, although it maintains less close relations with the other Communist countries than is typical of this group.

A second feature of today's world is the existence of already developed and developing countries, in both the Communist and the non-Communist sectors. The criterion here is mainly an economic one, although development in many other fields appears to be a related phenomenon. Of course, there is no sharp dividing line and one may wonder how to classify some countries, say Venezuela or Argentina. Roughly speaking, Asia, Africa, and Latin America, together with a number of countries or parts of countries in Southern Europe, are economically in the process of development. Although we are aware that it is a rather poor yardstick, the simplest criterion to apply is that of income per head. If income per head is above $250 a year, development may be said to be under way in the country concerned.

A third major feature of the political structure today is that colonialism is rapidly passing from the scene. To be sure, a number of countries in the non-Communist area are still under the rule of more developed countries, and a type of neocolonialism has come into being in the Communist area. Some very important former colonies, however, have changed their status and now have national independence. This is true of almost all of Asia and Africa.

Together with a number of developing countries which have been politically independent for a long period, the former colonies are to a considerable extent "uncommitted," i.e., not attached ideologically either to the Communist countries or to the developed Western nations. A country's ideological leaning is more difficult to determine than its development status or political system, and changes are more frequent. Leading countries of the uncommitted world are India, the United Arab Republic, and possibly Ghana; another important member of this group is Indonesia. Other coun-

tries may come to the forefront in the future. These countries maintain close ties with Yugoslavia, in a way also an uncommitted country. In some important Asian countries, like Japan and Pakistan, the close links with the West depend on the political preferences of a section of the community and may not persist. Most Latin American countries are in the process of transition and may increasingly feel uncommitted.

A final feature of our world, in the context of this section, is the tendency of some groups of countries toward integration, i.e., the giving up of some elements of their national sovereignty. This tendency is strongest in Western Europe, where close institutional links have already been established between the six countries of the European Economic Community (EEC, or the Common Market); discussions with the United Kingdom and other countries about their joining the Community are under way. The Community also has "associated countries," which include a number of African countries and Greece.

A start toward regional integration has been made in Central America and in Latin America generally, as well as in the Arab region. Still weaker tendencies can be observed in parts of Asia and Africa, but for understandable reasons most of the countries in these areas are not yet prepared to give up even small portions of their newly obtained sovereignty.

Today's most important tensions in the political and economic field have to do with the three main divisive factors indicated — communism, development, and colonialism. Of the problems involved some are economic while others are political and military, to mention only their most important aspects. The three main issues can hardly be separated and only a simultaneous solution will be satisfactory. Some problems, such as that of military security, seem almost insoluble in the situation which confronts us today. The problem of underdevelopment must have a central place in any attempt at "shaping the world." First of all, the problem concerns the basic human needs of large portions of the world population; secondly, its character is relatively clear and mainly economic — a

field in which mankind has made enormous progress; and thirdly, its solution may help to ease the other problems. For an elaboration of this last point see especially Chapters 2 and 10.

The problem of underdevelopment is aggravated by economic instability, especially in primary markets, and the shortsightedness of national policy-makers in matters of foreign trade. In the following chapters this theme will be developed further.

1.3 AN INCREASING GAP

The most basic and alarming feature of the underdevelopment problem is the fact that in the non-Communist area the gap between the developed and the less developed countries is, generally speaking, increasing in terms of real income per head.

It has been increasing if we make comparisons over a relatively long period, say the last fifty years. It must be admitted that no very precise figures are available for the majority of the underdeveloped countries around 1900; we must be content with crude estimates, except possibly for India. However, this should not prevent us from trying to get at least an impression of what the situation has been. Probably the most comprehensive and systematic student of the subject has been Professor Louis J. Zimmerman.[2] His data show that over the last half century there has been little change in real income per head in most of Asia, traditionally the home of over half the world's population. We all know that, by contrast, real income per capita has risen considerably in the West, especially in the United States, Western Europe, and a few high-income countries elsewhere such as Canada, Australia, and the white portion of South Africa. The picture with regard to these extremes in incomes is clear enough.

Less certainty exists about more recent developments and about countries not at the extremes of the distribution. In the last decade some success has been obtained with deliberate policies to promote economic development. In Latin America, which occupies an intermediate position, income has probably risen in the last half century

2. L. J. Zimmerman, *Arme en rijke landen,* Albani, The Hague, 1960.

Table 1–1

TREND OF PER CAPITA NATIONAL INCOME IN MAJOR AREAS, 1913–1957
(figures in dollars of 1952–54, not corrected for differences in price levels
between countries)

	1913	1929	1952–54	1957
North America (excl. Mexico)	$917	$1,243	$1,810	$1,868
Oceania	572	680	964	1,110
Northwestern Europe	454	528	681	790
Soviet Union (USSR)	162	178	535	750
Union of South Africa	177	221	300	318
Southeastern Europe	200	181	285	360
Latin America	170	196	260	300
Japan	85	152	184	240
Far East (excl. China and Japan)	93	106	109	115
Southeast Asia	65	68	64	67
China	50	50	50	61
		Index (1913=100)		
North America (excl. Mexico)	100	136	197	204
Oceania	100	119	169	194
Northwestern Europe	100	116	150	174
Soviet Union (USSR)	100	110	330	463
Union of South Africa	100	125	169	180
Southeastern Europe	100	91	143	180
Latin America	100	115	153	176
Japan	100	179	216	282
Far East (excl. China and Japan)	100	114	117	124
Southeast Asia	100	105	98	103
China	100	100	100	122

Source: L. J. Zimmerman, *Arme en rijke landen,* Albani, The Hague, 1960, pp. 29–31.

as well as lately. In addition, the recent economic development of the wealthiest among the big powers, the United States and the United Kingdom, has been relatively unimpressive. Recent movements are difficult to appraise because of the random variations occurring from year to year as a consequence of crop conditions, cyclical fluctuations, and so on. It is significant nevertheless that the

rise in real income per head in such an important country as India has been, in the last decade, definitely less than the rise in real income per head in the countries of the European Economic Community (EEC). While the former may be estimated at 1.5 per cent per annum, the latter has been over 3 per cent.[3] When appraising these data we should not forget that even an equal rate of growth would widen the absolute gap.

Table 1-1 summarizes some relevant information.

To understand what these figures mean in simple human terms, we must realize that most of the people in Asia and Africa and many in Latin America are living at a starvation level. Their consumption is some 10 per cent of that in developed countries and they are in a constant fight against hunger and illness. Everything in their budget — food, clothing, housing, education, amusement — is far below adequate standards as we see them. For a long time these people have been forced by circumstances and encouraged by philosophies, partly geared to their situation, to accept their condition as natural. Increasing contact with the wealthier parts of the world is now raising a question in their minds as to the necessity for their underprivileged status, and it seems clear that once this doubt has worked its way through the population we shall witness justified attempts to change the situation — attempts which may be carried out with an energy corresponding to the tensions endured. It is because such basic human issues are involved for such a large number of people that this problem is so important. It deserves to be our main preoccupation. We will try to analyze its causes, and then, in Part II, discuss possible remedial action.

1.4   BASIC CAUSES OF POVERTY

In itself the phenomenon of extreme poverty is not new. The less developed countries have been poor for a considerable period. For a very long time this poverty was the natural lot of a large

3. For 1950–1959: Federal Republic of Germany, 6.2 per cent; Italy, 4.6 per cent; the Netherlands, 3.5 per cent; France, 3.1 per cent; Belgium, 2.1 per cent. (See *Maandschrift van het Centraal Bureau voor de Statistiek*, W. de Haan, Utrecht, 1961, p. 220.)

section of the world's population. Any attempt to analyze its origins should distinguish between direct and indirect causes, i.e., the phenomena logically linked with it which are closest and those which are more remote. The best analogy may be that of a chain; the indirect causes are represented by all the links except the last, which is the immediate cause. The chain is no one-way avenue of causation, but shows numerous interconnections: the links are interwoven. While we know something about the strength, and so about the relative importance, of the direct causes of poverty, our knowledge about the more remote causes is qualitative rather than quantitative, and still very modest. Broadly we may say that the direct causes are more of a technological and economic nature, whereas the indirect ones, those farther back in the causal chain, tend to be psychological, historical, or geographic rather than economic in the strict sense.

We may consider as the central phenomenon to be explained by our analysis the low level of production per human being. The most important direct causes may then be listed as follows:

  (i) a low level of technical and organizing skill residing in the human factor of production; and

 (ii) a small quantity of the complementary factors of production, i.e., the total of land and capital.

Each of these direct causes stands for a complex of phenomena, since each of the factors of production may take a variety of forms. Thus, human skills are many-sided, capital may take a large number of concrete shapes, and "land," in the sense used here, embraces a range of soil fertility, climate, and mineral wealth.

Broadly speaking, the quantity of land and capital at the disposal of the less developed countries is much smaller than in developed countries, in roughly the same proportion as their incomes are related. There are considerable differences in the relative importance of land and capital among underdeveloped countries; in some, land is relatively abundant but capital very scarce. However, for most of the population in the underdeveloped sections of the world land is very scarce too, India and China being familiar examples. Skills, particularly the more relevant ones, are seldom the

subject of a census; nevertheless, indirect observations, such as the number of illiterates, clearly indicate a shortage in this area.

Both the skills and the capital available per head are linked logically with the indirect or deeper causes of the existing situation, and, in a general way, we may say that the latter are to be found in:

  (i) the more basic attitudes of the peoples considered; and
  (ii) a number of geographical and political facts, current and historical.

The basic attitudes relevant to economic development can be deduced from an analysis of the decisions or choices which human beings must take in order to establish or maintain a modern economy. Among these decisions, those concerning the use of durable means of production stand out. These only bear fruit in a more or less remote future about which there must always be some uncertainty, and they require co-operation between large numbers of individuals. The most important basic attitudes involved are:

    (i) an interest in material well-being;
   (ii) a willingness to look ahead;
  (iii) a willingness to take risks;
   (iv) an interest in technology;
    (v) a willingness to co-operate;
   (vi) an ability to persist;
  (vii) a willingness to accept the "rules of the game."

Students of the subject have chosen various formulations; some have left out a few of the attitudes listed and added others. But by and large there is a consensus of opinion about the sort of attitudes needed. There is also a consensus of belief that these attitudes are not sufficiently widespread in underdeveloped countries. Thus, business men in these countries often prefer quick profits from speculation to long-term profits obtained more patiently from mass production at relatively modest profit margins. Corruption often puts a brake on development. In a way, the population problem — which is rapidly becoming very pressing — may also be said to be due to a lack of willingness to look ahead, sometimes along with a lack of understanding of the operation of the economy.

The attitudes mentioned are not independent, however, of the

environment in which a population lives. They reflect the economic situation itself and are interdependent with it. Willingness to look ahead is slight with people living on the margin of subsistence, as can easily be understood. So also is the ability to persist. Corruption is partly a consequence of huge income differences.

The attitudes discussed also depend on more remote factors in the environment: geographic and political factors thus come in. These may have been at work for a long period. Surely the tropical or subtropical climates in which almost all the less developed countries are situated are not conducive to persistence or to productivity generally. The geographic environment may have deteriorated because of the exhaustion of natural resources: erosion may be cited as a specific example. Or it may have deteriorated because of a change in trade channels and traffic currents. The natural endowments of a people may be less favorable than those of other peoples. To be sure, our knowledge in this respect is very incomplete, but in a majority of the cases where variations in basic attitudes can be observed, it is probable that these variations can be explained by differences in the economic position of the individuals involved or their parents or even grandparents (see section 1.5). It is also conceivable that migration has systematically exerted a counterselective influence on a population. In a region where the economic situation was worsened by the factors just mentioned — e.g., exhaustion of natural resources or change in trade channels, phenomena which have appeared repeatedly in history — emigration often took place. Presumably the individuals who moved were more interested in material well-being and more willing to take risks than those who stayed behind. The remaining population was then, on the average, less gifted with the prerequisites of economic development. Thus emigration may have intensified the process of decay in the economy concerned.

Among the political factors which may have played a part, either recently or in the past, colonial rule may be mentioned. Such a political situation may suppress, or at least insufficiently cultivate, the forces making for development. This can happen when economic development is kept in the hands of foreigners and the fruits

of development — or of exploitation — are taken by a ruling nation. There are other possibilities too, some of which will be discussed below (in section 2.1). We may provisionally state that the effect of colonial rule depends on its character; the results may have been negative as well as positive. A broad comparison among countries within the same region does not seem to show that those which have been independent are better off than those which have been colonies. Consider, for example, Thailand compared with Malaya, Burma, and Indonesia; Ethiopia and Liberia compared with Kenya or Nigeria.

1.5 VICIOUS CIRCLES

The persistence of poverty in the less developed countries, and the difficulties involved in reaching a stage of self-sustained growth, must be attributed partly to the functioning of the socio-economic system itself. An easy way to visualize this operation is to use the term "vicious circles." Certain mechanisms tend to keep a system at the low level where it has been for inherent reasons or because of outside events, e.g., a deteriorated geographic position or some political development.

One example is the interdependence of income and capital: a low capital stock implies a low level of production, and so of income. But a low income does not permit large savings, and hence the capital stock cannot easily be increased.

A second example is the interdependence of income and health. Low incomes depress the level of nutrition and do not permit sufficient medical services to maintain good health. Ill health in turn depresses personal efforts in production and may keep down productivity.

A third example refers to the interdependence of income and education. Low incomes do not permit extensive educational facilities, and with inadequate education skill and productivity will tend to remain low.

Looked at in the reverse way these relations tell us that consider-

able effort will be needed to break these vicious circles. We will discuss this effort in section 1.7.

1.6 THE FATE OF PRIMARY MARKETS

It is in the nature of less developed countries that they are mainly producers of primary goods, i.e., agricultural or mining products. With a low level of human skill and capital, the types of production in which they will have a comparative advantage will usually be those dependent on natural resources. Not only the "supply side" but also the demand side is geared this way, for the poorer nations' greatest need is for food. To finance their imports underdeveloped countries will have to export primary commodities. The markets for such goods are often not such as to stimulate their development. There are of course some exceptions, of which petroleum is the best known: its production and export have, though not without foreign investments, led to rapid improvement in the economic position of a number of countries. Several other examples could be mentioned.

The majority of primary product markets, however, have two important drawbacks. First of all, their secular development is usually slow. The demand for basic commodities grows only slowly with increasing income, or, as the economist puts it, the "income elasticity of demand" is low. In addition, sellers of some important natural raw materials have experienced competition from substitutes such as rayon and other synthetic fibers, and artificial rubber.[4] The second drawback is the short-term instability of prices. The output of many primary goods is dependent on crop yields which vary erratically and widely. Also, market prices are in a sense a residual, and fluctuations in demand, mostly of a cyclical nature, will lead to much greater fluctuations in prices of raw materials than in prices of finished products. In addition, several primary products such as coffee and rubber show price cycles of a special

4. See *Trends in International Trade*, Report by a Panel of Experts, General Agreement on Tariffs and Trade, Geneva, 1958, especially pp. 43–44.

character due to the long period of production of existing trees and the time required for growing new trees.

Partly as a consequence of the slow pace of expansion of primary markets, and partly because of the efforts needed to shift productive factors to other occupations, the relative prices of primary goods (or their terms of trade) vis-à-vis those of industrial products are deteriorating. There have indeed been periods of improvement, as, for example, during and after World War II, but the prospects for the next decade are not too favorable unless action is taken.[5]

1.7 THE NEED FOR A BIG PUSH

We have already expressed our belief that the increasing gap in well-being between the developed and the less developed countries is one of the most important problems of today's world. We will pursue this line of thought more fully in Part II. In the present part of our analysis we merely want to set out in brief what is needed in order to improve the situation of the less fortunate nations.

From the preceding sketch it is clear that a deliberate effort will have to be made: it is improbable that an accelerated rate of development will come about spontaneously. In order to increase production in underdeveloped countries substantially, the quality and quantity of the factors of production — skills, attitudes, and the quantity of capital goods in all forms — will have to be increased. From our earlier analysis we can understand that it is very difficult for the economies and societies concerned to make this effort. The forces operating in the vicious circles described have a tendency to maintain the *status quo*. Only a considerable increase in each of the factors mentioned can produce a great enough response in national income to bring about the additional savings and educational facilities needed to sustain the process of growth. Small increases in product may prove ineffective if the random movements

5. See M. K. Atallah, *The Long-Term Movement of the Terms of Trade between Agricultural and Industrial Products*, Netherlands Economic Institute, Rotterdam, 1958, p. 74.

discussed previously happen to be adverse. For the process of growth to be self-sustaining, to use the customary term, there must be confidence that no setbacks will occur. This can only be the case if the trend of annual increases in production — the momentum — is sufficiently high to offset the effects of negative random movements.

The desirability of a considerable increase in production, and hence in the factors of production, is often referred to as the need for a "big push."[6] There are further reasons why a big push is desirable. These are to be found in the peculiarities of some of the capital goods needed in the process. If an economy is to diversify its production and introduce some types of manufacturing industries, there is a need for a so-called "infrastructure" of investments. This term refers to investments in the basic industries, especially energy and transportation, whose services are used by almost every other industry. Other investments are often included, such as outlays for schools and dwellings. Their common characteristic is that they do not usually yield quick and visible profits to their operators, either because very long processes of production are involved or because the end products cannot easily be sold. This characteristic holds especially for the product of roads but applies also in the case of education. These conditions suggest that the infrastructure is best taken care of by public authorities. Although this dictum does not necessarily apply to energy, the feature now to be discussed often makes it desirable for energy production to be organized in the public sector also.

This feature is the phenomenon of "indivisibilities." In most of the infrastructure, the units to be created must have a certain minimum size if they are to make sense at all. The clearest example is that of roads; the least that is needed in order to have a connection between two centers is the complete length of a road for at least one lane, which already represents a large investment. In hydraulic energy production often at least one dam is needed, or in thermal

6. P. N. Rosenstein-Rodan, "Notes on the Theory of the Big Push," *Economic Development for Latin America*, ed. by Howard S. Ellis, Macmillan, London, 1961, pp. 57 ff.

energy production, a plant of considerable capacity — smaller plants being substantially more expensive. Such indivisibilities constitute an important argument for a big push.

Indivisibilities are generally characteristic of heavy industries, such as steel and basic chemicals, which in a somewhat later phase of development may be important objects for investment. The very phenomenon of indivisibilities may be the reason why it is so difficult to enter the group of the developed economies: it establishes a sort of a threshold, in that below a certain level of industrial production costs are high and incomes low, while beyond that level the relationship is reversed. In order to get over the threshold a big push is necessary. Many of the now developed countries got "over the hump" only by a painful process: the big push is therefore an old problem facing the new countries.

It should not be concluded from the foregoing that a country in the first phases of development should concentrate predominantly on big projects. Smaller projects usually give quicker results which exert a stimulating effect on the economy. Starting with too many big projects may be unwise because of the discouraging effect of the long waiting period. It may also be unwise because of possible inflationary consequences. Often smaller projects can be linked up with existing production units (cottage industry with factories processing the same agricultural produce, for example) so that less sweeping physical changes and psychic switches are necessary. At the same time more people can be trained in managerial skills, and the projects can be spread over a wider area. Also, with smaller projects it is more feasible to experiment to determine which branches of production are particularly suitable for a given country. Therefore a wise choice must continually be made between projects of different size.

CHAPTER 2

TWO DOCTORS

2.1 MOTHER COUNTRIES AND
COLONIAL INVESTMENTS

The countries in need of development, and especially those that gained national independence only recently, are now eagerly seeking the means to further, or even start, their economic advance. In the present world they find two doctors who are willing to advise them on how to overcome the illness of poverty — the developed countries of the West and the Communist countries. Both have a record of development to show: the Western countries a long history of gradual advance and the Communist countries one of quicker progress more deliberately fostered, but partly based on Western experience. Both doctors will be judged by the prospective patient not only by their words or present-day policies but also by their historical record. This is only natural, since gaining any information takes time; it is even more natural if the patient's colonial history was painful in some respects. Here we must recall

19

Arnold Toynbee's analysis of how the West has been judged by the outside world.[1] The leading European countries of the West not only have a history of economic development; they have at the same time a history as colonial powers. And former colonies do not always have the feeling that their mother countries behaved like mothers. The memories of these former colonies have been helpfully nudged by the Communist countries, though in a somewhat one-sided way.

There is no need to make an apology for the Western countries here, since old-time colonialism is reaching its end in any case. For our purposes, however, it does make sense to analyze the colonial era in the light of development, asking whether colonial rule made a sufficient contribution to the development of the colonies, looked at in a modern way.

Economically, colonial rule was characterized by investments of considerable size. During the years from 1900 to 1914 annual capital imports into India from Britain amounted to about 1 per cent of Indian national income,[2] a figure that is doubled when reinvestment of locally made profits is included. It has been estimated that in 1938 about one-sixth of the total national wealth of the Netherlands was invested in Indonesia (then the Netherlands East Indies); this amount constituted roughly one-third to one-fourth of Indonesia's total capital stock.[3] As is well known, these investments were mostly directed to primary production and the infrastructure. A substantial portion of these investments was privately financed and the incentive was simply profits — higher profits than could be earned in the mother countries. The margin was not particularly great, however, as the following figures indicate:[4]

1. See Arnold Toynbee, *The World and the West*, BBC Reith Lectures 1952, Oxford University Press, London–New York–Toronto, 1953.

2. This figure may be compared with an inflow of public capital of 1.2 to 1.3 per cent of national income during the first and second five-year plans.

3. It may be held that the countries cited are relatively unfavorable examples as compared with some less populated colonies. We have chosen our examples precisely because the bulk of the population in underdeveloped areas lives in densely populated countries.

4. See Appendix V for sources and a discussion of the reliability of all figures mentioned in this paragraph.

Interest on Bonds			*Rate of Return on Shares*		
	UK	Colonies		Nether-lands	Neth. E. Ind.
1870–80					
Government	3.8	4.4	1900–12	5.7	6.5
Railways	5.3	6.3	1922–29	4.0	7.5
1900–09	3.4	3.6	1930–37	3.0	3.2
1921–30	4.5	5.3			

These investments, together with a flow of technical and commercial personnel, did increase colonial production and income. In the context of private enterprise it was natural that a part of the profits be paid to shareholders living outside the territories. Also, a substantial part of these profits was reinvested in colonial enterprises. Yet the increases in production and income definitely did not lead to the development of the colonies in a manner which we would consider satisfactory today. This may be illustrated by two studies which are in a way complementary.

D. H. Burger in a microanalysis of a region of Java[5] showed that the income increases were concentrated among a small group of producers, mainly immigrants, rather than spread over the indigenous population.

Professor Louis J. Zimmerman, whose figures we have already quoted,[6] uses a macroeconomic approach and confirms a conclusion reached by others, that production increased in proportion to population, leaving income per head unaffected. A fair presentation of the facts might be the statement that Western medical institutions and Western production increases made it possible for a larger population to live at a traditional level than might otherwise have been the case. Whether much has been gained thereby is a question of philosophy.

Having looked at the general quantitative features of development under colonial rule we may briefly discuss three qualitative aspects of colonialism which are of considerable importance to development policies. The first concerns the attitude of colonial gov-

5. D. H. Burger, *Vergelijking van den economischen toestand der districten Tajoe en Djakenan*, Kolff, Weltevreden, 1930.

6. L. J. Zimmerman, *Arme en rijke landen*, Albani, The Hague, 1960.

ernments with regard to industrialization. They have, to say the least, always been very hesitant to further industrialize their dependencies.[7] The idea prevailed that there was a natural division of labor, allegedly based on comparative advantages, making it at least doubtful whether the industrialization of tropical countries was advisable. It is true that some industries were developed in India during the colonial era, but these were not exactly furthered by the British government.

This brings us to a second aspect of colonial rule, trade policy. This has repeatedly been used in favor of the industries of the ruling country and to the disadvantage of local industries or consumers. The record with regard to textiles makes this abundantly clear.[8] As a rather recent example, the quantitative restrictions of the nineteen thirties against cheap Japanese textiles in the Netherlands East Indies may be mentioned.[9]

A third feature refers to the choice of institutions and technologies made by Western technicians working in the colonies. There was an understandable tendency for outside technical and administrative experts to be guided by their own experience, and this was bound to be to some extent an experience gained in their own countries. Thus one is struck by the parallelism in the institutions and techniques of the mother country and the colonies. This often resulted in the imposition of a technology which was not optimal for the economies concerned: it tended to be too capital-intensive. The same error has since been made — and perhaps to an even greater degree — by some American experts working in developing countries. In this case it has little to do with colonialism; it merely reflects the orientation of technology toward the economic conditions prevailing in the developed countries.

7. See, e.g., Benjamin Higgins, *Economic Development*, Norton, New York, 1959, pp. 316, 352–353, 371; J. A. Wartna, *De Indonesische nijverheid—verleden en toekomstmogelijkheden*, Excelsior, Rijswijk, 1961, Ch. 1; P. Prasad, *Some Economic Problems of Public Enterprise in India*, H. E. Stenfert Kroese, Leiden, 1957, Ch. 4.

8. K. M. Panikkar, *Asia and Western Dominance*, Allen and Unwin, London, 1953, pp. 65 ff.

9. G. Gonggrijp, *Schets ener economische geschiedenis van Indonesië*, F. Bohn, Haarlem, 1957, p. 188.

While recognizing that the colonies were primarily governed in the interest of the mother countries, one can at the same time admit that in many instances it was the colonial tie that introduced into the thinking of the colonies a number of Western elements which are basic to a positive attitude toward economic development. This may help them in their further development. It will also make it easier to bring about a "real meeting" between these countries and the West, which is to say a contact in a broader and deeper sense than in economic terms alone. And this will be necessary in view of the ultimate aim of world-wide co-operation.[10]

An important element of Western thinking transmitted by colonial rule was that of geographic integration, the creation of relatively large politically unified areas. The significance of this element will become clear when we discuss (in Chapter 8) some of the tendencies toward disintegration now visible in Africa.

2.2 WESTERN HELP AND ADVICE

Although understandable, it would be a mistake for legislators in developing countries to base their judgment of the potentialities of Western-type societies on the colonial experience only. There are two more pieces of evidence. First, the Western countries' own development should be considered, especially the later stage when the pure laissez-faire and capitalistic features were tempered — mostly by the influence of labor movements — and social relations improved. It should be remembered too that in this stage several groups and individuals became increasingly conscious that "social relations" with the nations which up to then had been colonies should be promoted. The second piece of evidence is the West's changed approach to developing countries after World War II.

The more farsighted among Western politicians and experts understood fairly early that after World War II colonialism would be in the process of liquidation. Relations between India and the United Kingdom are the standard example of the new attitude. To

10. See H. Kraemer, "Grootheid en ellende van het Vasco da Gamatijdperk," *Wending*, Boekencentrum, The Hague, 1959, pp. 403–415.

be sure, less fortunate examples are numerous and often the problems to be solved are more difficult while the skills available for the task are less.

The governments responsible for the creation of the United Nations organization and a number of their specialized agencies were aware, individually and collectively, that other means would have to be made available in the interest of a successful development policy. Assistance in the public sphere with capital and technical knowledge coming from the developed countries was the main element in these new means. The International Bank for Reconstruction and Development (IBRD, or World Bank) was established and various agencies, especially the Food and Agriculture Organization (FAO), organized technical assistance. Somewhat later, when still other specialized agencies, including the United Nations Educational, Scientific and Cultural Organization (UNESCO), as well as the UN Secretariat had organized technical assistance, an attempt was made to co-ordinate these activities. Since 1950 this co-ordination has been in the hands of the Technical Assistance Board (TAB) of the United Nations. Financial assistance is now also given by the International Finance Corporation (IFC), the International Development Association (IDA), and the UN Special Fund (UNSF). An idea of the order of magnitude of the means made available in this way can be obtained from Tables 2–1 and 2–2.

In addition to the preceding activities, usually described as multilateral assistance, so-called bilateral assistance is granted by many countries (see Table 2–3). For Southeast Asia, a special co-ordinating organization has been formed for this purpose, working mainly with the financial support of the Commonwealth — the Colombo Plan. Huge programs of bilateral assistance are those of the United States — formerly the International Cooperation Administration (ICA), now the Agency for International Development (AID) — and of the French Community.

An intermediate position is taken in the case of the assistance given by the European Development Fund (EDF) and the European Investment Bank of the European Economic Community, and by the Inter-American Development Bank (IADB). Some figures

Table 2–1

MULTILATERAL CAPITAL AID TO NEWLY DEVELOPING COUNTRIES,
1954–1961 (in millions)

Total	$1,817
IBRD	1,270
IFC	23
UNSF	131
IDA	101
EDF	162
IADB	130

Note: For IBRD and IFC, estimated net disbursements; for other agencies, loans or grants approved. Years indicate fiscal periods ending that year.

Source: United Nations, *Statistical Yearbook 1960,* New York, 1961; and Annual Reports of the organizations involved.

Table 2–2

MULTILATERAL TECHNICAL ASSISTANCE, 1960[a]

	Expanded Program (in millions)	NUMBER OF EXPERTS		NUMBER OF FELLOWSHIPS	
		Expanded Program	Regular Program	Expanded Program	Regular Program
Total	$ 32.3	2,258	1,046	2,745	4,002
UNTA	7.3	522	331	817	412
FAO	8.4	553	68	408	17
WHO	5.5	430	471	518	2,364
UNESCO	4.9	302	93	321	662
ILO	3.2	251	65	453	203
ICAO	1.5	116	—	54	—
WMO	0.5	35	—	62	—
ITU	0.4	27	—	27	—
IAEA	0.6	22	18	85	344

Note: Expenditure on the regular program is included in the normal budget of the agencies concerned; expenditure on the expanded program is separately budgeted in the Expanded Program of Technical Assistance.

a. For abbreviations, see List of Abbreviations.

Source: United Nations Technical Assistance Committee, *Annual Report of the Technical Assistance Board for 1960,* New York, 1961 (Doc. E/3471).

Table 2–3

BILATERAL ECONOMIC AID TO NEWLY DEVELOPING COUNTRIES,
1954–1959 (in millions)

	Total	Grants	Net Loans
Total	$13,537	$10,366	$3,171
Australia	185	183	2
Belgium	66	10	56
Canada	244	207	37
France	4,117	2,982	1,135
Germany (Fed. Rep.)a	76	5	71
Italy	161	42	119
Japan	179	179	—
Netherlands	105	119	14
New Zealand	27	26	1
Norway	4	4	—
Portugal	15	1	14
Sweden	2	2	—
United Kingdom	869	615	254
United States	7,476	5,991	1,485
Yugoslavia	11	...	11

Note: Years indicate fiscal periods ending that year.
a. 1959 only.
Source: United Nations, *Statistical Yearbook 1958,* and *1960,* New York, 1959 and 1961.

concerning the latter type of assistance were given in Table 2–1.

While the activities just summed up are of a public character, private investment continues to contribute considerably to the flow of investment funds as Table 2–4 shows. A large percentage of this investment has been concentrated in the oil industry.

Some figures summarizing all these activities in the field of capital aid are presented in Table 2–5.

The nature of the technical assistance, as well as the conditions sometimes set for the capital aid granted, were inspired by what Western experts and government and financial circles believed to be

Table 2–4

NET FLOW OF PRIVATE CAPITAL TO NEWLY DEVELOPING
COUNTRIES, 1956–1959 (in millions)

	Total 1956–59	1956	1957	1958	1959
Total	$11,273	$2,975	$3,514	$2,506	$2,278
United States	4,639	1,251	1,827	872	689
United Kingdom	1,998	402	690	518	388
France	1,622	461	359	378	424
Germany (Fed. Rep.)	1,086	275	247	240	324
Netherlands	588	215	124	145	104
Other developed countries	1,340	371	267	353	349

Note: The figures exclude short-term capital (less than one year). They include guaranteed export credits and reinvested earnings.

Source: **OEEC,** *The Flow of Financial Resources to Countries in Course of Economic Development 1956–1959,* **Paris, 1961.**

the most efficient policy of development. Since ideas are free in Western countries, the advice reflected various shades of opinion ranging from a strong recommendation of private initiative, wherever possible, to the suggestion of a mixed system adapted to the potentialities of the recipient countries. Much advice was given also on the financial and monetary structure and more particularly on the type of foreign exchange policy to be adopted. This advice usually centered around "orthodox" financial policies and the abolition of multiple exchange rates and discriminatory trade practices. It is only natural that the experts and government representatives should benefit from experience, and a clear development is apparent in the content of their advice (see Chapter 6).

Apart from recommendations believed to be in the interest of the countries helped, the West's policy has also been characterized by some less fortunate features, intentional and otherwise, which have changed recently. In the beginning, rather stringent political ties were a prerequisite to the aid given. For years India was not offered much assistance because her "neutralist" attitude was dis-

Table 2–5

TOTAL FLOW OF CAPITAL TO NEWLY DEVELOPING COUNTRIES,
1956–1959 (in billions)

Total	$28.6
Contributions to multilateral agencies	1.9
Bilateral contributions:	
Official	15.5
Grants	9.6
Net lending	5.9
Private	11.2
Guaranteed export credit	1.5
Other new lending and investment	6.1
Reinvested earnings	3.6

Note: The figures exclude short-term capital (less than one year) and military expenditures. Contributions to multilateral agencies as reported here are higher than actual disbursements of these agencies as given in Table 2–1, because of the balances accumulated by the agencies. The figures given in this table for Official Bilateral Aid differ from those given in Table 2–3 mainly because of differences in the definition of assistance and in the basis of reporting. For further discussion of these points see the Annex to *International Flow of Long-Term Capital and Official Donations 1951–1959*, United Nations, New York, 1961 (Sales no.: 62.II.D.1).

Source: OEEC, *The Flow of Financial Resources to Countries in Course of Economic Development 1956–1959*, Paris, 1961, and estimates of the Netherlands Economic Institute, Rotterdam.

liked, especially by the American public. Smaller countries were given aid with political conditions. A most unfortunate game was played with the United Arab Republic (then Egypt) in the withdrawal of a proposal to finance part of the Aswan High Dam project.

Apart from governmental intentions, some experts did violence to the intentions of the aid programs by a personal attitude irritating to the recipient countries. In some cases it was an attitude of knowing everything better; in others, a lack of adaptability to the circumstances of the country, and a tendency to luxurious living. It is a tribute to the American way of life that such attitudes were publicly ridiculed and criticized,[11] and it should not be overlooked

11. See W. J. Lederer and E. Burdick, *The Ugly American*, Norton, New York, 1958.

that many other American experts did very good jobs. Moreover, errors were certainly not committed only by the foreign visitors. It is part of the phenomenon of underdevelopment that many things are done, individually and collectively, in developing countries which are, to say the least, not helpful in attaining the desired goal.

One of the important developments during the relatively brief period under review is the changed attitude of Western experts toward economic planning. While planning at a project level was seen as necessary from the start — bankers usually like planning for their clients better than planning for their own governments — the planning approach for a nation as a whole was not given its proper place. Thus the programs recommended by IBRD missions in the earlier years often fell short of what was needed to attain real development.[12] Nowadays it is generally recognized by organizations like the World Bank and the ICA and by most individual Western experts that a developing country must have a development plan to serve as a framework for the program of projects to be carried out. Several countries understood this necessity soon after independence; some countries, particularly in Asia, already have an interesting record in this respect. Planning techniques evolved quickly and a reasonably good set of not too complicated techniques is now available.[13] At the same time the staff needed for such planning is rapidly increasing, although there is still a definite shortage. Also, it has become clear that to have a plan is not enough; it must be effectively implemented. This means that instruments must be chosen to influence the actual course of development when it is not in conformity with the plan. In order to judge the efficiency of such instruments so-called short-term decision models or policy models of the particular economy are very useful: these summarize the most important forces in the economic mechanism relevant to short-term policy.

12. F. T. Moore, *The Failures of the World Bank Missions*, RAND Corporation, Santa Monica, Calif., 1958.

13. An outstanding survey of the most important techniques available may be found in H. B. Chenery and P. G. Clark, *Interindustry Economics*, Wiley, New York, 1959. See also H. B. Chenery, "Development Policies and Programmes," *Economic Bulletin for Latin America*, March 1958, pp. 51 ff.

Planning techniques, as just advocated in a general way, are also very useful in the preparation of the many types of education and training processes needed for development. The latest step in techniques and activities applied by experts assisting developing countries is directed at using planning techniques in these areas.

2.3   THE RUSSIAN PERFORMANCE

The economic history of the countries united in the Soviet Union (the West continues to speak of Russia, which is by far the most important country in the Union) since the 1917 October Revolution has been dramatic. Strong forces have been involved on various sides. This was true of the circumstances in which the Revolution took place; it was true of the attempts made by reactionary forces from outside to interfere with the political situation in Russia; it was true of the opposition from certain groups of the population, especially of the peasantry; it was true of a number of measures instituted by the regime. Russia also went through the Second World War and suffered tremendous losses in people and material wealth which required huge efforts at reconstruction. Accordingly, the economic history of the Union has not been uniform; it has been marked by serious setbacks. Only a brief summary and appraisal of this unprecedented attempt to reshape an economy can be given here.

An outstanding question which must be answered in order to make such an appraisal is, of course, whether Russian development has indeed been more rapid than the development of the Western countries, as the Communist Party claims — and as a number of Western economists deny. The comparison, to begin with, is not an easy one. The statistical evidence available is based on concepts and sometimes on methods which are different from those used in the West. A vast literature has come into existence on this subject. Another major difficulty is the choice of comparable periods. Simply to compare the Soviet Union with the United States over the same period is to compare a developing economy with one which is highly developed. A more appropriate comparison may be to take

periods starting with the same quantity of production. That is what G. Warren Nutter has done;[14] he compared industrial production as a whole and in a large number of industries by determining the lag of Russia behind the United States in years. Nutter finds that for steel ingots the Soviet Union lagged 21 years in 1913, 32 years in 1937, and 29 years in 1955. Using the same benchmarks the median figures for 37 industries are 28, 36, and 35 years. For per capita production there is an increase in the lag between 1913 and 1937 of 10 years; between 1937 and 1955 the increase amounts to 4 years.

For more recent years R. Wagenführ has made a comparison between the industrial production of the USSR and of the United States.[15] This shows that in 1956 the industrial production of the USRR was from 44 to 48 per cent of that in the United States while in 1959 the range was from 57 to 62 per cent.

Nutter's figures over the period starting in 1913 are not too helpful since in that period, ending in 1937, the Russian economy went through the destruction of the revolutionary and antirevolutionary fighting following the First World War. The figures over the 1937–1955 period are more significant, but here the Second World War is involved. This certainly brought about much more devastation in the Soviet Union than did the First World War in the United States, which was then at a comparable stage of development. If anything can be concluded from the figures then, it is that Russian over-all development has been more rapid than American development.[16]

Further analysis is required, however, before it can be concluded that the Communist regime is more effective in bringing about growth. Effectiveness can be determined by a comparison between

14. G. Warren Nutter, "Some Observations on Soviet Industrial Growth," *American Economic Review*, May 1957 (Papers and Proceedings of the Sixty-ninth Annual Meeting of the American Economic Association, 1956), p. 618.

15. R. Wagenführ, *Croissances industrielles comparées de la Communauté Européenne, des USA et de l'URSS*, Centre de Recherches Européennes, Université de Lausanne, Lausanne, 1961.

16. The same conclusion is reached in more elaborate studies; see, for example, Abram Bergson, *The Real National Income of Soviet Russia since 1928*, Harvard University Press, Cambridge, 1961, Ch. 14.

output on the one hand and efforts and sacrifices on the other. Among the efforts and sacrifices are the means used, in the narrower sense — including goods and the human capital invested in education. Possibly more of these means could have been used to good effect by the Western economies. Before dealing with these comparisons we must first consider the most characteristic features of the Communist economies — called, as we know, "socialist" by their leaders. They may be listed as follows:

   (i) most of the means of production are community property;

  (ii) the economic process is centrally planned in considerable detail;

 (iii) a large portion — of the order of 25 per cent, in Western concepts — of national income is saved and invested, meaning that consumption is kept at a lower level than income permits;

 (iv) the educational system tries, more deliberately than in Western societies, to use individual talents for the furtherance of economic and scientific development;

  (v) deviations in economic behavior from the official policy are severely punished.

Many more features might be worth recalling for the reader, but we believe that the five mentioned are the most important ones. Some others can be deduced from those listed. Thus it is a consequence of (i), (ii), and (v) that there exists considerable central guidance with respect to the choice of technology and the size of productive units. A corollary is the avoidance of waste due to uneconomically large or small plants. Other key central decisions relate to the division of production between capital goods and consumer goods and between different kinds of consumer goods. The latter at the same time influences the relation between individual consumption and saving as well as the individual pattern of consumption. An interesting example of the allocation system is the fact that means of mass transportation have been emphasized while few resources — in contrast to the situation in the West — are used for the production of private cars. Another example is found in com-

munications: advertising is practically absent, except for extensive official propaganda.

Depending upon ideology, there is a definite difference in the appraisal of the role played by the five main features in the success of the regime with regard to development. Official Communist opinion emphasizes (i), (ii), and (iv) as the main factors. Western opinion tends to attach primary importance to (iii) and (v), some importance to (ii), and increasing importance to (iv). Western opinion is not unanimous on the question of government owner-ship of the means of production. Thus conservatives hold that (i) is indeed an adverse influence while more progressive circles do not think that it has much connection with development, except for a number of key industries which in many Western countries are also publicly owned (infrastructure and some heavy industries). West-ern opinion is fairly uniform, however, in considering (v) a far more serious drawback of the Communist system, mainly for non-economic reasons, than official Communist opinion admits.

If we now want to compare the economic value of the two sys-tems with respect to growth we must start by considering the ratios between output and means in the narrow sense; in other words, the ratios between increased production obtained and capital invested (including education). It is a pity that precise and comparable estimates of this yardstick, which in its crudest form coincides with the output-capital ratio, do not exist. The available figures tend to favor the Communist countries, but this is partly because invest-ment in housing, which is known to be characterized by a low out-put-capital ratio, was for a long time neglected.

The relatively high level of capital investment in the Communist economies must then — evidently — yield relatively impressive re-sults. So we think the most appropriate Western comment on Com-munist development may be that it is only natural that develop-ment can be speeded up if a sufficiently large portion of national income is invested and, further, that account must be taken of the sacrifices made in the form of a low level of consumption and the restraint of freedom.

Apart from the main features of communism already discussed one other feature may be of increasing importance, namely change. The Soviet system does not remain the same, any more than the Western system. Both are moving and the movements are, generally speaking, converging ones.[17] Thus some ideas which sprang from early Communist preferences but proved difficult to apply have been given up. It is no longer held that workers can manage productive units by themselves, that all incomes should be more or less equal, or that money is superfluous. Incomes are geared to productivity and money concepts are increasingly used in planning. Interest, though not recognized as a possible source of private income, has gradually been accepted as representing a real cost element. The value of an international exchange of products has been increasingly understood and some autarkic preferences weakened. Some decentralization in economic decision-making has been introduced and consumption has been given more attention in the new party program. Mathematical methods in economic planning, at first considered "bourgeois," are now increasingly applied.

2.4 THE GROWTH OF EASTERN EUROPE AND CHINA

Since World War II the Soviet Union has not been the only country under Communist rule. At various moments and in various ways a number of Eastern European countries together with China and some smaller Asian nations have come under the dominance of their Communist parties. Some of these economies, especially Czechoslovakia and the German Democratic Republic, were more developed than the Russian; China was probably the least developed major country in the world. In all of them a vigorous policy of economic reconstruction and economic development has been applied, using Russian experience, suggestions, and methods along with domestic resources.

The economic development of these countries has been quick,

17. See J. Tinbergen, "Do Communist and Free Economies Show a Converging Pattern?," *Soviet Studies*, 1961, p. 333.

largely for the same reasons as in the Soviet Union. Underdeveloped regions, such as Slovakia, have been developed. Heavy industries have been established in practically all of the countries, partly for armament purposes and partly because of the belief that every country should have its own heavy industry. The process has been accompanied by a tendency toward autarky, although the size and character of the Eastern European countries has not permitted the full application of this principle. More recently the economic policy and planning of these countries has undergone some clear changes with respect to international trade. While the international exchange of products was in the beginning a matter for bilateral negotiations, more co-ordination and international planning have been introduced. No important powers in these fields, however, have been given to supranational agencies: national autonomy is guarded very carefully.

Gradually some differences have evolved between the systems of the countries under Communist rule. Yugoslavia was the first country to follow its own course and it has devised a system with some remarkable features in line with the national character of the Republic. A high degree of decentralization has been introduced in production and in investment decisions and pricing. It may be said that Yugoslavia now is a competitive economy of factories owned by the various lower and higher public authorities or by the workers as a group, with an interventionist central policy. Large numbers of small enterprises are, in practice, private.

After 1956 the other Eastern European countries introduced changes in their economic regimes and their economic policies. Like Yugoslavia, Poland adopted more decentralization, though not in pricing. More emphasis was laid on indirect influences on management and central planning was done in less detail than before. In all of these countries consumption was given more attention.

Since 1952 China too has shown a rapid development. The character of the country and its culture makes it very difficult to compare its development with that of the European countries. China's income per head is extremely low and a very large portion of its

production is still agricultural. In consequence China is even more susceptible to random changes in crop yields than the other Communist countries. As in Russia, there have been rather violent alterations in the approach of the regime to agriculture. But China develops her own ideas with regard to the agricultural system as well as in many other fields. Differences in emphasis in matters of foreign policy clearly illustrate this point. While the progress in production made by China has been one of jumps and setbacks, it has been sufficiently large to impress neighboring countries like India and Indonesia.

2.5 COMPETING DOCTORS

As is now generally understood, the Western and the Communist systems are in a competitive position vis-à-vis the developing countries. It is in the interest of the latter that objective judges make as precise an appraisal as possible of the relative merits of each. This means, first of all, that objective information must be abstracted from the influences of propaganda and emotion. Both of these play a considerable role, as can be understood only too easily. To the extent that they cannot readily be eliminated, the West must try to make its propaganda as effective as that put forth by the Communist countries. The best means of protection against the influence of propaganda which is not based on facts is the nurture of critical abilities in the developing countries.

An evaluation of the two systems should entail:
  (i) a statement of the differences and their probable influence on development; and
  (ii) an appraisal of these differences and influences by the value standards of the developing countries.

The fundamental difference between the two systems from the standpoint of economic policy lies in the disparity between the number of instruments of economic policy at their disposal. The number is much larger in the case of the Communist countries. In general, a larger number of instruments makes it possible to reach a set of goals with more precision than a smaller number of instru-

ments. In plain terms, Western economies may more easily get out of control. They may and generally do reveal instances of individual interests being served in opposition to community interests and of very unequal income distribution, partly as a consequence of private ownership of the means of production.

The main drawback — in the restricted economic sphere — of the Communist system and the corresponding advantage of the mixed system of the West is to be found in the level of efficiency of the instruments available. A multiplicity of instruments necessarily leads to red tape and friction; it discourages quick action at the lower level, say the level of the single factory or the single man. Free enterprise and private ownership of the means of production do, in contrast, stimulate action at the lower level. An appraisal of the relative effectiveness of the two systems turns on estimates of the strength of these opposed forces: more precise guidance with perhaps less stimulus in the Communist system, less precise guidance with perhaps more stimulus in the mixed system. Unfortunately our knowledge of the quantitative effect of these forces is still so rudimentary that no clear judgment is possible. It was stated earlier that one of the first crude criteria, the output-capital ratio, has not yet been measured accurately enough to draw conclusions.

Apart from these objective measurements, the appraisal by developing countries is different from that by developed countries, for the latter attach a much higher value to freedom as such. The weight given an increase in production, on the other hand, will be greater in developing countries than in developed countries, because of the lower level of consumption.

The foregoing makes it understandable that the Communist system has a considerable attraction for certain groups of politicians in developing countries. The most important contribution the economist can make is to point out that the choice is not necessarily a choice between the extremes, rather it is one of an optimum combination of institutions and instruments in every case.

There is a second form of competition now going on between the two systems or rather, in this case, the two groups of developed

Table 2–6

GOVERNMENTAL AID TO NEWLY DEVELOPING COUNTRIES: A
COMPARISON OF THE WEST AND THE SOVIET AREA, 1956–1959
(in billions)

	THE WEST				SOVIET AREA		
	Total	Grants[a]	Net Loans		Total	Grants[a]	Net Loans
Total	$14.64	$10.16	$4.48	Total	$0.60	$0.03	$0.57
United States	8.42	5.57	2.85				
France	3.36	2.73	0.63				
United Kingdom	1.03	0.72	0.31				
Germany (F. R.)	0.48	0.13	0.35				
Other West	1.35	1.01	0.34				

Note: The figures are estimates of actual disbursements. They exclude military aid, private financing, postwar reparations and indemnification payments. It should be noted that Sino-Soviet area commitments (as distinct from disbursements) for credits and grants, excluding military aid, totaled $2.3 billion for the same period. Both figures exclude aid transactions inside the Sino-Soviet bloc.

a. Including contributions through multilateral agencies.

Sources: "Aid in Perspective," *The Economist,* August 16, 1961, pp. 788–790; OEEC, *The Flow of Financial Resources to Countries in Course of Economic Development 1956–1959,* Paris, 1961, p. 9.

countries — competition in financial and technical assistance. The common philosophy evidently is that the process of development can be accelerated if foreign capital is added to domestic savings and foreign knowledge is offered to build up production units and train people. In addition it is believed that such help will be appreciated by the countries receiving it.

The West has an advantage in this type of activity in that it has more resources at its disposal. Accordingly the total aid given by Western countries greatly surpasses the help given by Communist countries, as Table 2–6 shows. Despite this, the West has not fully utilized its potentialities. This not only hurts the competitive position of the West but, what is worse, it does a disservice to the underdeveloped countries, and hence to the cause of international solidarity. In addition the publicity — or propaganda — accom-

panying the foreign aid struggle has been more effective on the Communist side.

The competition between the two systems as well as the decisions which the underdeveloped countries will finally take are of great importance to the upcoming economies and to the world at large. As already observed, there should be an awareness on all sides that the decisions are not necessarily between black and white alternatives. It is not true that the systems are diametrically opposite, nor even that they are unchanging and unchangeable. The two already have many features in common; elements from each can be combined, leading to new mixed systems. The present Western economies are themselves a mixture between pure 19th century capitalism and socialism. Both systems will continue to learn from experience, and from each other, and will continue to change. Economic science teaches us[18] that the optimum probably is a mixed system. Economic forces will therefore be at work tending to move both systems toward the optimum. It is of extreme importance that further research be undertaken to develop this theme and to collect more precise information.

18. See J. Tinbergen, "The Theory of the Optimum Regime," *Selected Papers*, North-Holland Publishing Company, Amsterdam, 1959, p. 264.

THE CRUSADE AGAINST PROTECTION

3.1 THE OLD CONTROVERSY: STATE OF THE DEBATE

Our analysis of the world's tensions led us to concentrate on the problem of underdevelopment. So far we have discussed this problem in terms of the economic conditions prevailing in the less developed nations. Now it is time to turn to the external conditions confronting the developing countries, and we will begin with a discussion of trade policy. The postwar era has been characterized by a crusade against protection. This has taken the form of an organized attempt to reduce trade barriers, against the opposition of manifold forces and interests.

The controversy between advocates of free trade and advocates

of protection is one of the oldest in modern economics. Trade policy is among the important instruments of economic control, and what form it takes is of significance to today's underdeveloped countries. More than a century of experience, intensive discussion, and analysis has left us with relatively sophisticated and temperate views on the subject; hence more agreement is possible than in the past. In this section an attempt will be made to summarize the current state of the debate over theory. Subsequent sections will be devoted to the practical arguments.

We must realize that the concepts of free trade and protection are not equally definitive. Free trade is a more precise term than protection, for protection is a relative matter. There may be a greater difference between a high-tariff policy and a low-tariff policy than between a low-tariff policy and a free-trade policy. For policy-making purposes, the significant need is to indicate what level of protection is optimal; as a limiting case this level may be zero, meaning free trade. It must be added that there is a clear asymmetry in the assumptions made when a protectionist as opposed to a free-trade policy is recommended. Protection is usually advocated as a second-best solution. This may be illustrated by the "optimum tariff" thesis. According to this thesis a relatively large country can maximize its real national expenditure by the imposition of an import tariff which will favorably affect the terms of trade, i.e., the price ratio between export and import goods. The case for an optimum tariff can only be proved in terms of the national interest of the country under consideration, that is, in terms of a restriction — which makes it a second-best policy. The infant-industry argument also rests on a restrictive assumption, namely the impossibility that industrial growth can be better promoted by other means, such as lump-sum subsidies. Actually, such subsidies have the advantage of not distorting the marginal decisions of producers and consumers, and in this respect they permit a closer approach to the optimum of well-being. Finally, it should be realized that mixed solutions are possible, a fact which deprives the issue of much of its clarity.

The position can best be characterized by stating the conditions

which must obtain in order to prove the case for free trade. Protection will then emerge as the second-best solution in a number of exceptional cases, covering an important segment of reality.

Free trade can be shown to be compatible with maximum well-being for the world provided that:

(i) income is sufficiently redistributed among citizens within each country and among countries themselves;

(ii) temporary subsidies are given to young industries which have not yet reached a normal level of productivity (infant industries);

(iii) subsidies are given to support industries so vital that no interruption of supply can be tolerated;

(iv) subsidies are given to retrain workers, and to facilitate the transfer of capital from declining industries to new and profitable ones.

As indicated, free trade can exert a favorable influence only within the framework of other institutions; it may not be the best regime if certain conditions are not fulfilled. Condition (i) is the most fundamental; it implies that in the absence of sufficient income equality some protection may yield a better result.[1] Of course the question is, what is a "sufficient" degree of equality? Theoretically, it would be such as to equalize the marginal utilities, or the satisfactions, derived from the last dollars of all personal incomes. Practically, this must be interpreted to mean the maximum degree of income equality which is compatible with the other aims of economic policy. As for the distribution within national boundaries, the income distribution of the socially most advanced countries may serve as an immediate objective for developed societies and as a long-term goal for developing societies. The socially most advanced countries may be Scandinavia in the Western world and Poland or Yugoslavia in the Communist world. The question of the income distribution among countries will be taken up in Chapter 6.

1. See J. Marcus Fleming, "The Optimal Tariff from an International Point of View," *Review of Economics and Statistics,* February 1956, pp. 1 ff. Fleming makes this point a main issue in his plea for protection by underdeveloped countries — considered as a group.

Condition (ii) expresses the belief that it is in the general interest that industries which in the long run will become competitive be supported in their early stages. As stated above, lump-sum subsidies are theoretically the best type of help because they do not falsify the marginal decisions of producers and consumers. In plain language this means that it is better to keep prices at a competitive level and subsidize producers than to protect them by an import duty to be passed on to consumers in the price they pay. High prices reduce consumption and promote undesirable substitutions.

Condition (iii) refers to the fact that since international trade is subject to interruption in times of stress, a country is well advised to produce essential commodities at home even though this is more costly than acquiring them abroad.

Because capital goods are long-lived and skills are difficult to acquire, changes in data over time are likely to lead to a sub-optimal use of the factors of production. In condition (iv) we take the position that subsidies may reduce these losses by bringing about a quicker change-over than would otherwise occur.

In cases (ii)–(iv) the point is that free competition, and thus free trade, will not by itself lead to an optimum use of resources; other devices must be incorporated and subsidies are preferable to protection. The case for some protection can be made only if the "cost" of subsidies (including all of the sacrifices connected with them) is greater than the cost of protection (including the consequences stemming from the falsification of marginal decisions).

This means that protection — at a level to be specified later — can be defended (a) for underdeveloped countries:

(i) if they have an insufficient share of the world's income; and
(ii) if it is difficult or impossible to organize subsidies for industries which have not yet reached their optimum size;

and (b) for all countries:

(iii) if it is difficult or impossible to organize subsidies for vital industries, such as agriculture, which have to be operated even at a loss to guard against any interruption of supplies; and
(iv) if it is impossible to finance measures designed to enhance the mobility of capital and labor in any other way.

In some circumstances protection can also be defended as an instrument of retaliation, or as a means of improving the bargaining position of a victim of unfair practices by others.

As an indication of the state of the debate in practical policy we may consider the rules of the General Agreement on Tariffs and Trade (GATT) and their application. These involve the acceptance of tariffs for infant industries in underdeveloped countries. They permit quantitative restrictions in the case of balance of payments difficulties in developed as well as underdeveloped countries, although the rules are more lenient with regard to the latter.[2]

The GATT rules concerning government assistance to economic development are to be found in Article XVIII of the General Agreement. In paragraph 1 of this article in the original text (1947) it is stated that: "The Contracting Parties recognize that special governmental assistance may be required to promote the establishment, development or reconstruction of particular industries or branches of agriculture and that in appropriate circumstances the grant of such assistance in the form of protective measures is justified." Tariff protection therefore is accorded complete recognition by the Contracting Parties.

Remarkably, this article was rarely applied though it was discussed in detail during the preliminary consultations. The explanation is probably to be found in the many possibilities of escape via other articles. In the ninth session (1955) a completely new Article XVIII came into being. Again a large number of specific regulations were added in order to give a precise meaning to this exception to free trade. The main improvement, however, is the more positive phrasing employed, as follows: "The Contracting Parties recognize that the attainment of the objectives of this agreement will be facilitated by the progressive development of their economies, particularly of those Contracting Parties the economies of which can only support low standards of living and are in the early stages of development." Means available for developmental purposes are described in paragraph 2, viz.: "(a) sufficient flexibility in

2. See Articles XII and XVIII.

their tariff structure to be able to grant the tariff protection required for the establishment of a particular industry and (b) quantitative restrictions for balance of payments purposes in a manner which takes full account of the continued high level of demand for imports likely to be generated by their programmes of economic development."

The new text makes a clear distinction between countries which have "low standards of living and are in early stages of development" and other countries.

Article XIX deals with "emergency action on imports of particular products": "If, as a result of unforeseen developments and of the effect of the obligations incurred by a contracting party under this Agreement, including tariff concessions, any product is being imported into the territory of that contracting party in such increased quantities and under such conditions as to cause or threaten serious injury to domestic producers in that territory of like or directly competitive products, the contracting party shall be free, in respect of such product, and to the extent and for such time as may be necessary to prevent or remedy such injury, to suspend the obligation in whole or in part or to withdraw or modify the concession."

Although this article specifies rather narrowly the situations for which it is intended, it could probably also be invoked to cover cases of temporary protection during a transition period in which resources are shifted to other occupations.

Thus the GATT rules are in line with our cases (ii) and (iv) in which protection can be defended. As for case (i), developing countries usually will have balance of payments difficulties as a consequence of a "continued high level of demand for imports likely to be generated by their programmes of economic development" (Art. XVIII, 2, b), so that as a general rule this case will be covered too.

3.2 ITO, GATT, AND REALITY

The actual situation with regard to trade policy is rather different from the ideal situation and from the aims of GATT. It is

well known that the GATT aims are a more modest edition of the original aims of the International Trade Organization (ITO). In fact, ITO as first proposed paid more attention to the relationships between trade policy and general economic policies than did its successor, GATT.

An analysis of the postwar history of trade policy and negotiations in the international field may help us understand some of the present difficulties, but it should not induce a feeling of resignation. The trade policy of the past has been characterized by a considerable degree of protection, protection invoked by countries not justified by circumstances in employing it. Apart from the war, which made trade impediments temporarily unavoidable, tradition in several important countries must be blamed for this unhappy situation. Whenever technical and economic development led to the rise of new industries in some countries, vested interests in other countries asked for protection. Governments have not, as a rule, been the strong counterforces to the protectionists which they should have been in the interest of consumers and export industries. This is partly because a considerable interest is involved in the industry seeking protection, whereas for consumers and export industries smaller interests are at stake in any one case of protection, though consumers are numerically the largest interest group. The protection-seeking industries have also been successful because they have maintained better lobbies than the other interested parties. In general we may say that governments have made a mistake in not granting protection on a temporary basis and at a decreasing rate. Infant industries should be protected only until they attain sufficient scale to enable them to compete.[3]

Governments have been slow to participate in the postwar crusade against protection. Because of political pressures, governments were not given wide powers to reduce tariffs. Also, many governments were themselves unwilling to permit international discussion of some of their restrictive measures, such as internal taxes on specific products. Discriminatory internal taxes were not admitted

3. It may be stated here that the Dutch government only grants protection to new manufacturing industries on the basis of such a scheme.

to be negotiable in GATT, although their restrictive effect is much the same as that of import duties. This is not to say that no results have been obtained. There have been several encouraging developments, but they have been confined to relatively small groups of countries or have required a disproportionate amount of effort.

As an example of a laggard attitude the policy of the United States government may be mentioned. This policy precludes over-all tariff reductions and requires item-by-item negotiations, often with one government at a time. It is therefore very time-consuming and inefficient — even when the most-favored-nation clause general-izes the result. Other countries, like the United Kingdom, are not much better as a rule. This is evidence of a "fear of commitment" which inhibits the West in matters of foreign trade. It is a fear which takes various forms and affects other policies besides those pertaining to trade.

Another example of an unsatisfactory policy is to lower import duties while increasing internal taxes. Such a policy was applied by Germany in the case of coffee.

A particularly unsatisfactory aspect of trade policy is the imposi-tion of quantitative restrictions on goods from low-wage countries, especially Japan, India, and Hong Kong. Two elements must be distinguished when considering the problem of this policy. One encompasses the trade between Communist and non-Communist countries. This problem will not be specifically dealt with in this study; it will be mentioned only in Chapter 10, where the relation-ships between these two groups of countries are given some atten-tion. The other element is the one of trade, within the non-Com-munist area, between developing and developed countries, or, as it is sometimes put, of "trade with low-wage countries."[4] The idea that a special policy is necessary in dealing with low-wage countries rests on an erroneous interpretation of economic relations and facts. Low wages by themselves are not a threat, since they are usually the consequence and expression of a generally low level of produc-

4. For both elements see Harlan Cleveland, ed., *The Promise of World Tensions*, Macmillan, New York, 1961, p. 54; the remarks made there seem pertinent.

tivity and, for all industries combined, just compensate for this lack. As a normal phenomenon this implies that industries which are more productive than the national average will have lower prices while industries which are inferior in this respect will have higher prices.[5]

When Japan joined GATT in 1955, a number of countries reserved the right to maintain quantitative import restrictions on the ground of Article XXXV.[6] Member countries not invoking this privilege felt the full force of Japanese competition. As a consequence, Germany, which had not taken advantage of Article XXXV, resorted to "administrative restrictions" with regard to the import of Japanese cotton fabrics. After she was reproved in GATT meetings she gradually reformed. Italy applied similar restrictions.

5. Interesting examples have been given by Sir Donald MacDougall in "British and American Exports," *Economic Journal*, 1951, pp. 707 ff. At the time of this investigation the average level of productivity of the United States was double that of the United Kingdom. In pig iron, motor cars, and machinery the United States was from 3.6 to 2.7 times as productive, and accordingly it had a much larger share of the world market. In cement, woolen, worsted, and cotton spinning and weaving, on the other hand, the United States was less than twice as productive as Britain, and here American shares in the world market were very small in comparison with British.

The Japanese situation is just as diversified. While the prices of some commodities are much lower than in the United States, in many other instances Japanese prices are higher than American. This is shown by a table presented in a study by C. Tsukuda ("The Role of Wage Costs in Japanese Exports," *Selected Papers*, Six-Month Diploma Course in Economic Planning and National Accounting, Institute of Social Studies, The Hague, 1961, Part II, Table 5):

Price Ratios (Japan/USA) for Selected Commodities, 1954–1955

Motor gasoline, etc.	2.167	Canned tuna	0.337
Refined sugar	1.947	Socks for men	0.565
Zinc ingots	1.577	Viscose rayon	0.613
Ammonium sulphate, etc.	1.561	Cotton fabrics, standard type	0.700
Wire	1.343	Urea resins, etc.	0.740
Newsprint, wrapping paper	1.330	Cordages (sisal)	0.803
Caustic soda, soda ash	1.273	Cotton yarn, 20, 30, 40	0.820

6. Art. XXXV: "This Agreement, or alternatively Article II of this Agreement, shall not apply as between any contracting party and any other contracting party if:
"(a) the two contracting parties have not entered into tariff negotiations with each other; and
"(b) either of the contracting parties, at the time either becomes a contracting party, does not consent to such application."

Toward the end of 1960 a provision concerning "market disruption" was accepted by GATT. It may be considered a refinement of Article XIX on emergency action. In cases of market disruption the contracting parties are empowered to seek constructive solutions consistent with the basic aims of GATT. This decision led to the acceptance of a "short-term agreement" on trade in cotton fabrics in 1961. It provides that during one year importing countries can limit their purchases from the various supplying countries to the amount taken in the previous year. An element of discrimination is implicit here. It is true that the exporting low-wage countries themselves signed the agreement, but it seems clear that if they had not done so some importing countries would have interpreted the decision on market disruption to mean that they had the right to autonomous discriminating protection.

The 1961 agreement was followed by a long-term arrangement which will be discussed later (see section 8.7, p. 158).

Our thesis that there is no need to be "afraid" of low-wage countries is illustrated by the fact that these countries are just as afraid of us as we are of them — and with a bit more justification, since we enjoy the advantage of increasing returns on indivisibilities much more than they do. As long as prices are calculated correctly — and here we face another question — there is no point in excluding low-wage products from foreign markets. It is precisely from such comparative advantages that international trade derives its *raison d'être*.

Measures against dumping can be justified, but as temporary measures only. Dumping is an expression of disequilibria which will not as a rule persist. It is necessary, from an industry point of view, only as long as capacity surpasses demand at normal prices. It may be used as a means of entering a certain market, but it is not in the interest of a country to dump persistently or on a broad scale. A condition of overcapacity in one industry will automatically stimulate the development of other industries, provided general depressions are avoided. Also, with the over-all development of a country, wages will rise. All these considerations tend to support provisions against dumping, but on a short-term basis only.

The trade policies and, closely linked with them, the exchange policies of many underdeveloped countries are complicated and un-satisfactory. High import duties, severe and changing quantitative restrictions, multiple exchange rates, and long payment delays are some of their best known features. This situation has one central cause: a balance of payments deficit on current account, which is identical with a surplus of national expenditure over national in-come. This must be understood in the light of the desire of the economically lagging countries to develop more quickly, and the well-known slow growth of their export markets. Part of the pro-tectionism of these countries can be justified on the basis of the infant-industry argument, although one doubts whether some of the industries concerned will ever become competitive.

Western experts and international agencies like the IBRD and the International Monetary Fund (IMF) usually advise underde-veloped countries either to reduce their expenditures or to raise more taxes. This is technically correct, but it underestimates the institutional difficulties which these countries face. The simplest solution, namely more foreign aid, is not altogether a bad one, since it is desirable in itself and may help in the long run to elimi-nate the institutional problems.

3.3   BIG POWERS AND GIANT POWERS:
THE NUISANCE OF *KLEINSTAATEREI*

The reduction of trade impediments among smaller groups of countries constitutes a separate chapter in the story of world trade since the war. Europe has been particularly active in this field. The movement toward European integration originated because coun-tries previously considered "big powers" felt that the world was be-coming dominated by "giant powers," nowadays the United States and the Soviet Union, soon possibly China and India.

France, Western Germany, and Italy, and also to some extent the United Kingdom, became more and more conscious of this shift in emphasis. Smaller countries had already realized that their influ-

ence could only be exerted through some form of co-operation.[7] After World War II Western European countries generally felt that for political and economic reasons some form of integration was desirable, if not imperative. Politically, only a unified Europe could play a role comparable to that of the two giants — and the possible future giants in Asia; economically, the idea was that prosperity depends on the size of the market. To be sure, the popular idea sometimes expounded, that America's prosperity is mainly due to the size of its market, is grossly exaggerated. By far the most important factors are capital per head and technical and organizational skill. Both are considerably higher in the United States than in Europe and probably explain most of the difference in well-being. But it cannot be denied that a big uniform market will stimulate competition, specialization, and productivity. It will also reduce the waste inherent in a large number of small political units. The phenomenon of fragmentation was characteristic of 18th century Germany, where it was known as *Kleinstaaterei;* it was overcome toward the end of the 19th century — though imposed on Germany again to a degree after the Second World War for fear of Germany's power. It exists today in Western Europe if that area is considered as a whole. No doubt the phenomenon has some advantages from a humanistic point of view; it has deep cultural roots which cannot, should not, and need not be cut off.

The process of European co-operation and partial integration was greatly stimulated by the European Recovery Program (Marshall Plan), which with unprecedented farsightedness and generosity first helped the war-stricken countries to gather momentum in their efforts at economic reconstruction and development. It is an example of the type of approach now needed in other fields.

The appeal of a big market was mainly responsible for the efforts made by the Organization for European Economic Co-operation (OEEC) and the European Payments Union (EPU) to reduce the trade and payment barriers built up during the war. Quotas were

7. The prewar activity of the so-called "Oslo states" may be cited in this connection.

abolished and payments facilities broadened. This latter move helped to re-establish the multilateral character of European trade and production. However, liberalization occurred only with regard to quantitative restrictions; it did not include import duties. In this respect the small-scale experiments of the Benelux countries and the European Coal and Steel Community (ECSC) were pioneering efforts. Later the Rome Treaty laid the basis for a customs union among the six countries of the European Economic Community (EEC). This is to take shape over some twelve years, starting in 1958.[8] Actually, the Rome Treaty envisions more than a customs union; the intent is to create an economic union with several elements of positive integration, i.e., supranational agencies and common policies. While other factors are undoubtedly involved, it is significant that the countries participating in this scheme have experienced an unprecedented rate of economic growth. Since the reconstruction period, the annual rise in real income in the region has been some 5 per cent per annum.

Although the changes under way are rapid and remarkable from a historical point of view, against the background of the needs of our times they are less impressive. The fear of commitment is at work at many spots and in many minds. It holds up a really forceful integration of Europe's economies and, even more, of its political units. The only way to make Western Europe really strong is to create supranational agencies for tasks which technically can best be carried out at a European level. Agencies such as the Coal and Steel Community, the European Defense Community, the European Economic Community, and Euratom have been opposed by forces of an irrational nationalist or isolationist character, which are not even culturally significant. The only issue involved is a somewhat egoistic desire not to bind one's hands. This attitude has been particularly strong in the United Kingdom and the Commonwealth, areas well known for their preference for very loose forms of co-

8. The progress made since 1958 is illustrated by the following figures, expressing internal tariffs between EEC member countries on January 1, 1962 as a percentage of the initial level: industrial products, 60; nonliberalized agrarian products, 65; liberalized agrarian products, 70.

operation. It is cause for great satisfaction that the United Kingdom has now applied for membership in the Common Market.

The attitude just criticized is by no means restricted to British politicians and British public opinion. In France forces are at work which may damage the true interests of that country and of Europe, forces which have been well described by Lüthy.[9] One may contend that the signatories to the Rome Treaty have sometimes given in to conservative forces, as in the financial and monetary sectors (see Chapter 9). But the construction they accepted is far superior to the inconsistent structure of a free-trade area with its red tape as to the origin of commodities, and it is much closer to what an objective analysis of the requirements of the situation would show to be necessary in the interest of maximum efficiency.

The slowness of the negotiations centering around European unity, especially those concerning the interests of third countries, has given rise to some apprehension in the countries most affected by European integration. Two groups of countries are involved: those having a large volume of trade with the European Economic Community and those competing in export markets against the privileged associated territories. The outside world as a whole will hardly be affected by the establishment of the EEC since average import duties have not been increased.[10] A temporary decline in the competitive position of outside producers can be expected; prices of EEC products may become lower, but the resulting disequilibrium in the balance of payments of the EEC with the rest of the world will eventually eliminate this differential. The process of adjustment may be helped by the measures of "social harmonization" (increase in women's wages, overtime payments) required by the Rome Treaty.

There will, however, be cases — mostly industrial — where product prices will not return to their former level. They will settle at

9. H. Lüthy, *A l'heure de son clocher — Essai sur la France*, Calman-Lévy, Paris, 1955.

10. J. Tinbergen and associates, "The Impact of the European Economic Community on Third Countries," in *Sciences humaines et intégration européenne*, A. W. Sijthoff, Leiden, 1960, pp. 386 ff.

Table 3–1

OVER-ALL INCIDENCE OF TARIFF DISCRIMINATION
BY THE EEC AGAINST CERTAIN OUTSIDE COUNTRIES
(discrimination as a percentage of the total value of exports of the outside country)

Australia	0.03	Iraq	0.26
Austria	1.52	Liberia	0.00
Brazil	0.73	New Zealand	0.13
Burma	0.07	Nicaragua	0.39
Ceylon	0.21	Pakistan	0.00
Colombia	0.59	Portugal	0.50
Costa Rica	1.38	Salvador	0.88
Cuba	2.82	Saudi Arabia	0.00
Dominican Republic	3.52	Spain	1.49
Ecuador	1.47	Thailand	0.08
Greece	1.89	Turkey	1.19
Guatemala	0.50	United Arab Republic	0.11
Honduras	0.60	Uruguay	0.08
Iceland	0.80	Yugoslavia	0.88
Iran	1.12		

Note: By tariff discrimination the authors mean the difference between the tariff paid by the country considered and the average tariff paid by all importers. Among the latter the imports from other EEC countries are included; since no tariff is paid on these imports, the average tariff is always lower than the tariff paid by outside countries.

Source: J. Tinbergen and associates, "The Impact of the European Economic Community on Third Countries," in *Sciences humaines et intégration européenne*, A. W. Sijthoff, Leiden, 1960, p. 393.

a lower level,[11] and competing outside countries will have to adapt themselves to this condition. This is one way in which consumers in the outside world will profit from the increase in productivity brought about by European integration. At the same time the higher level of economic activity in EEC countries will create a greater demand for imports, especially since the EEC region is highly dependent on foreign sources for many of its industrial inputs.

11. In contrast some underdeveloped countries fear price increases, because of decreased competition as a result of the formation of EEC cartels. Whether or not this fear is justified will depend on EEC antitrust policy.

Even though the outside world as a whole may not be unfavorably affected by the establishment of the EEC, some individual countries will suffer. This is true of those countries that supplied relatively more commodities to the low-tariff constituents of the EEC like Benelux than to the high-tariff members like France. The equalization of duties damages them more in their Benelux exports than it helps them in their exports to France. It is also true that the structure of the EEC implies discriminatory treatment of outside countries, a policy which is indefensible even though grounded in the past. An over-all picture of the discrimination implied in the tariff structure is given in Table 3–1.

3.4 ECLA LEADS THE WAY

The tensions created by European integration are understandable. They should not, however, lead to any retreat, for the creation of bigger economic and political units will contribute to the well-being of the world as a whole. There are two positive and constructive developments one must hope for: a reduction in the outer tariffs of EEC, and similar acts of integration in other parts of the world. This topic will be discussed more fully in Part II of this study. Here we will merely recount the current status of efforts to integrate elsewhere in the world.

A remarkable example of continental thinking has been given by the Economic Commission for Latin America and its (former) Executive Secretary, Raúl Prebisch. ECLA has been a leader among the international agencies in the field of pure research: it was the first to apply comprehensive input-output analysis to countries and linear programming to industries of the continent. In suggesting development plans and policies ECLA has been more advanced and more courageous than any other international agency, even though the suggestions made by GATT have been more acceptable politically. Because of Latin America's cultural and economic solidarity some progress toward political integration has also been possible, although, as in Europe, vested interests have reacted adversely and governments have been loath to commit themselves. A long distance

will have to be covered before substantial results can be obtained. Yet a beginning has been made in the co-operation of the five Central American states and in shaping a Free-Trade Area in Latin America as a whole.

The main tensions in Latin America today may be summarized under the following categories:

(i) in general the desire for rapid development stands in contrast to the slow expansion of world markets for primary goods; thus it creates balance of payments difficulties and the phenomenon of inflation;

(ii) the difference in the economic development of the United States and Latin America has given rise to economic tics which sometimes have political overtones: the Latin American countries, and especially Cuba, have rejected the hegemony of the United States, but Latin America regards the United States as an obvious source of financial assistance;

(iii) Europe's association with overseas territories tends to accentuate a certain discrimination against Latin American products, e.g., coffee, cocoa, bananas, meat;

(iv) within the continent there is some difference in attitude toward co-operation; the biggest country, Brazil, is inclined to go its own way while the other nations are more inclined toward a common policy.

It is only to be expected that in the remaining regions of the world — in Asia (including Australia, which cannot be considered a region by itself) and Africa — integration would be in a less advanced stage. Since many countries in these areas only recently became politically independent, they are not yet ready to consider giving up a measure of their national autonomy.

This is not to say that co-operation is unknown. In the Arab region it exists to a modest extent in the Arab League. This had initially a political and a defensive character, and thus it has a Joint Defence Council and a Permanent Military Commission. But there is also an Economic Council and some economic achievements can be recorded. Import duties on agrarian products have been abolished between most of the members, and the tariff on a

number of industrial articles has been reduced (25 per cent to 60 per cent below the general tariff). This liberalization was meant to pave the way to a customs union, but import license requirements substantially mitigate the influence of the tariff reductions.

Some years ago the League members agreed upon the formation of an Arab Development Bank ("Arab Financial Institution for Economic Development") with a capital of 25 million Egyptian pounds. This bank will have many features in common with the IBRD. Recently agreement was achieved on the countries' capital participations and the institution is now being set up. After the United Arab Republic, Kuwait will be the largest single contributor. It is hoped that the Bank may lead to further investments in the region for development purposes by the oil-producing members of the Arab League (see Appendix II, p. 213).

The League has organized regular Arab Oil Conferences ever since 1959. Representatives of other oil-producing countries and of oil companies are invited to these congresses.

The Arab League has been active in the cultural field too. The Institute of Advanced Arab Studies, the Centre of Registration of Arab Publications, and the Cultural Museum, all in Cairo, attest to this fact.

The formation of EEC appears to have stimulated attempts at economic co-operation in Arabia. In all of the Arab countries studies have been made as to how this co-operation can be expanded. At the same time it is realized that there will be many political and institutional roadblocks; the tendency to domination by the United Arab Republic is a case in point. There is a great difference of opinion concerning the length of time it will take to achieve far-reaching economic co-operation in the Arab region.

In Africa the economic desirability of some form of co-operation is clear enough. European integration might bring about some disintegration in this area because countries linked to the EEC by economic ties are in a somewhat privileged position in comparison with other African nations and trade between these two groups may be less than optimal. As far as the countries formerly or still in the Commonwealth are concerned, some solution to this problem will

soon emerge, as will be seen in Chapter 8. The situation in Africa changes so rapidly that it is difficult to pin down the causes of tension. However, it is worth noting that many of these new countries are so politically conscious that economic interests are often subordinated to political ends. This can be illustrated by the controversy between two important groups of African countries, the Casablanca Group and the Monrovia Group. Mali, the principal hinterland of Senegal, is a member of the Casablanca Group, while Senegal is a member of the Monrovia Group. This difference in political orientation has led to the official disruption of economic relations. Ghana's economic policy is to improve the trade position of Upper Volta vis-à-vis the Republic of the Ivory Coast, because the Ivory Coast belongs to the Monrovia Group while Upper Volta is a potential member of the Casablanca Group to which Ghana belongs.

Similar problems exist in Asia, where political issues have also done damage to the cause of economic co-operation. Many political obstacles must be overcome before co-operation can materialize. The greatest of these is apparently the contrast between the Communist and the non-Communist nations of the region. Even in the long run, there seems to be little hope for close co-operation — on a voluntary basis — between these two groups. The schism between the uncommitted and the pro-Western countries, and antagonisms caused by more down-to-earth matters, such as boundary disputes and personal relationships among political leaders, are other sources of trouble.

The Asian countries also face difficult problems in the economic field. Most of these stem from differences in development level and competitive strength. In this respect Asia is certainly less homogeneous than Africa. Some countries already have a fairly well developed industrial sector; Japan is essentially an industrial country. The least advanced economies are afraid of the more developed ones, and any co-operative scheme must take this into account. Also, because several countries have at present no foreign trade problems or balance of payments difficulties, they are not particularly inter-

ested in plans to expand intraregional trade — a clear case of myopia in the underdeveloped world.

Instances of successful regional co-operation exist, but most are limited in the nature of the activities co-ordinated and the geographical scope of the arrangement. Familiar cases are the lower Mekong River development scheme — in which Cambodia, Laos, Thailand, and southern Viet-Nam participate — and the Indus Valley project, a joint undertaking of India and Pakistan. In recent years the ECAFE Secretariat has increased its activities in the field of regional collaboration, and has made more attempts to strengthen economic co-operation among its member states.

Among the more ambitious co-operative schemes, the plans for deepening and widening economic co-operation between the Asian Commonwealth countries would seem to be the most realistic, especially as trade between them is already given preferential treatment. India is the great sponsor of this idea. On a more modest geographical scale the Federation of Malaya and Singapore want to integrate their economies and to extend this co-operation to Greater Malaysia, which includes some smaller Borneo territories. Outside the Commonwealth sphere, another co-operative group must be mentioned: the Association of Southeast Asia. This newly established association is made up of Thailand, the Philippines, and (again) the Federation of Malaya. So far, only a very loose form of co-operation is envisioned.

3.5 A SURVEY OF TODAY'S TRADE STRUCTURE

It seems desirable to find out, with the aid of objective criteria, in what respects today's pattern of international trade deviates from the most desirable quantitative structure: between which pairs of countries do we actually find much less trade than an optimum division of labor would suggest?

Data on duties and quantitative restrictions do not by themselves provide an answer to this question. The effect of duties and restrictions on trade must be determined. In principle this quantity

should be measured by comparing actual trade flows with those which would occur in an optimal situation. Quantitative restrictions may be harmless if they permit a volume of trade not much lower than normal. The effect of duties depends on the price elasticity of demand for the goods concerned, and the same duty level may have different consequences for different commodities. The imposition of a uniform level of duties may simply lead to an adjustment of the country's exchange rate; it need not reduce the volume of trade at all.

The optimum pattern of trade can be defined in various ways. If all of the conditions enumerated in section 3.1 are fulfilled, optimum trade will be identical with free trade. Otherwise it may differ from free trade in ways not easy to estimate.

The problem has a micro and a macroversion: it may be posed for individual goods or for trade as a whole. The microversion would require many difficult operations; the macroversion seems more practicable, and at the same time more pertinent. The macroversion of the problem entails estimating the optimum volume of total trade between any two trade partners. The most practical way to do this is to assume that this figure depends on a few general characteristics of the countries considered, and to estimate the numerical parameters of this relationship from actual trade figures. This implies that trade between most of the pairs of countries is not restricted and can therefore be considered as an indication of the most desirable volume of trade. Alternatively, the relationship can be estimated on the basis of the trade figures between selected pairs of countries which apply no restrictions.

On the basis of earlier and more detailed empirical studies[12] as well as theoretical analysis, it was concluded that the most significant determinants of optimum trade were the size of the two countries forming each pair, and their geographic separation. The measure chosen to represent size was gross national product. The size of the receiving country plays a twofold role: it is an indication of the country's general volume of demand and also of its degree of diver-

12. Conducted by Mr. G. J. Aeyelts Averink, at the Netherlands Economic Institute.

sity of production. For this reason one should expect the influence of size to be less than proportionate: the greater a country's diversification, the less its need for imports. The size of the supplying country is an indication of its capacity to provide goods for export. Geographic separation is relevant for the obvious reason that it costs to move goods from one place to another. Since this cost is higher the farther the goods have to travel, distance must be expected to have a negative effect on imports. In the tradition of economic research, the explanatory variables have been assumed to influence the volume of trade according to a constant-elasticity function.

In some of our calculations we used money incomes; in others, real incomes, i.e., money incomes divided by a price index. It will be seen that this distinction had little effect on the results.

Three sets of calculations were made: one using figures for 18 countries (i.e., 306 pairs), another using figures for 42 countries (1,722 pairs), and a third using figures for 28 countries (766 pairs). The results of the calculations are shown in Table 3–2. A more detailed account of the material used and the calculations made will be found in Appendix VI. Before summarizing the conclusions to be drawn from the results we will make a few prefatory remarks.

Figures pertaining to the balance of payments for services given in Table VI–10 of Appendix VI show that in the majority of the cases this item is far less than the difference between the actual trade and the calculated "ideal" trade. Moreover, most countries are either mainly exporters or mainly importers of services. Our main conclusions therefore will not be changed substantially by the neglect of service imports and exports, even though trade in services will change the picture for individual countries.

As will be set forth in more technical detail in Appendix VI, deviations between the actual trade and the calculated "theoretical" trade may be due to import and export restrictions in all of the countries concerned. Import restrictions will as a rule operate most intensively on the trade flow they are applied to, but there will be indirect repercussions on the imports of the affected exporter since that country must try to maintain equilibrium in its balance of

Table 3–2

DEVIATIONS FROM STANDARDIZED INTERNATIONAL TRADE FLOWS, FOR COUNTRIES HAVING A SMALLER VOLUME OF TRADE THAN EXPECTED

(deviation as a percentage of actual trade)

	DEVIATIONS OF EXPORTS, ACCORDING TO SEVEN CALCULATIONS							DEVIATIONS OF IMPORTS, ACCORDING TO SEVEN CALCULATIONS						
	A-1	B-1	B-2	B-3	B-4	B-5	C-2	A-1	B-1	B-2	B-3	B-4	B-5	C-2
1. Argentina	..							..						
2. Brazil	-42							-46						
3. Chile	..						..	..						..
4. Cuba	..				-124	-66	..	..				-204	-150	..
5. Mexico	..						..	..						
6. Peru	..							..						
7. Uruguay	..	-11	-28		-13		..	..						
8. Venezuela							..	..				-60	-8	..
9. Belgian Congo	..							..						
10. Ethiopia	..								-10	-8				..
11. Ghana	..							..						

#	Country												
12.	Morocco	:											
13.	Nigeria	:											
14.	S. Africa	−73					−9						
15.	Sudan	:											
16.	Fr. W. Africa	:											
17.	Afghanistan	:						−6	−5	−8	−25	−2	−19
18.	Ceylon	:											
19.	India	−4	−8	−81	−42	−217	:	−6	−33	−34	−24	−18	−121
20.	Indonesia	:					:		−34	−34	−18	−19	
21.	Japan	−144					−128						
22.	Malaya	:					:						
23.	Pakistan	−3	−18	−43	−159	:	:		−39	−10	−104		
24.	Philippines	:	−49	−9	−9	:	:		−103	−59			
25.	Thailand	:	:	−9	−9	:	:						
26.	UAR (Egypt)	−29	−23	−21	−9	−9	:	:					
27.	Iran	:	:	:	:	:	:	:					
28.	Turkey	−27	−23	−21	−1	−8	−22	−57					
29.	Canada	−13	−33	−23	−18	−40	−65	−62	−44	−78	−13	−65	
30.	USA	−64	−55	−81	−55	−73	−28	−42	−21	−32	−13	−43	−76

Table 3–2 (continued)

	DEVIATIONS OF EXPORTS, ACCORDING TO SEVEN CALCULATIONS							DEVIATIONS OF IMPORTS, ACCORDING TO SEVEN CALCULATIONS						
	A-1	B-1	B-2	B-3	B-4	B-5	C-2	A-1	B-1	B-2	B-3	B-4	B-5	C-2
31. Austria	–35			–14		–2	–18	–41			–21		–8	
32. BLEU		–1	–11	–42	–85	–97	–23		–10	–23	–62	–102	–112	–27
33. Denmark														
34. France	–108	–102	–136	–115	–267	–80	–194	–95	–129	–160	–152	–296	–120	–150
35. Germany (Fed. Rep.)		–11	–27	–92	–93	–62	–11	–4	–44	–62	–139	–147	–101	–67
36. Italy	–79	–37	–49	–96	–113	–68	–82	–51	–23	–34	–75	–106	–49	–24
37. Netherlands				–26	–33	–78	–27				–37	–28	–64	
38. Norway	–24													
39. Sweden														
40. Switzerland	–2		–13				...	–2		–11				...
41. UK	–10	–25	–8	–65	–18	–109	–45	–4	–19	–4	–105	–10	–91	–36
42. Australia	–44							–68						

... means no figure available.   A blank indicates a positive deviation.   For further explanation see text and Appendix VI.

payments. Conversely, if we find that the imports of any country are below the theoretical value, the explanation may either be that this country applies restrictions or that the restrictions it experiences in its export markets indirectly influence the size of its imports.

Trade restrictions are most damaging when they prevent developing countries from importing a sufficient volume of the goods necessary for economic expansion. In this sense the negative deviations recorded for imports are more telling than those noted for exports. In cases where a "too" low level of imports is coupled with a "too" low level of exports, the deficiency must be ascribed mainly to the import restrictions of other countries. The typical "victim" of such import restrictions therefore must be characterized by too low figures on both sides of the trade balance.

The main conclusions to be derived from our inquiry may be summarized as follows:

First of all there emerges a normal pattern of trade; in all of our calculations we find a correlation coefficient of about 0.8 and fairly stable regression coefficients.[13] Roughly speaking, the standard pattern implies that the "normal" (or "theoretical," or "ideal") trade flow between any two countries will be proportional to the gross national products of these countries and inversely proportional to the distance between them. The first surprise is that the income of the importing country has a proportionate influence, notwithstanding the fact that some correlation might be expected between size and self-sufficiency. This seems to have a direct bearing on another surprise, namely that the only group of countries showing a consistently (and considerably) subnormal volume of trade (on the import as well as the export side) are the large industrial countries. This can only be ascribed to the restrictive practices of these countries or to their greater diversity of production, but the latter apparently is not so highly correlated with gross national product as we had expected. In fact, for 28 countries where a concentration

13. The correlation coefficient is a measure of the degree of similarity in the movements of two sets of figures. Completely parallel movement is reflected in a value of +1, completely opposite movement in a coefficient of −1; a zero value indicates absence of similarity.

coefficient for exports — which may be considered a crude indication of a country's "lack of diversity" — was available, the correlation between that concentration coefficient and gross national product amounted to only 0.54.

Our main result stands at variance with the belief that there is more trade between industrial countries than between nonindustrial countries. To be sure, this notion is correct in an absolute sense, but it is not correct if proportionality with gross national product is taken as a criterion of the normative level of such trade. Among the big industrial countries it is interesting to note that France — and to some extent the Belgo-Luxembourg Economic Union — is more restrictive and the United States less restrictive than the average. The smaller industrial countries including Japan do not show marked deviations from the theoretical norm; this implies that Japan is not a victim of the import restrictions of others.

We do not find clear examples of trade victims among the developing countries either. It is true that India, Pakistan, the United Arab Republic, and Turkey show a negative deviation on the export side (less exports than expected theoretically) in at least four calculations, but in some instances the deviation is barely significant. Pakistan shows a negative deviation on the import side in three calculations, India in two calculations. Afghanistan and Indonesia show subnormal imports in at least three cases, but they do not show subnormal exports — which may mean that it is their own autonomous restrictions which are at issue. Several other countries — Cuba, Venezuela, Ethiopia, and the Philippines — show too low imports in two cases. The only clear-cut cases where import restrictions reduced purchasing power are therefore Pakistan and, possibly, India.

It is clear that more research will be needed before firmer conclusions can be drawn. For what our conclusions may be worth, it follows that trade policies should not be overemphasized as an instrument in development; thus, we do not think the slogan "Trade, not aid" a proper guide to action.

D A M P I N G
T H E   W A V E S

4.1 THE GREAT DEPRESSION, KEYNES,
AND TODAY'S CYCLES

The environment in which developing countries have to conduct their affairs is affected by a number of political decisions pertaining to stabilization as well as by trade policy. Most but not all of these decisions are made by the big countries of the West. They center around two main objectives, nowadays generally recognized as desirable: the stabilization of general demand, and the stabilization of the prices of certain key primary products. In this context, stabilization means the avoidance of cyclical variations; it does not encompass the elimination of secular trend or seasonal pattern.

In this section methods of stabilizing general demand, usually described as anticyclical policies, will be discussed. Our approach to economic cycles has changed drastically during recent decades.

It was the tragedy of the thirties that many economists and politicians failed to understand the mechanism of cycles. One general misunderstanding was the idea that cycles were unavoidable. This probably arose because cycles had persisted for over a century; it was reinforced by a strong belief in laissez faire. Since the great depression, which greatly stimulated economic thinking, economists have isolated the main factors involved and traced their relationship. It is now clear that there exist instruments of economic policy that can be used to damp strong fluctuations in total demand, and to avoid the cumulative effects of disturbances which are unavoidable in a dynamic society. It is also apparent that while there is scope for government action in this field, government can be given a well-defined and limited task; there is no reason for business to fear large-scale intervention. The instrumentality is mainly public finance, and the method is to make compensatory changes in net public demand, i.e., government expenditures minus taxes.[1]

Of course, problems remain, but they cannot be compared with those that existed during the great depression. Then the role of government was imperfectly understood, and mistakes were made. Too much importance was attached to the restoration of "confidence" as a factor making for investment demand. Building faith in the government's fiscal position was thought to be the key to recovery. Public expenditures were reduced in the erroneous belief that the solvency of the state depended upon a balanced budget. However, the decline in public spending undermined confidence in the future because of its direct impact on demand.

As long as the forces making for cycles were poorly understood, governments resorted to regulation of the markets for single products strongly affected by the decrease in demand. Such regulation was highly esteemed and ironically some business groups willingly gave up more freedom of action than was actually necessary. A more stable flow of total demand, to be obtained with the aid of general anticyclical policies, will make future stabilization arrangements less complicated.

---

1. A more sophisticated approach would take into account the fact that the multipliers for expenditures and for taxes are not equal and that hence it is not strictly the difference between the two that matters.

John Maynard Keynes was without doubt the greatest single contributor to our knowledge of the nature of cycles. Granted that not all his arguments were accurately presented and his method sometimes stimulated the adoption of inappropriate policies, and that many other economists have made important contributions to our understanding of cycles, the vision of Lord Keynes and the terms he coined in order to popularize his views left a decisive imprint on modern theory.

In the present connection the most important lesson to be learned from the unhappy thirties is the failure of nationalism in economic policies. Much damage was done by policies which sought to enhance one nation's interest at the expense of others. This was true of trade restrictions and devaluations, both applied frequently and intensively in that period. These measures were designed to alter the balance of trade in favor of certain countries rather than to improve the position of the world at large.

On the whole the lessons of the thirties have been understood by economists and politicians. The anticyclical policies embraced by governments today differ widely from those of the thirties. Deficit spending was then considered a major sin; it is now accepted as a natural means of combating depression. It must be admitted that politicians do not always reject deficit spending in boom conditions as strongly as they should, and that the problem of creeping inflation is partly due to this attitude. One must hope that the proper discipline and flexibility will eventually develop in this field, but it should never be forgotten that unemployment is much worse than overemployment or inflation since it places a heavy burden on the economically weakest segment of the population.

The proper anticyclical policies are also the first line of defense against price instability in primary markets — a main problem for developing countries. It is significant that these policies are now accepted in the developed countries. Certainly our changed attitude toward stabilization is one of the reasons why we have been relatively free of cycles since the end of World War II. It is worth noting that in a period of equal length after World War I two major depressions occurred. The argument that our recent stability is simply the consequence of favorable long cycles, and that the

danger has not vanished, is not convincing, for the instruments which have been used successfully to compensate for minor cycles can be used just as well in the event of any longer-term decline in private investment. We are now much better equipped to face set-backs. If private investment should weaken as a result of some saturation of the motor car or television markets, or as a result of a reduced need for reinvestment, or lower armament expenditures, our annual analysis would make it possible to apply compensatory measures which would keep total demand at its trend value. There is nothing mysterious about such a policy; therefore it need not affect confidence in the future. This is certainly one of the advantages of commodity flow analyses and central plans.

Policy-makers in the trade and monetary sphere also benefited from the lessons of the thirties. It is largely because of this that the IMF policy of prohibiting competitive devaluation and co-operative bans on trade policy weapons have been widely accepted.

4.2   THE NEED FOR A DOUBLE LOCK ON COMMODITY MARKETS

As noted above, better anticyclical policies of a general character will reduce the wide price fluctuations characteristic of primary markets by stabilizing demand. The main reason for the excessive disorganization of these markets in the thirties — prices fell to about one-third in many of them and huge stocks accumulated in others — was doubtless a failure of demand. But other factors also contribute to the instability of individual markets. The following may be mentioned:

> (i) variations in crop yields are considerable and random, i.e., they are unpredictable a year ahead;
>
> (ii) since the production processes of many primary commodities (coffee, rubber, cattle, pigs, and in a way all crops) require a considerable length of time, varying from six months to more than seven years, supplies cannot be rapidly accommodated to changes in demand;
>
> (iii) the elasticities of demand and supply are often low;

(iv) several primary products are objects of speculation, a phenomenon that sometimes accentuates price movements.[2]

The need for special measures to stabilize price formation in primary markets has been widely felt, and a number of proposals have been made. Even though action is not as urgent as it was in the thirties, there are important reasons to provide primary markets with a "second lock," just as engineers are accustomed to work with safety factors of two or three. Indeed, the regular and orderly development of many countries depends so much on primary markets that their stabilization — within reasonable limits — is an important aspect of development policies.[3]

More stability may be obtained in a variety of ways, each of them beset by difficulties. Simple price setting will not work as a rule; it must be supplemented by quantitative regulations. Regulations on the demand side include rationing in times of scarcity and an obligation to buy more than would otherwise be the case in times of abundance. Such a program can be enforced with the co-operation of government agencies, but it has clear limitations.

Regulations on the supply side may be applied either in the sphere of trade, mostly foreign trade, or in that of production. In times of abundance supplies in trade can be restricted by stock accumulation on the part of a public or private organization. When not backed by restrictions in production such a program may soon lead to heavy financial burdens. The regulation of production requires more elaborate organization since it depends on the co-operation of individual producers, who usually are very numerous. Measures to enlarge supply in times of scarcity include subsidies of many kinds, commitments to purchase a certain quantity of a certain product, and obligations to produce certain minimum quantities; they have either financial or psychological drawbacks.

All of the measures mentioned may be applied to a market as a

2. See H. Rijken van Olst, *Prijsstabiliteit en speculatie* (unpublished doctoral thesis), Netherlands School of Economics, Rotterdam, 1948.

3. This is illustrated by the fact that a 10 per cent decline in the value of the exports of less developed countries offsets all aid received. See H. W. Singer, "Trends in Economic Thought on Underdevelopment," *Social Research*, Winter 1961.

whole or to only a portion of it, for example, to some of the large supplying countries. Practically, they have to be international in scope; they require the agreement of a number of governments on certain specific quantities, i.e., the level of prices or the volume of demand or supply. Such agreement is difficult to obtain since governments often have conflicting interests.

Occasionally, control is so centralized that agreement between governments is unnecessary. One case is that in which one country supplies a sufficiently large part of the total supply to enable it to dominate the market. A traditional example is that of Brazil and the coffee market; a less important one is that of Indonesia and the kapok market. Such situations are rare nowadays, but there is another possibility. If a single agency has the financial means to buy all the temporary surpluses that may develop, it can, by well-devised speculation, stabilize the market by itself.

Each kind of regulation has been applied recently, and some of the results will be discussed briefly in the next section.

4.3 THE FEAR OF COMMITMENT: POSTWAR MUDDLING

In general, the progress made in the field of international commodity agreements since the war has been disappointing, the more so since the world should have benefited from prewar experience in this area. The almost fatal price instability of a large number of primary international commodities during the period 1901 to 1951 has been documented by the United Nations.[4]

Perhaps the circumstances after the Second World War have been less pressing; among other things, anticyclical policy in several countries has had a stabilizing effect, and demand has only occasionally slackened. But uncertainty continues to plague international trade in primary products, mainly because of the factors mentioned in section 4.2. Therefore governments might have been

4. *Instability in Export Markets of Underdeveloped Countries,* United Nations, New York, 1952 (Sales no.: 1952. II.A.1.).

expected to show more alertness and co-operation in negotiating and implementing new commodity agreements. However, negotiations have often been lengthy and abortive because of the fear of commitment. Short-term national interests have prevailed. In a rising market sellers have not been interested, in a falling market buyers have not been interested, and few countries have shown interest in markets in which they were not immediately engaged.

One might attribute shortsightedness and irresponsibility to many of the governments concerned. Yet it must be admitted — especially in the case of agreements where both importing and exporting countries are represented — that there are quite understandable impediments to progress. Countries may hesitate to commit themselves because of the complexity of the subject. They may fear that a lack of balance between producing and consuming countries will weaken the force of the agreement. Such fears have sometimes proved to be justified, as in the case of the Wheat Agreement where, as will be shown, exporting countries increased their export prices to such a high level that they impaired the Agreement's flexibility. Countries that are very susceptible to outside competition are most concerned about the number of prospective signatories to an agreement. An agreement may serve the interest of an exporting country that is strongly dependent on a single commodity, but there are many cases in which a country's import and export interests conflict. Compromise solutions may be difficult to arrive at unless the agreement is extended to a range of commodities, a move which would give rise to more complicated and costly administrative arrangements. The number of single-commodity agreements could be extended, but not all commodities are adaptable to this purpose and, again, this would involve higher costs. Then there is uncertainty as to the actual influence on prices and incomes of the regulations contemplated in the agreement. Finally, there are technical problems — centralized or decentralized storage, the capacity of the storage facilities, financing methods, etc. — which are not always easy to solve. All these factors explain why it is often very difficult to come to an agreement. Yet they do not provide sufficient justification for a fear of commitment.

4.4   A BRIEF SURVEY OF IMPORTANT
COMMODITY MARKETS

The commodity agreements in operation are the Wheat Agreement, the Sugar Agreement, the Tin Agreement, and the Coffee Agreement. We will discuss these pacts briefly in the light of the problems mentioned above and then consider the prospects for agreements in other areas.

In their study *Trends in International Trade*, a panel of experts[5] gave considerable attention to international commodity agreements and found that there were three methods of implementation in general use. Thus the Wheat Agreement is mainly based on the principle of the multilateral long-term contract, the Sugar Agreement and the Coffee Agreement on the principle of quota restrictions on exports, and the Tin Agreement on the buffer stock principle.

The International Wheat Agreement

Wheat is the most important internationally traded agricultural commodity. Changes in the wheat market have repercussions on the world markets for most staple products. The International Wheat Agreement attempts to stabilize world grain markets by assuring wheat supplies to importing countries and markets for wheat to exporting countries at equitable and stable prices. The Agreement came into being in 1949 after long negotiations; it was revised in 1953, 1956, and 1959. In 1956 the participating exporting countries were Argentina, Australia, Canada, France, Sweden, and the United States; participating importing member countries numbered 44. In 1959 Italy, Mexico, and Spain joined the exporting countries. The United Kingdom refrained from participation until 1958 because she was opposed to the onesided price fixing of Canada and the United States, which resulted in high prices and surplus stocks.

The terms of the Agreement are such that as long as prices on the international wheat market remain between a specified maximum and a minimum level (the former being about 30 per cent higher than the latter), trade is entirely free. If in a given year the free world market

5. *Trends in International Trade*, a Report by a Panel of Experts, GATT, Geneva, October 1958.

price exceeds the upper limit, exporting countries are obliged to sell a certain quantity of wheat (so-called guaranteed sales) at the maximum price to member importers in the same year. On the other hand, if world market prices fall below the lower limit, importing countries have to make "guaranteed purchases." Total guaranteed sales are equal to total guaranteed purchases. The Agreement is administered by the International Wheat Council, which was set up in 1942. The importing countries together hold the same number of votes as the exporting countries. Voting rights are distributed according to the quantities guaranteed. This means that the United States and Canada, the largest exporters, are in fact the administrators of the Agreement.

The results of the Wheat Agreement have been disappointing. In the period 1949–1953 free world market prices were so high that the Agreement's prices were at their maximum. After 1953 free world wheat prices decreased substantially but the Council's prices were maintained at a relatively high level despite accumulating world surpluses. In fact prices were fixed by the United States and Canada on the basis of national price regulations, through operations with local wheat stocks.[6] This situation still persists. The Wheat Agreement did not result in an elimination or reduction of national price regulations for wheat. On the contrary, the international price structure of wheat has been greatly disturbed by government interference in all important wheat-producing countries.

The 1959 agreement is somewhat more flexible than the original agreement. Importing countries guarantee to buy not fixed quantities but a percentage of their total wheat imports. In order to give more attention to the surplus problem, and perhaps in order to counteract the price regulations of the United States and Canada, the United Kingdom joined the Agreement. This is an obvious gain in coverage. But although the participating countries account for about 85 per cent of the world's wheat trade, only half of the world trade is subject to the rules of the Agreement, for the rules apply only to commercial transactions between member countries; "special transactions" such as bilateral agreements, credit and barter arrangements, and gifts are excluded. So far there is no indication that the Agreement has contributed to the substitution of multilateral for bilateral trade; the latter is on the whole even preferred by the participating countries.

6. The fact that the governments of these exporting countries are in a position to control the world price of wheat by local stock manipulations and other means would make it difficult to apply the international buffer stock principle to wheat (see *Trends in International Trade,* p. 76).

Serious concern for the future is expressed in a report of an FAO Committee on Commodity Problems.[7] The report states that the world grain situation is characterized by an imbalance between supply and consumption. It further observes that the situation is most serious with regard to wheat, although increasing concern is felt over coarse grains. The rise in consumption is not keeping pace with the rise in production, so that stocks continue to pile up. Wheat prices have been fairly stable, but prices of coarse grains have shown a downward trend. A need for more effective international co-ordination of governmental action is apparent.

The United Nations Wheat Conference met in January 1962 to discuss the content of a new agreement, as the present one expires on August 1, 1962. Apart from a number of technical and administrative matters, attention was focused on the problem of exporting surplus wheat to underdeveloped countries without disturbing the normal commercial trade. It is hoped that more countries will participate and submit to the regulations of the Agreement.

The International Sugar Agreement

The International Sugar Agreement uses quota restrictions on exports to regulate the volume of trade in the free market, i.e., that segment of the world not covered by special trading arrangements. It seeks to stabilize world sugar prices within a given range by adjusting the quotas granted to exporting countries.

The first agreement was concluded in 1937; it was ratified by 21 countries and covered a period of five years. In 1942 the commercial rules of the Agreement were suspended as a consequence of the war. The International Sugar Council remained active and made a sustained effort to draft a new agreement. This agreement came into force on January 1, 1954. The present International Sugar Agreement which became effective on January 1, 1959 is a continuation of it and also runs for five years. There are 44 members: 18 importing countries and 26 exporting countries. The general objectives of the Agreement are: to assure supplies of sugar at stable prices which are acceptable to consumers and producers alike; to increase the consumption of sugar; and, by providing adequate returns to producers, to maintain the purchasing power of countries and areas which are dependent upon the production or export of sugar. It is recognized that a fair return is also desirable so that fair wages and decent working conditions can be maintained.

The world sugar market is characterized by preferential blocs. A

7. *Report of the Thirty-fourth Session of the Committee on Commodity Problems to the Thirty-fifth Session of the Council of FAO*, Rome, 1961 (Doc. C 61/8).

large part of the world sugar trade takes place within the confines set by the preferential regulations of the United Kingdom, the United States, France, and Portugal. The rest of the world sugar market, about 40 per cent, is known as the "free market." Only this part falls under the jurisdiction of the Agreement.

The initial export quotas are based on yearly estimates of the needs of the participating importing countries. The Council can make new estimates before April 1st of each calendar year and change the quotas accordingly (the maximum reduction is 20 per cent). Exporting countries are expected to retain minimum stocks at the beginning of the crop year amounting to 12.5 per cent of their basic export tonnage. Members of the Commonwealth Sugar Agreement reserve a special stock for the free market. If the market price rises above a certain level (at present $3.75 per 100 lbs.), stocks must be reinforced. Exceptions are made for the British Commonwealth, the United States, the USSR, France, and Portugal. Basic export quotas are also set by the Council for the USSR, France, and Portugal. A combined export quota for the Commonwealth is fixed by the British Commonwealth Sugar Agreement. Estimates are made of the USSR exports.

There is a certain understanding and complementarity between the "free market" and the preferential blocs.[8] Thus, although the Sugar Agreement covers less than half the world sugar market, it has undoubtedly had a stabilizing effect.

Many serious problems remain nevertheless. Although consumption is rising, particularly in some low-income areas, the increase is slower than the increase in production.[9] Moreover, production during the last ten years increased most in importing countries, which means that international sugar trade has grown at a much slower rate than world production and consumption. There is also a tendency for individual importing countries to become more self-sufficient and even to become net exporters. All of these matters have the full attention of the International Sugar Council. In accordance with a decision of the 1961 UN Sugar Conference, and with a view to the preparation of a new Sugar Agreement, the Council is going to undertake an extensive study of the stock problem; it will also make recommendations designed to increase

8. This is probably one of the reasons why the Agreement has been fairly successful. With regard to quota arrangements in general, a panel of experts is of the opinion that "they are liable to break down unless the agreement covers virtually all exporters or unless the importing countries in the agreement take effective measures to limit their imports from outside countries." (See *Trends in International Trade*, pp. 75–76.)

9. See *FAO Commodity Review 1961*, Rome, 1961 (Doc. CCP 61/9, p. 61).

consumption, including non-human consumption. However, the Council has not yet succeeded in fixing new basic export quotas adapted to the radical change in the pattern of international sugar trade caused by the end of trade relations between the United States and Cuba.[10]

The International Sugar Agreement expires in 1963. It is hoped that the new agreement will cover a larger part of the sugar market[11] and be less complicated than its predecessor.

The International Tin Agreement

The most important producers of tin ore are the Federation of Malaya, Bolivia, Indonesia, Congo, Thailand, and Nigeria. These countries produce most of the world's tin excluding the Sino-Soviet area. There have always been problems in the tin market. Production costs vary widely and vested producing interests have often suffered as a result of severe competition from newcomers. On the demand side, there have been marked fluctuations in consumption due to cyclical movements, technical difficulties, and stock problems. Still greater swings have occurred in prices, even if we consider yearly averages.

From the beginning of the twenties until 1953, when the International Tin Agreement was concluded, several attempts were made to stabilize the world tin market (Bandung Pool, 1921; Tin Producers Association, 1929; in 1931 the International Tin Committee and an International Tin Pool; in 1935 a buffer stock). All were based on co-operation between producers only. When the London Metal Exchange reopened after the war, the price of tin showed excessive instability. This led to more intensive contacts and consultations between producers, but it was not until 1956 that the International Tin Agreement came into operation. The Tin Agreement, which was revised in 1961, is the third international raw material agreement to come under the auspices of the United Nations. The governing body is the International Tin Council.

The International Tin Agreement is the only commodity agreement which utilizes the principle of buffer stocks. The buffer stock is controlled by the Council. Producing countries contribute to it, a maximum of 75 per cent in tin metal and the rest in cash. The function of

10. The most striking development during the discussions on this subject was that Cuba, which lost about 3 million tons as a result of being shut out of the American preferential market, claimed a basic tonnage of 7.3 million tons for the free market, covering its original quota of 2.4 million tons and total deliveries of 4.9 million tons to the Communist countries.

11. South Africa relinquished its share in the Commonwealth combined export quota and obtained an independent quota in the free-market sector of the Agreement.

the buffer stock is to keep tin prices between certain limits. If the price of "cash" tin at the London Metal Exchange is equal to or higher than the upper limit (in 1961, £880 per ton, now £965), the Council must sell tin until the cash price is lower than the maximum price or until the buffer stock is exhausted. If the price of cash tin is lower than the minimum price (during 1961, £730, at present £790), the Buffer Stock Manager will try to purchase tin until the cash price is above the minimum or his money resources are exhausted. The Manager also has discretion to sell or to purchase if the price is approaching the upper or the lower limit, respectively. The Council can impose quota restrictions on exports if the buffer stock exceeds 10,000 tons (the maximum buffer stock is 25,000 tons) in order to maintain the price of tin metal within the set range. Its decisions are based on estimates of future demand, stocks, prices, and so on. The total export volume agreed upon is shared between the producing countries according to their percentage shares in total production.

The International Tin Agreement has no doubt contributed to price stability. It has done so without extensive government control, although the Manager has considerable authority to act. The system is regarded as workable even if not all producing and consuming countries are participants (it covers about 80 per cent of world production and about 50 per cent of world consumption, both excluding the USSR and Communist China). It would be gratifying if the United States and Germany, as major consuming countries, joined the Agreement. The United States reportedly is opposed to any extension of systems based on buffer stocks. According to recent information, however, it is prepared to discuss terms on which it might join the International Tin Agreement. The United States has built up an enormous strategic stockpile of tin, but it has announced that it will not disturb the market by selling large quantities of surplus metal.

That the present situation vis-à-vis the United States is unsatisfactory is indicated by recent developments. One of the problems of the Tin Council is the prompt adaptation of maximum and minimum prices to changes in supply and demand. The price of cash tin had risen to £830 per ton in April 1961; by June 1961 it was £880 per ton and the Manager's Buffer Stock was being exhausted. The tin price continued to rise, reaching £992 per ton in September 1961, a level in excess of the ceiling set by the Agreement. Export controls have been in abeyance since October 1960 but producing countries feel that the existing price range is unfair to the industry. Although their proposal to raise the floor and ceiling prices (to £800 and £1,000 respectively) has been rejected by the Council, the matter is still undecided. As long as there is

uncertainty about the possibility of releasing tin from the United States stockpile in order to help regulate prices and as long as the Buffer Stock Manager has no tin to sell, the Council finds it impracticable to raise support prices. The present agreement expires on July 1, 1962. Producing countries have announced that they will withdraw from the Council and form a separate pool if their proposal is rejected again.

Behind all this muddling and horse-trading is the fact that market conditions have changed. A lag in production has been apparent for some time. No new fields have been found in the non-Communist world in recent decades so lower-grade deposits have to be explored despite the high initial costs. At the same time consumption is steadily increasing. International co-operation should be adapted to the new market situation.

The International Coffee Agreement

According to a study made by the Food and Agriculture Organization,[12] coffee production since 1930 falls into three distinct periods. The first (1930–1939) was characterized by slowly increasing production and the accumulation of surplus stocks; the second (1940–1947), by declining production; and the third (1947 to date), by rapidly expanding plantings stimulated by postwar price increases and, since 1957, the growth of massive surplus stocks.

The FAO notes that the pattern of world production changed considerably after 1947. During the 1947–1959 period production increased in Brazil by 84 per cent, in Colombia by 27 per cent, and in other Latin American countries by 66 per cent. At the same time production in Africa and the other continents increased by 150 per cent. The increase in tonnage in Brazil was, however, greater than that in all other coffee-growing countries combined. At present coffee is produced in over forty countries; Brazil accounts for about 50 per cent of world production, Colombia for some 15 per cent, and African producers for about 25 per cent.

During the period 1946–1949 prices rose due to increasing consumption and the reduction of stocks; it was a period of renewed planting. The 1950–1957 period saw unprecedented price increases, and a boom in coffee tree planting. Since 1958 there has been a period of adjustment and prices have declined. For the first time since the Second World War the coffee industry is faced with a serious problem of overproduction and stock accumulation caused by the maturation of trees in substantial quantities. World coffee consumption at present is at a record level and

12. *Bulletin No. 31,* FAO Commodity Series, Rome, 1959.

may increase still further, especially in the producing countries of Latin America. It is improbable, however, that the increasing supplies can be absorbed by consumers at prices acceptable to producers.

The increasing need for integrated programs for the improvement of the coffee industry has led to the establishment and strengthening of several multilateral bodies concerned with coffee in Latin America and Africa. In 1959 the International Coffee Agreement, combining Latin American and African producers, came into force; it was renewed in 1960, with only slight modifications, for a period of one year. There are 28 participating countries, accounting for over 90 per cent of world output. The Agreement is based on the principle of export quota regulations. According to the 1960 agreement, countries may choose between export quotas equal to the quantities shipped by them in their peak export year during the past ten years and quotas amounting to 88 per cent of their exportable production during one of the two years the Agreement has been in force. Brazil and Colombia have fixed quotas. Since world consumption continues to lag far behind production, the export restrictions of the Agreement are not sufficient to stabilize the market although they do prevent major price declines.

The International Coffee Study Group is now studying the possibility of a long-term world-wide Coffee Agreement between producing and consuming countries, with export quotas and a common policy toward stocks. The existence and even the extension of the regional organizations in Africa and Latin America dealing with coffee (for instance, the Inter-African Coffee Organisation, which was founded in December 1960 by six independent African countries, the United Kingdom, and Portugal, recently embraced closer co-operation with Brazil) does not affect the general support for such a long-term agreement. As a result of discussions in September 1961 a committee was set up by the Study Group to draft the text for a new agreement to be discussed at an intergovernmental meeting early in 1962. Meanwhile the existing International Coffee Agreement was renewed for another year. It is hoped that the new agreement will be signed by participating countries before the expiration of the present agreement on August 1, 1962.

The International Tea Agreement

During the past ten years there has been a divergence between the increase in tea production and the growth of international tea trade. Calculations by the FAO show that during this period production rose by 35 per cent and trade by 30 per cent. The gap, however, was filled by increasing consumption in the producing countries. As a result the international tea market is a stable one. Because of these benign cir-

cumstances the International Tea Agreement was not renewed in 1955 though the International Tea Committee was kept in being.

Probably the rate of increase of consumption in producing countries will be somewhat lower in the future. World production is expected to continue to increase at about the same rate. Sooner or later, therefore, a situation may develop which will call for a revival of the International Tea Agreement.

Cocoa

International governmental discussions are under way in order to arrive at an agreement to stabilize cocoa prices. One might wonder why an international agreement did not emerge earlier — especially in the fifties — since cocoa has long been subject to severe price fluctuations. One reason is that the fluctuations of the past were mainly due to sharp year-to-year variations in yield caused by weather conditions and the incidence of plant diseases. Another reason is that demand is virtually incalculable; there has been little uniformity of trend in the main consuming areas. Some producing countries have attempted unique solutions. Thus the Ghana Cocoa Marketing Board makes payments to producers which are not directly linked to export prices. However, most producing countries simply did not pay sufficient attention to the problem of long-term price stability.

In recent years the picture has changed. With the gradual perfecting of production methods, better control of diseases and pests, extension of planted areas, and the maturation of earlier plantings, world production has increased substantially. But since consumption has not kept pace, prices have declined and stocks have accumulated. Producing countries realize that continued low prices threaten their national economies. In October 1960 the FAO Cocoa Study Group set up a working party on price stabilization and one on the promotion of consumption. The first committee prepared a draft agreement to stabilize cocoa prices, which has been sent to the interested governments. The proposed agreement is based on the principle of export quota regulations.

Bananas

About 85 per cent of world output of bananas originates in Latin America. Outside of this region the Canary Islands and Africa are the main producers.[13] Production is strongly susceptible to fluctuations. Although statistics are inadequate, it is apparent that there has been a steady increase in production which is likely to continue in years to

13. See *FAO Commodity Review 1961*, pp. 104–105, and *International Trade 1960*, GATT, Geneva, 1961, p. 31.

come. World exports have increased accordingly; Ecuador's share in the total rose from 1.5 per cent before the war to 25 per cent in 1961. Major importing areas are North America and Western Europe. As a result of growing supplies from low-cost areas, especially Latin America, and increasing competition from other fresh fruit, banana prices have shown a downward tendency.

Although there seems to be no serious disequilibrium between supply and demand at present, the upward trend of production and the competition prevailing seem to warrant the establishment of more contacts between producing and consuming countries. However, although an International Meeting on Banana Production was organized by the FAO in 1960, it dealt only with technical and statistical matters. The Inter-American Banana Organization, which was established in August 1961, is not equipped to control production, trade, or prices, because no agreement was reached with regard to these matters.

Citrus Fruit

An international agreement for citrus fruit is under study. In 1961 the FAO Group on Citrus Fruit made a special investigation of the long-term prospects of these commodities. They found a distinct upward trend in world citrus fruit production in spite of setbacks due to unfavorable weather conditions and competition from other types of fruit. This will most probably be strengthened in the future because of new plantings during recent years and planned further expansion.[14]

It is generally recognized that consumption must be stimulated. Better-organized international co-operation is also felt to be necessary. In view of the complexity of the marketing problems to be expected in the near future as a result of production increases in individual countries, co-ordination of national policies is being studied. Attention is also being paid to the improvement of statistics, standardization, and quality control.

Olive Oil

As for olive oil, the initiative for an international conference was first taken by the FAO early in the fifties. In 1956 a conference was held, on the initiative of the United States, which led to an International Olive Oil Agreement. This covers a number of arrangements with regard to the stimulation of consumption, standardization, the preparation of market surveys, and so on. The Agreement was signed by 14 countries, and has been ratified by nearly all of them. No agreement

14. See *Report of the Fifth Session of the Committee on Commodity Problems*, p. 37; *FAO Commodity Review 1960*, p. 58, and *International Trade 1960*, p. 31.

has yet been reached on organizing the international olive oil market.

However, annual fluctuations in olive crops remain the principal matter for concern. In 1961 the International Olive Council set under way a study of an international price stabilization scheme, which would include financing of stocks. This study is now in progress.

Cotton

The outstanding fact about the international raw cotton market is that the United States is by far the world's largest exporter, accounting for about 40 per cent of world exports. The growth of world cotton trade depends on consumption in industrialized countries and, to a large extent, on import demand in developing countries. Cotton consumption has risen slowly during the last decades, and its role in total fiber consumption has decreased because of competition from rayon and synthetics. If cotton succeeds in remaining fairly competitive with other fibers it may maintain its relative market share.

The United States is the price leader in the raw cotton market. Its export policy ultimately determines world cotton prices. United States policy is characterized by a system of domestic support prices, acreage allotments, marketing quotas, stockpiling, and export subsidies. Admittedly, this system has helped to stabilize world cotton prices. But, being a high-cost producer, the United States has not only imposed relatively high prices on the importing countries, it has also created export and surplus-stock problems for itself. The International Cotton Advisory Committee, which was established at the end of the thirties, repeatedly tried to bring about an international cotton agreement. Many consuming countries took part in the discussions, but in 1954 the question was removed from the agenda. It was felt that no serious overproduction existed, and that United States agricultural policy was a stumbling block. The United States system of export subsidies was censured.

Over the years the Committee has been studying the world cotton economy, production and consumption trends, the exchange of technical information, the problem of cotton surpluses, and so on. Recently it has devoted much attention to the international repercussions of the United States cotton policy, and a study group has been established to look into this question.

Copper

The United States is the main copper-producing country and at the same time the main copper-importing country. The pattern of world trade is distinctly influenced by the fact that there are strong, decen-

tralized but integrated companies, chiefly in the United States and Western Europe, that own mines in the exporting countries and refineries in the importing countries. World demand for copper is expected to increase considerably, mainly because of its use in the electrical engineering field, where technical considerations give it a strong competitive position.

Although there will be short-term changes in world supply-demand relations, which will vary from one area to another, it seems reasonable to assume that future demand will be able to keep pace with supply. In 1958 the UN Exploratory Meeting on Copper concluded that there was no need for further action. Since then no consultations at the governmental level have been initiated. Although there may be voluntary restrictions on production, there is no indication that an international long-term agreement will be effectuated in the foreseeable future. Because of the predominant position of a high-cost developed country and the typical structure of the copper market, the terms of an agreement would have to be most carefully studied.

Lead

The United States consumes about 40 per cent of free-world lead supplies, the United Kingdom about 17 per cent, and the EEC countries 25 per cent. The United States is also the biggest importer. The main exporters of ore and metal are Australia, Canada, Mexico, Morocco, Peru, and some Western European countries. The international trade pattern of lead is, again, partly determined by property rights. American, British, and French industrial concerns have interests in Peruvian, Mexican, Canadian, and African lead production.

The production of lead and zinc is often closely related, especially in Australia. Lead prices are below zinc prices, however, and the market prospects for lead are less favorable than those for zinc. In recent years lead prices have been depressed by a continuous oversupply, resulting in increasing stocks. In September 1960 the UN International Lead and Zinc Study Group decided to continue voluntary curtailments in market supplies. The result was unsatisfactory. In March 1961 the Study Group agreed on curtailments of mine and/or metal production by a number of producing countries. These reductions have not been put into effect, and world demand has continued to lag behind production. Meanwhile partial solutions have been considered. In the United States financial aid to the lead and zinc mining industry has been proposed and is a subject of discussion in Congress. Barter transactions between the United States and Canada and Australia have provided only temporary relief. There is of course general agreement as to the

need to encourage consumption. Exports from the centrally planned countries are an uncertain factor, but this applies to most commodities.

Zinc

As is true of lead, zinc has end uses in which it is not substitutable, and others in which its position is less secure. But on the whole the prospects for zinc are better than those for lead. Zinc prices have been relatively stable, and consumption is developing satisfactorily. The stock position differs from that of lead in that zinc stocks are only excessive locally. The United States holds the largest part of world zinc stocks, but most American producers have brought about a reduction in surplus stocks. Although the situation is not entirely satisfactory, the International Lead and Zinc Study Group decided at its 1961 meeting that for the time being there was no reason to take action to reduce zinc supplies. The group felt, however, that long-term studies should be undertaken and that the search for new applications should be pushed. A working party has been established to go into these matters; it will also make inquiries into the possibility of intergovernmental agreements.

4.5   SOME ATTEMPTS AT SHORTCUTS

As should be clear from the preceding section, the road toward stabilization of commodity markets with the help of international agreements is not an easy one. A large number of organizational steps must be taken, and agreement is sometimes difficult to obtain. Many years of administrative work are involved. Experts and politicians have occasionally asked whether simpler solutions are not possible. One simpler solution has already been mentioned: a large buffer stock operated by a single agency. Three other proposals have been the subject of thorough discussion by expert groups established by the Secretary-General of the United Nations.

The first of these proposals was formulated in a report of 1949[15] in the context of a general anticyclical policy. Its purpose is to compensate countries that are unable to maintain their imports because of a decline in their export income. These countries would be entitled to draw the necessary currencies from the IMF. The

15. *National and International Measures for Full Employment,* United Nations, New York, 1949 (Sales no.: 1949, II.A.3). Members of the group were J. M. Clark (working in association with A. Smithies), N. Kaldor, P. Uri, E. R. Walker (chairman).

IMF would obtain these currencies from the countries whose imports had fallen in the first place if, and only if, the fall was a consequence of inadequate anticyclical policies on their part. The adequacy of anticyclical policies would be judged on the basis of employment figures.

The second proposal was formulated by a member of another group that published a report in 1953.[16] It was taken up again and unanimously accepted in a form worked out in a report of 1961.[17] The aim is roughly the same as that of the proposal just described. The means is an insurance scheme comparable to the unemployment insurance plans in industrial countries. A fund would be created which would be fed by contributions from all countries adhering to the scheme. These contributions would amount to a few tenths of 1 per cent of national income, or about 1 per cent of exports if all countries should participate. Benefits would be paid to member countries that experienced a decline in exports amounting to more than 2.5 per cent of the moving average of the three preceding years; they would cover the loss beyond this percentage to the extent of 50, 75, or 100 per cent. These figures have been so calculated as to leave a favorable balance in the fund for most years, a balance which could be invested in developing countries by the purchase of government bonds. Alternative setups are described in the report, and the characteristics of the benefits are flexible: they may be grants as well as loans.

The third proposal was put forward by the chairman of the second group, Professor Goudriaan. It may be summed up as a joint stabilization scheme for a number of raw materials by the monetization of these goods. It has been referred to as the raw material standard, and has also been advocated by Mr. Benjamin Graham.[18] The main idea is that a certain cocktail of raw material property

16. *Commodity Trade and Economic Development*, United Nations, New York, 1953 (Sales no.: 1954, II.B.1). Members of the group were C. F. Carter, Sumitro Djojohadikusumo, J. Goudriaan (chairman), K. Knorr, F. G. Olano.

17. *International Compensation for Fluctuations in Commodity Trade*, United Nations, New York, 1961 (Sales no.: 1961, II.D.3). Members of the group were I. H. Abdel Rahman, A. Carillo Flores, Sir John G. Crawford (chairman), A. G. Hart, S. Posthuma, M. L. Qureshi.

18. B. Graham, *Storage and Stability*, McGraw-Hill, New York, 1937.

rights (a set of fixed quantities of each of about twenty raw materials) would be accepted by a few of the main central banks as cover for their monetary circulation at a fixed price. Such raw material packages would be purchased by the banks whenever the joint free-market price of the commodities involved fell below the fixed price, and sold by the banks in the opposite case. The stock with the central bank would regulate joint supply and demand in such a way as to keep the average price (weighted according to the composition of the package) constant. Although this scheme would certainly stabilize the average position of all the primary producing countries, it does not exclude the possibility of serious difficulties in single markets.

The first and third of the proposals described have been criticized on technical points. No doubt many difficulties would have to be solved before any of them could be applied. Nevertheless, commodity agreements also present difficulties, and the situation that would exist in the absence of any co-operation would be even more troublesome. Before engaging in activities to stabilize more raw material markets, governments might do well to ask for a comparative study of the schemes presented.

TOMORROW'S WORLD ECONOMY

Policy Suggestions

B R O A D E R   H O R I Z O N S

5.1 ONE WORLD OR NONE: THE NEED FOR WORLD AIMS

In Part I we tried to isolate and analyze the main sources of tension in today's world economy. We found that these could be grouped under the following categories:

    (i) the underdevelopment of a large part of the world;

   (ii) competition between different economic systems;

  (iii) the passing of colonialism;

  (iv) economic instability, especially in primary markets; and

   (v) national shortsightedness, especially in trade policy.

Underdevelopment was considered to be the main problem, and the other problems were discussed in relation to this central issue. In Part II we will attempt to suggest a coherent international economic policy. The world problems involved are closely interrelated and will not necessarily be dealt with one by one.

We must bear in mind that economic policy is formed at many

levels in many countries and international bodies, and that it is interwoven with policies directed at noneconomic aims, such as power, security and many lesser objectives. The motivations of nations are based largely on traditions and historical facts, and they differ widely. Even if it is intellectually clear that important changes are needed, inertia must be reckoned with. The best we can hope for is that political activity can be more systematically directed at the urgent goals of today, that it can be streamlined and made more consistent. In this part of the book we will often suggest what seem to us to be ideal policies or institutions. Nobody could expect these suggestions to be carried out immediately. They may, however, serve as a guide for policy-making at various levels in the longer run. It is the task of the economist to make clear what is the best technical solution to an urgent problem, even if that solution seems at the time "politically impossible." Political opinion is not invariable, nor entirely autonomous; it can be changed by economic arguments, if only with some delay.

This chapter will discuss the principles which should inform a consistent set of policies; it will be a reasoned plea for as broad a point of view as possible. Our attitude may be summarized by the assertion that we can no longer afford the luxury of national autonomy. With regard to security we have already accepted the truth of the warning, "One world or none." We must accustom ourselves to the same idea with regard to economic conditions. Economic policy should serve the ends of the world at large — or, if agreement with the Communist bloc cannot be reached, the ends of the non-Communist world.[1]

We may begin our argument by reminding the reader of past experience with autonomous national policies, economic as well as other. Early in the 20th century, world affairs depended upon the interaction of the national policies of a small number of powerful nations. In economic terminology it was a game of oligopoly. As

1. On this subject see H. W. Singer ("Trends in Economic Thought on Underdevelopment," *Social Research,* Winter 1961), who in addition quotes Arnold Toynbee to the effect that ours is the "first age since the dawn of civilization, some five or six thousand years back, in which people dared to think it practicable to make the benefits of civilization available for the whole human race."

such it had no stable solution, but resulted in a series of conflicts of which World Wars I and II were the most momentous. To be sure, these conflicts were not solely economic, but economic forces played an important role. More recently social factors have become more important — on a national and an international level — but social and economic factors are intimately linked.

Besides contributing to wars and colonial conflicts, economic nationalism severely aggravated the economic difficulties of the thirties, as was pointed out in Chapter 4. During the great depression governments tried to solve their difficulties by measures damaging to other countries' interests, such as trade restrictions and devaluations, instead of adopting a common anticyclical policy of deficit spending. In principle it is clear that a system of autonomous national policies, like an oligopolistic market structure, does not lead to an optimum situation for the group. This optimum requires the general acceptance of a goal which is to the advantage of all concerned. In other circumstances, world policy might soundly be based on the interest of some dominant country; but in the present world it can only be based on the interest of all.

The need to break through narrow nationalist concepts has been increasingly felt for a long time. To illustrate the point we may remind the reader of American participation in two World Wars which initially did not affect the United States, and of the Marshall Plan. The process of broadening the horizons of Western policy-makers is a complicated and irregular one, but it has been gaining momentum and has recently affected economic affairs. To a considerable extent it is a natural development, even from the national standpoint, for with decreasing transportation costs and the increasing interdependence of national economies it is in the national interest to take a broader view. The contrast is less between national and international interests than between a narrower and a broader view of national interests. When national, or even regional, economies could be considered as isolated entities, one country's suffering did not affect the well-being of others. In an interdependent system, economic ills are generalized. Even more important is the possibility that economic distress in one major coun-

try might have an adverse effect on the political stability of the whole world. Violent actions by desperate people may easily lead to widespread conflicts.

In some measure the obligation of one country toward others was understood during the period of colonialism. Most ruling powers felt it their responsibility to fight famines and to enact certain basic laws in the interest of the colonial peoples. This sense of responsibility may be illustrated by the Netherlands Indies law prohibiting the sale of land by Indonesians to foreigners. There are other examples. Nevertheless, the sense of responsibility did not go very far, and it was too weak to prevent happenings which were against the interest of subject peoples.

Since World War II a new sense of responsibility has become apparent, as evidenced by the Colombo Plan and the Point Four Program. These are isolated examples; the most important example of a more systematic approach was, of course, the establishment of the United Nations and its specialized agencies. In the United Nations Charter broad tasks were formulated which may be regarded as an acceptance of world aims for economic policy. Thus according to Article 1, one of the purposes of the United Nations is "to achieve international cooperation in solving international problems of an economic, social, cultural, or humanitarian character . . ." and "to be a center for harmonizing the actions of nations in the attainment of these common ends." Further, Article 55 states that "the United Nations shall promote a) higher standards of living, full employment and conditions of economic and social progress and development. . . ." Article 56 adds that "All members pledge themselves to take joint and separate action in cooperation with the Organization for the achievement of the purposes set forth in Article 55."

Granting that the United Nations Charter is important as the bearer of new responsibilities in the field of economic policy, we must immediately add that it represents only a beginning. The aims are so vague and general and are formulated in such nontechnical language that only a foundation has been laid, no building erected. If the charter is to be taken seriously, we must specify in technical

terms the aims of the organization. We must also indicate the instruments[2] and other means to be employed and to what extent they should be international or supranational in character. In other words, the whole complex of economic institutions and measures needed to achieve the general aims set forth in the charter should be designated by experts in the field to make its implications clear to the political community. So far, this natural follow-up to the work of the founders of the United Nations has been undertaken only in a very partial way.[3]

It is true that some important specialized agencies have been created; some of them even antedate the United Nations. We now have the International Monetary Fund, the International Bank for Reconstruction and Development, the International Finance Corporation, the International Development Association, the Special Fund, the Food and Agriculture Organization and some more specialized agencies in the noneconomic field. Also, the International Labor Organization (ILO), the oldest of the international institutions, has been given the status of a specialized agency. All these institutions are doing important work in their own fields. They all report to the Economic and Social Council of the United Nations, and this council meets twice a year. Much interesting information is being made available by these agencies and by the Secretariat of the United Nations. The latter also undertakes technical assistance operations and the Technical Assistance Board co-ordinates this work with similar work undertaken by the specialized agencies.

It cannot be said, however, that this loosely connected set of agencies is inspired by a well-defined policy, or that it represents the most efficient machinery for the execution of such a policy.

A policy, if it is to deserve the name, must be defined in terms of

2. Instruments are a class of means. They are of a quantitative nature and are used for the adaptation of the economy to small and frequent changes in certain data, e.g., tax rates, discount rates, reserve ratios, and foreign exchange rates. See J. Tinbergen, *Economy Policy: Principles and Design,* North-Holland Publishing Company, Amsterdam, 1956, p. 5.

3. Today some of us doubt whether the United Nations is still the most appropriate organ for an international economic policy. This question will be considered in section 6.4.

qualitative and quantitative aims, and in terms of certain means of carrying it out. It must also embody a decision as to what degree of decentralization is to prevail, that is, the division of labor between lower and higher echelons. Our present arrangements fall far short of this concept. For example, as early as 1951 a group of experts appointed by the Secretary-General expressed the opinion that the amount available for aid to underdeveloped countries was far below the amount necessary to reach reasonable goals. Today this is generally admitted and considerable action has been taken to relieve the situation. However, it is unfortunate that clear goals have never been established by any international agency. Nor has an attempt been made to determine what organs are needed in order to organize an international economic policy effectively. It is our contention that there is an urgent need to remedy these deficiencies, and that a committee should be established by the Economic and Social Council or by the General Assembly to investigate this subject. This committee should take the interests of the world at large as its frame of reference.

5.2 A ROLE FOR THE WEST: BUILDING AN INTERNATIONAL ECONOMIC ORDER

What role can the West play in constructing a new international community? Clearly the position of the Western nations has changed; no longer are they the masters of the world. Yet they may still play an important role if they have a real understanding of the new situation and of their own potentialities. Western leaders, first of all, must accept the fact that all peoples have a natural right to choose their own way of life. They must also concede equal political rights to all those who represent national interests. Within this framework we have to find the most appropriate contributions the West can make to the construction of a world economic order. These contributions must be made predominantly in those fields where the Western countries have special abilities and assets.

In economic terms, the significant factors are the "comparative advantages" — in the broadest sense — enjoyed by the Western

countries. During the last century there has been a clear shift in the sort of activities in which highly developed countries excel. Before the industrial revolution production everywhere was predominantly agricultural with some handicraft and there was not much international division of labor, except as determined by climate. With the industrial revolution manufactured products became the specialty of developed countries. As industrial activity spread, developed countries tended to concentrate on the production of capital goods. Today we observe that more and more developing countries are starting to produce capital goods while the most developed countries are tending to specialize in information services and research. The same trend can be observed within the developed group, where the leading country, the United States, devotes a relatively larger share of its resources to activities requiring specialized knowledge and experience, ordered in a scientific way, than the others do.

Apart from contributions to the knowledge of production processes, it seems that the Western advisers can contribute to shaping the economic policies of the less developed countries, domestically as well as in the international field. Here the possible contributions of the West are twofold. In the first place, the West has acquired a certain experience in international economic co-operation. It gained this experience from steps taken toward integration at various levels of economic operation in Europe and, to some extent, in Latin America. It has proved itself willing to give up elements of national sovereignty at a time when the young Asian and African countries are still too chary of their independence to enter into integration schemes. Remarkably enough, the West is more willing to undertake economic integration than the Communist countries seem to be. The situation is changing, however, and the comparative advantage of Western countries in this respect may not last long. On the other hand, Western experts have developed a high degree of objectivity, and they try not to prejudge any particular doctrine. Undoubtedly it is the spirit of Western science which gives them this comparative advantage.

The second current comparative advantage of the West lies in its

wealth. Because of their relative affluence the Western countries are in a position to make a unique contribution to one of the most pressing problems of the underdeveloped world. The underdeveloped countries, we may recall, are caught within a vicious circle of low incomes and low savings. They must either resign themselves to their predicament or apply authoritarian political methods to the problem of capital formation. They could be saved from this painful choice if considerable additional investment funds and technical assistance were made available by the wealthier countries. The benefits flowing from such a contribution would be incomparably larger, humanly speaking, than the sacrifice involved in making it. This follows from the simple fact that an additional dollar's worth of goods means much more to a man with a low income than to a man with a high income.

5.3 APPLICATION OF OUR OWN PRINCIPLES TO THE WORLD AT LARGE

Once it has been agreed that a stronger and better international order should be built, and that the West should offer its advice and services to the world's political leaders, it is necessary to decide upon the leading principles of the new international order.

It is only natural that in giving advice the West will be guided by its own experience with economic and social institutions and policy. Western society has since its inception been guided by the principle of efficiency.[4] It was the claim of those who defended the capitalist free-enterprise system in its early stages that it was far more efficient than its predecessor, feudalism. Capitalism led, however, to appalling contrasts in well-being and as a result of these contrasts the labor movement came into existence and flourished. Labor was severely critical of the free-enterprise system. Socialist thought assumed significant proportions in Western Europe in the beginning of the twentieth century; it developed somewhat later

4. "Efficiency" is used in the sense of the Western business-like approach of doing the best job possible once the aim has been defined.

and less vigorously in the United States. This influence led to a gradual change in institutions and policies, and these changes were governed by another principle which may be called solidarity.[5] Many measures were introduced to help those unable to help themselves: children, widows, victims of accidents and illness, the old, and the unemployed. Social insurance in its manifold forms and progressive taxes were some of the new institutions which evolved. More recently education has been made more accessible to groups of the population previously unable to afford it, and greater responsibility has been assumed by public authorities for general economic development.

The public sector was enlarged to include an increasing number of activities which, because of their external effects and increasing returns, could not be operated by private entrepreneurs in the interest of society as a whole. Other industries showing these characteristics were regulated to ensure that their operation would conform to the general interest. So mixed systems came into existence which are a far cry from 19th century capitalist economies.

There is, at the present moment, a marked difference between our domestic and our international policies. Only a small part of the institutions and instruments just mentioned have been applied in the international field. For reasons of political tradition the movement toward true community has stopped at national frontiers. Political convention has vested responsibility for community action in the hands of national governments, and these are anxious to avoid commitments. Even Social Democrats, by origin internationalists, have largely ceased to take guidance from international political programs, since their representatives in national governments — burdened with heavy responsibilities, often relatively new to them — are afraid to tie their hands.

This is one of the forms in which the "fear of commitment" has shown itself, leaving a vacuum in international economic policy. This fear constitutes a grave danger to our future. Using an

5. "Solidarity" refers to a willingness to regard the interests of others as being of equal importance to one's own.

ominous formula of Marx, we may say that history will eliminate systems which are not technically able to solve their problems. We are neglecting the interests of the world as a whole and those interests are becoming inseparable from our own.

We can no longer afford to disregard these interests, lest the world end in disaster for everyone, including ourselves. It is high time to apply the principles of efficiency and solidarity to the formulation of a world economic and social policy.

5.4 BROADENING OUR TIME HORIZONS

In reconstructing our economic order and our economic policy we not only need broader spatial horizons; we also need broader temporal horizons.

We are often guilty of shortsightedness with the result that Western policy, especially in international matters, tends to "run behind the facts" and lose initiative. It should not be overlooked that economic processes as well as processes of education and policy-making are time-consuming. Some of them extend over very long time periods. Decisions taken today will influence conditions for years to come. This is true of decisions on building and education, for instance; it is also true of decisions which, though they have technical consequences extending over shorter intervals, have a psychological aftermath. If our present decisions are to be correct they must take into account possible future developments. Often an awareness of the distant future exists only subconsciously, so that unrecognized sources of error are present in our calculations. But there has been a tendency recently to think more consciously about the future and to base business decisions on open forecasts instead of hidden assumptions. If this is good sense for business, it is also good sense for economic policy.

In technical language our last recommendation means that international economic policy must be based on forecasts and plans which are international in scope, and must be carried out by the appropriate United Nations organs.

Of course, projections or forecasts (which we consider synony-

mous[6]) can be based on varying assumptions about some of the data of the problem. These assumptions must be stated in order to avoid confusion. A very common assumption is that no change in policy will occur. For decision-making purposes this is a useful assumption. The forecast can then be compared with what we will call a "plan." This is another forecast, based on the assumption that the best policy feasible is followed. The word plan does not imply a policy of imposing a certain behavior pattern on private business. The best policy will have to be defined in terms of admissible aims and means.

5.5 BROADENING OUR OPINIONS ON SYSTEMS

The policies to be devised must be based not only on a wide range of interests and a long-run view of the future but also on a broad view of the relative merits of various socio-economic systems of which we have knowledge.

There is a tendency in popular propaganda to speak about the economic and social regimes of the Western countries and the Communist countries as if they were in sharp contrast to each other. The dichotomy is emphasized by labels such as "free" and "authoritarian" and "capitalist" and "socialist." There is a danger that top-ranking politicians and diplomats who do not have expert economic knowledge will also think in these black-and-white terms, which are not in conformity with the facts.[7] In other words, there is a danger of doctrinaire thinking which may do great harm to the world. We should be aware of the existence of a whole range of

6. It may be worth while to clarify a few concepts about which some confusion exists. Some technicians in this field distinguish between forecasts and projections. If we exclude operations which are designedly below the standard of scientific work, we may define projections as estimates of future levels of relevant variables; it goes without saying that these estimates can only be based on our knowledge of the forces operating. Unexpected forces are by definition not taken into account. A distinction between projections and forecasts, which do contain random elements, does not seem to serve any particular purpose if forecasts are supposed to be "exact" estimates of the future. Because of unforeseen forces, such exact estimates are not possible.

7. See Gunnar Myrdal, *Beyond the Welfare State — Economic Planning in the Welfare States and Its International Implications*, Duckworth, London, 1960.

possible systems using institutions and instruments of varying character; our aim must be to find the best system without reference to preconceived ideas. To choose, on doctrinaire grounds, a system which is not optimal would be stupid.

The problem can, of course, be more easily posed than solved. Our knowledge is only partial and must be augmented by intuitive beliefs, a condition which necessarily introduces differences of opinion. But at least it is now certain that the best system cannot be found at the extremes of the scale. Free enterprise in its older, 19th century form is not the best system; neither is complete regulation of all details. It is mainly a question of degree. Some activities are best carried out by public means while others can best be handled by private means. It makes sense to leave many markets free and to regulate quite a few others. Taxes are necessary; even relatively high income taxes do little harm while making possible many benefits. Incomes cannot all be equal, but extreme inequality so spoils the team spirit in society that it is highly dangerous, aside from being contrary to humanitarian principles. Thus on almost all counts the golden mean seems to be what we seek.

Much more analytical and empirical work must be done to define the optimum for economies in differing circumstances. This is just as much a work of careful engineering as is any industrial process, except that the subject matter is more flexible, and sometimes more evasive; seldom will heroic simplifications be of much help. The optimum is characterized by more interference in times of war or other emergency than in times of prosperity. Developing countries are in a desperate state of poverty and their optimum is not identical to ours. As countries, Communist and non-Communist, become more prosperous and mature, their optima will change.

Summarizing the points made in this chapter, we indicated that future socio-economic policies should be based on the interests of the world at large, which must be stated in terms of certain well-defined aims. These aims and the most important means to be used should be specified by the United Nations. Suggestions on the pos-

sible choice will be made in section 6.2. The means consist of a number of institutions and instruments, at various levels: international, national and local. The degree of centralization and the type of political instruments to be used should be pragmatically determined, so as best to serve the interests at stake. Because of special experience in related fields, Western experts may play a useful role in advising policy-makers on the optimum regime. Efficiency and solidarity should form the cornerstones of international policy. Some of the instruments which Western countries have employed in order to remedy the deficiencies of the free-enterprise system may be extended to the international community. Income transfers, for example, might help developing countries to break out of the vicious circles which bind them. Future policies should also be based on long-range forecasts and plans.

CHAPTER 6

THE JOB
AND THE TOOLS

6.1 THE SETTING OF GOALS

We will assume in the following discussion that the principles set out in Chapter 5 are to act as a guide for Western politicians anxious to give a new shape to the world economy. In this chapter we will specify more concretely the contents of an economic policy for the world at large and the machinery necessary for attaining the goals of such a policy. In so doing we will make a number of suggestions designed to elaborate a policy for the United Nations, the need for which was expressed in section 5.1.

First, the United Nations should be explicit about the goals that are to be pursued in international economic policy. Economic policy-making is a job just as any other, and a job cannot be done efficiently if no clear goal exists. Efficiency is a relative concept; it can

only be measured by making regular checks on the progress made toward set goals. No large business enterprise would have any doubts on this score, and politicians can no longer be an exception to the rule. It is true that public policy-making involves risks, but the same is true of business policy-making. Moreover, there are also advantages in having goals clearly in mind in that it paves the way for a public announcement of intent. It has become increasingly apparent that there is an announcement effect in matters of economic policy. In our frame of reference we contend that it is a favorable effect. Developing countries are likely to be impressed by an advance announcement of a well-conceived development policy.

The setting of goals for an international policy is possible because there is considerable parallelism in the goals countries set for themselves. With some degree of central economic planning going on in most countries nowadays, under a variety of names, goals at the national level are more clearly formulated. Usually national policy-making focuses on production in general, employment, the balance of payments, prices, and, in some cases, the distribution of income among social groups or regions. It is true that the emphasis given to the individual goals differs; developed countries emphasize employment, the balance of payments, and distribution, whereas developing countries stress productivity and sometimes prices. There are also differences of emphasis among the developed countries and differences in the levels and rates projected. Thus the goals set for production (or income) increases by some developing countries, e.g., the United Arab Republic, Japan, or Turkey, may be as high as 7 or 8 per cent per annum. They are more modest for developed countries; for example, the OEEC countries as a group aimed at 5 per cent for 1955–1960. This same increase was projected by India in her last three plans, because internal saving and expected external aid would not permit a higher figure. The formulation of goals for the world at large might bring these figures into a more reasonable alignment.

Even though there is considerable uniformity in thinking about the objectives of economic policy, the formulation of goals for the international community will be a major job. To go into great de-

tail would be impossible and unwise. The best procedure is to try
to arrive at a courageous but realistic set of central aims.

These central aims must include development targets for national income over a period of five years, not necessarily for all
countries, but for the larger ones and for groups of the smaller ones.

These income targets imply employment targets; for developed
countries they may mean the avoidance of cyclical unemployment
and the rapid elimination of structural unemployment. For developing countries they may mean the elimination, after a certain
period, of structural unemployment.

Balances of payments are a second element of the aims; by and
large the target must be the equilibrium of all balances. A third
element is price stability, which may be defined in terms of maximum deviations to be tolerated for a number of main trade products, much as in the case of the Wheat Agreement. For the industrial countries targets may also be set with regard to the general
price level; perhaps this would provide an example for the main
developing countries. Finally, income distribution targets can be
set or, alternatively, this can be left to the national economies. As
far as the international distribution of income is concerned, some
change will be implied in the national income targets. Basically
these figures should indicate a convergence rather than a divergence
of real incomes per head.

We stress the word convergence because we do not think that a
rise in incomes of underdeveloped countries beyond the subsistence minimum would suffice to make the world stabler. It is true
that the worst thing to be removed is incomes below the level of
subsistence; but the concept of subsistence level is a relative one. As
productivity grows so does the conception of what is necessary in
life. What makes people unhappy is large differences in income;
poverty is more easily borne if everybody is poor than if differences
are large. What irritates people is that the same kind of work is
paid so much better in one country than in another, and the
smaller the world becomes, the more important will these comparisons become. It will be wise policy to understand this in advance.

6.2 SOLIDARITY IN INTERNATIONAL POLICIES

In this section we will elaborate on the means whereby an international economic policy can be implemented. The choice of means must be based on the general principles of solidarity and efficiency, attributes in which nations are seriously lacking today.

The separate nations will have to show a sense of common responsibility for the definition of international aims and the implementation of world policies. Solidarity has to express itself in the introduction, on the international level, of the sort of agreement which exists among the various political units of a large decentralized country. Although state or provincial governments are not always fully co-operative, they at least have an understanding of the corrective role of the central government. Similarly, national governments and their citizens must accept co-responsibility for the correct execution of a program for the world at large. This sense of responsibility must reveal itself in the means chosen for a common development policy. As an illustration of the proper attitude, an American senator in judging an aid program proposed by his government should not ask whether it is in the interest of the United States, but whether it is an example of how a country should behave if we want to make this world a proper environment for a thoughtful and broadminded international regime.

What is needed in concrete terms is a system of capital flows — in the form of grants, loans, and participations — sufficient to attain the goals of a converging development of incomes and equilibrated balances of payments. More particularly, a sense of common responsibility requires that the various countries contribute according to their "ability to pay." Professor Rosenstein-Rodan, in a study for the Center for International Studies of Massachusetts Institute of Technology,[1] has proposed that relative contributions be based on a fictitious income tax applied equally to all countries. His proposal is the best basis for discussing this important instrument of economic policy.

1. "International Aid for Underdeveloped Countries," *Review of Economics and Statistics*, May 1961, pp. 107 ff.

It is a question of semantics whether grants should be called capital transfers or not. Probably the simplest way of looking at grants is to regard them as current contributions to an international development budget. They are analogous to current budget items for development purposes inside a country in that the location of the projects bears no necessary relation to the geographic source of the funds expended. Current transfers are a normal phenomenon within each nation as the result of social and educational policies backed by the theoretical teachings of welfare economics. Even though welfare economists are not yet able to indicate the optimum level of income transfers, and even though the particular type of transfer implied in income taxes does not conform with the conditions for a welfare optimum, income taxes can be shown to contribute to social welfare.[2] If solidarity is to become a reality not only within the frontiers of each country but in the world at large, current transfers, organized under a current international budget, will have to be accepted as a natural phenomenon too. The existing United Nations budget is one example in existence; for many reasons we should wish it to grow considerably. There may be a need for a current budget for IDA or OECD as well.

A common development policy will require not only a larger international investment scheme than has hitherto existed but also an international education scheme. In part this is a question of money, and so falls under the preceding subject, but in education the financial question is relatively less important than it is for material needs in general. An education program will call for considerable efforts in manpower, since in the initial period teachers will not be available in sufficient number in the developing countries. International solidarity here translates itself into a sizable program of technical assistance in its many different forms. Difficulties are created, however, by language barriers. Except for the relatively modest number of foreigners who have learned the language of the trainees, the possibilities for active outside participation are limited to those pro-

2. See J. Tinbergen, "Should the Income Tax be Among the Means of Economic Policy?," in *Til Frederik Zeuthen,* Nationaløkonomisk Forening, Copenhagen, 1958, p. 351.

grams of advanced training which can be conducted in international languages. The situation can be improved, of course, by teaching more languages at Western universities.

Solidarity also can and must play an important part in the implementation of stabilization policies. The achievement of price stability requires the institution of more commodity agreements and of an international insurance scheme against heavy declines in export receipts. Governments of the developed countries can show their community feeling by entering into such schemes with fewer reservations than in the past.

Finally, trade policy is another area where a higher degree of solidarity can be displayed. Sizable reductions in trade impediments are necessary if we are to arrive at a situation more in conformity with world interests. The spirit which led to the European Economic Community and to the proposals for Latin American integration or for the integration of the Arab region must be extended to wider areas if we are to approach more closely to the world optimum.[3]

6.3 EFFICIENCY IN INTERNATIONAL ECONOMIC POLICY

Efficiency means the most favorable ratio between ends and means. As long as only one end is aimed at, say a given increase in production, the attainment of maximum efficiency depends upon finding the cheapest method of accomplishing that task. In single-purpose problems efficiency can be expressed in physical units, as we know from simple applications in industry. If multiple ends and multiple means are involved, there must be a common measure to enable us to compare the various ends and means. The final criterion will always be social utility, a familiar but difficult concept of welfare economics. In practical cases we can sometimes use

3. A convincing plea for fewer restrictions on imports from developing countries is made by ECE in its *Economic Survey of Europe, 1960*, Geneva, 1961, Ch. 5, p. 48, where it is argued that in the next twenty years developing countries must increase their exports to Western Europe by some $5 billion if their balance of payments is to be in equilibrium.

money as a common denominator. Often, however, "shadow" prices, i.e., prices equating demand and supply, must be used in place of actual prices if we are to acquire an insight into benefits and sacrifices.

Some knowledge has recently been gained as to the relative efficiency of the alternative instruments of economic policy available for short-term adjustments to changes in exogenous factors. In anticyclical policies meant to stabilize total demand, changes in public finance (public expenditure and taxes) are considered more efficient than changes in factor prices (interest and wage rates) because the former have a strong and clear influence on total demand while the influence of the latter is weak and uncertain. For the stabilization of prices, on the other hand, wage rates are an efficient instrument because of their direct influence on the price level. If it is desired to pursue two targets simultaneously, it will be necessary to use two instruments at the same time; the best combination consists of a fiscal policy measure and a wage rate change. To refrain from using the wage rate and to use instead two instruments of public finance or budgetary and credit policy would mean that in some cases very big changes in these instruments in opposite directions would be necessary, which would meet with many difficulties.[4]

Less precise knowledge is available with regard to long-term economic adjustments. Yet some insight has been gained concerning such matters as how to restore a fundamental disequilibrium in the balance of payments and how to further industrial development. In connection with balance of payments problems it is known that the adjustment of exchange rates is a more efficient policy than the adjustment of wages in that it requires less violent changes and less disturbance of social equilibrium.[5] To promote industrial development, that is, to increase the capacity of the economy to absorb more assistance in this field, public investment in the sphere of infrastructure and subsidies and technical assistance to stimulate

4. For a more detailed analysis of the highly technical problems involved, see J. Tinbergen, *Economic Policy: Principles and Design,* North-Holland Publishing Company, Amsterdam, 1956, Chapters 3 and 4.

5. See *ibid.,* p. 113.

private investment will in many circumstances be an optimal combination of means. If private initiative is weak, public investment in basic industries may be useful too.[6] Clues to the optimum regime, i.e., the most efficient set of institutions, can be obtained from welfare economics with the aid of econometric studies (see sections 2.5 and 5.5 for examples). Welfare economics is that branch of economics which tries to determine what conditions must be fulfilled by the economic institutions in order to permit the economy to attain the maximum of well-being consistent with the natural, psychological, and technical data. The term welfare economics is sometimes confused with the term welfare state, but the latter does not necessarily fulfill the conditions formulated by welfare economics. Even though there are many unsolved problems in the field of welfare economics, some generally accepted propositions have been formulated.

Some useful information, then, has been accumulated concerning the most efficient set of institutions and instruments which a single country can use to achieve a given set of aims. A further point to be decided is how to organize the use of these means in an international community. The core of this question is the appropriate degree of decentralization, or the division of labor between supranational, national, and lower-level authorities.

Here we come to a very important question. In order to arrive at an optimum organization from the world's point of view, we must disregard traditional preferences for narrow national autonomy and concentrate on the technical aspects of the international task to be performed. Again welfare economics can help us. We want to know which organization will result in the purest decision-making, and welfare economics provides us with criteria for making a choice.[7] Decisions will be closest to optimum when the benefits and costs involved are properly estimated by the policy-makers. It is the drawback of national administrations that they are responsible

6. See J. Tinbergen, *The Design of Development*, Johns Hopkins Press, Baltimore, 1958, pp. 63 ff.

7. See J. Tinbergen, *Centralization and Decentralization in Economic Policy*, North-Holland Publishing Company, Amsterdam, 1954.

to national parliaments in which, in principle, only the national interests count. As often as a decision has to be taken affecting benefits or costs outside the national boundaries, there is a possibility that the national government will not take an objective decision. The history of the thirties is eloquent in this respect, as section 5.1 shows; it is characterized by a considerable overemphasis on instruments of economic policy not in the international interest ("conflicting instruments") and a considerable underemphasis on instruments in the international interest ("supporting instruments"). The history of European co-operation after World War II is also illustrative; as long as only unanimous decisions were effective, the pace of integration was slow.

While the preceding considerations were recognized when trade policy was made a matter of international concern — in GATT and in EEC — they have not been taken sufficient account of in financial and monetary policy or in price stabilization. If the job of international economic policy is to be carried out efficiently, stronger supranational agencies must be created particularly in these fields, and more power must be given to agencies already existing in other fields — including trade policy — which handle instruments affecting the well-being of the outside world.[8]

While our analysis implies that in the long run supranational agencies will be needed to handle such instruments as public finance, trade policy, and commodity agreements, it is clear that tradition as well as sectional interests may oppose such a development. Probably the wisest course is gradually to reinforce co-ordination in the use of these instruments by national governments. This can be done by using weaker forms of co-ordination at first and applying stronger forms only to the most urgent portions of the apparatus of economic policy. Thus a start could be made with a modest international budget for development which might be gradually expanded. Because of its impact on cyclical movements, public finance could be co-ordinated in a weaker way by extending existing consultations — e.g., in the EEC Monetary Committee —

8. See Gunnar Myrdal, *Beyond the Welfare State*, Duckworth, London, 1960.

both as to subject matter and as to the group of countries involved. It would be of great importance to have the United States participate in this co-ordination.

6.4 THE ROLE OF INTERNATIONAL AGENCIES

If the need for more centralization in the use of some vital instruments of economic policy is accepted in principle, questions arise of the utilization of existing agencies and the scope of the new agencies which may be needed. The major alternatives are the United Nations agencies and agencies covering smaller groups of countries, such as IBRD and, with the same membership, the International Finance Corporation (IFC) and the International Development Association (IDA), or OECD.

In making a choice some elements must be considered which go beyond the purely economic sphere. The main difference between the United Nations and the other groupings is, of course, the membership of Communist countries. Co-operation with Communist countries has sometimes been difficult if not impossible. Must we risk the failure of the policies advocated by trying to institute them in co-operation with Communist countries? There is one cogent reason why we should accept some risk. The world as a whole is in vital need of a way of peaceful coexistence. While the most urgent problem is that of security, an international order will have to bear on economic and social issues as well. These issues may be good issues on which to try out peaceful coexistence. Proposals for universal co-operation on matters such as trade and development can be considered as proposals for coexistence. For one thing, an elaboration of the meaning of coexistence is badly needed. Our suggestions regarding an international economic policy as given in the preceding sections may be considered as such an elaboration. We will add some extra-economic suggestions in Chapter 10. For the moment we wish only to say that it is worth while giving more tasks to the United Nations.

This does not mean that United Nations organs — that is, organs ᵗ the highest international level — should have complete control

of all the instruments of economic policy which need centralized handling. If it is agreed that capital and income transfers for developmental purposes are such an instrument, it does not necessarily follow that all these transfers should be made through the United Nations. Two minimum conditions must be fulfilled if the instrument is to be properly used: all transfers at lower levels must be recorded at the "center," and the center must be able to supplement these "lower-level" activities so as to make the total investment pattern optimal from the international standpoint. If existing "lower levels" such as IBRD, IDA, EEC, the Colombo Plan, the United States government, and so on, together with private investors, do not make sufficient means available to, say, Southeast Asia, supplementary means must be on hand to fill this "gap" so that the total pattern is acceptable. This may be possible with relatively modest means, the more so where the lower-level institutions are already aware of their world responsibilities. Considerable decentralization in the execution of policy may therefore go hand in hand with centralized supervision and supplementary action.

A major decision confronting the non-Communist countries concerns the organ which will have to disburse the considerably larger development funds to be advocated below (see section 7.1). For the time being the International Development Association (IDA) seems to be the most appropriate organ, since it is operated by the experienced staff of IBRD. Its policy will have to diverge from the Bank's at several points, however, and it may turn out that an independent organ would be better suited to the task.[9]

Another possibility is that OECD be given this responsibility. OECD has the advantage of experience in handling problems of international economic co-operation. On the other hand, it is exclusively a Western organization, and the inclusion of developing countries in the disbursing agency would seem to be a condition for a successful common development policy.

Many tasks in economic policy can be left to autonomous action at still lower levels. Most matters of public finance can and must be

9. See Andrew Shonfield, *The Attack on World Poverty*, Random House, New York, 1960, p. 156.

handled at national and sub-national levels. There is a long list of public activities which can best be carried out at the local, the provincial, or the state level.

There is scope for simplifying the organizational structure of international co-operation. The pattern of organization is almost chaotic, especially in Europe where co-operation is strongest. Efforts to unify the operation of the governments in EEC are highly desirable and are already under way. If the United Kingdom becomes a member of EEC, the Western European Union (WEU) may become superfluous. In principle, Benelux should also become superfluous. We must even hope that OECD may become a duplication of an Atlantic Union.

There is reason, however, to maintain and even to strengthen co-operation in other continents. For several activities it would seem useful to have bodies intermediate between the national governments and the United Nations. Here the agencies could be the existing United Nations regional commissions: the Economic Commission for Africa (ECA), the Economic Commission for Asia and the Far East (ECAFE), the Economic Commission for Europe (ECE), and the Economic Commission for Latin America (ECLA). Of course, it is conceivable that smaller groups of countries will form agencies to carry out such tasks, and that these groups will later merge. It is also possible that permanent groups with a membership different from that of the existing regional commissions will appear (see section 8.4).

The last question to be examined in this section concerns the need for specialized agencies. These already exist in several fields; examples include IMF, IBRD, IDA, IFC, FAO, GATT, ILO, and UNESCO. While there is no need at the moment to create a new specialized agency for industrialization, this idea may be worth further exploration.[10] The question whether the activities of the specialized agencies are already sufficiently co-ordinated may be recommended for exploration at the same time.

In conclusion we would like to stress the need for a strong

10. See Shonfield, *op. cit.*, pp. 237–239.

United Nations Secretariat, endowed with substantial funds and charged with some important tasks, including the making of forecasts (discussed in the next section) and the elaboration of targets for international economic policies in the fields of income transfers, development financing, and stabilization (see section 5.1). These tasks cannot be carried out and the co-operation of governments cannot be sufficiently enlisted if the Secretariat does not command considerably more financial means, particularly for supplementary action in the field of development, than in the past.

6.5 FORECASTS, PLANS, AND ANNUAL DISCUSSIONS

An efficient international economic regime not only requires aims and means and appropriate agencies to handle them; it also requires a planning apparatus, as any complex activity does, and it requires supervision. These needs should be carried out by the highest economic organ in the international hierarchy, which is the Economic and Social Council of the United Nations (ECOSOC). This council should be the place where world economic policies are fruitfully discussed, both in prospect and in retrospect. The traditional discussion of the world economic situation must be made more operational. This means that the *World Economic Survey* should bring out the main deviations between desirable and actual development and should be supplemented by a document containing international economic plans or programs. In comparable documents prepared by some countries (see section 5.4) one usually finds a forecast of probable developments without a change in policy, and a plan indicating the developments most desired. Here, too, world aims should be formulated (section 5.1).

The task may seem to many an impossible one. Will it be possible to arrive at any consensus among the main governments? Will not the debate become a propaganda show for Communist and non-Communist countries, or even just for Communist countries? Does it make sense to discuss government policies in a meeting without any competence to act in the field?

Much depends on the way the discussion sessions are developed

and on the manner in which competences in the international field are acquired. As a general rule, it probably would be wise to start on a modest scale. This means that in the first years of this experiment only a few extremely important areas would be discussed, namely the desirable levels of aid and development per continent, and anticyclical policy for the world at large. The establishment of an international development budget may give some direct operational sense to the debate. In addition, OEEC's tradition of examining member countries' policies may be introduced, if the atmosphere permits.

One of the important factors in the effectiveness of international discussions will be the position of the United Nations Secretariat. As was advocated in the preceding section, the Secretariat should become more independent; it should change from a "servant," as it has often considered itself, to an authority. In several fields it already acts as an authority because of the quality and experience of its staff. However, tasks must be assigned to it in the field of development policy.[11]

Some remarks may be added on the methods and procedures to be used in preparing the forecasts and plans. The methods might consist, to begin with, of the simple models proposed and elaborated by Professor J. J. Polak of IMF.[12] These models are an international version of some of the post-Keynesian econometric models. Many opportunities exist to make these models more precise, as witness the work done at national levels; but in the beginning simple approaches must be recommended. In order to use these models it is necessary to estimate the so-called extra-economic phenomena influencing the economic situation, and the so-called coefficients,

11. It may be mentioned here that the Second (Economic and Financial) Committee of the UN General Assembly adopted a draft resolution on November 16, 1961, requesting the Secretary-General among others to establish an Economic Projections and Programming Centre — with sub-centers as appropriate in the regional economic commissions — to intensify development planning activities already under way and to make long-term projections. (See *United Nations Review,* December 1961, pp. 29 ff.) This resolution was adopted by the General Assembly at the December 1961 meeting.

12. See J. J. Polak, *An International Economic System,* University of Chicago Press, Chicago, 1953, and numerous later publications in the IMF Staff Papers.

i.e., the intensities with which such influences (and mutual influences of economic phenomena) are acting. Among the extraeconomic phenomena government expenditure and investment stand out; crops are very important for annual forecasts, but for longer-range forecasts their role is negligible. An increasing volume of international comparisons is available which may make it possible to estimate coefficients for countries not yet able to make such estimates for themselves.

The procedure would consist of the following steps:

(i) some central directives with regard to the assumptions to be made and the figures to be used are formulated and forwarded by the UN Secretariat to the Regional Commissions;

(ii) the Commissions forward this information to their member governments, asking them for the figures needed;

(iii) incoming figures are evaluated, and perhaps supplemented, by the Regional Commissions and forwarded to UN Headquarters for further evaluation;

(iv) the resulting set of forecasts for national income, imports, exports, investments, and consumption (public and private) are made available to all governments;

(v) UN Headquarters uses these figures to estimate the development of world demand in certain main sectors of production, with regional subdivisions.

Among the figures should be ones — to be estimated by Headquarters on the evidence received — on financial aid, subdivided according to supplying and receiving countries and including both a forecast and a set of goals.

A discussion of these figures might be an outlet for national tensions and irritations. As we have suggested, much will depend on the approach chosen for such a debate, and on the personality of the debaters.

INVESTMENT

CRITERIA ON A

WORLD SCALE

7.1 INVESTMENT IN EQUIPMENT AND IN MEN

The main groups of means or instruments of international economic policy described in Chapter 6 will now be taken up one by one. Since investment policies are of primary importance they will be taken up first.

A number of the criteria for an effective investment policy are already known from national development policies. These criteria need to be formulated for use on a world-wide scale. They should help to solve a number of important problems related to the size of the program and its distribution over contributors and recipients, over branches of the economy, and over the public and private sectors. The distribution of individual projects will tend to be a domestic matter, but if large projects are at stake, some interna-

tional co-operation will be necessary, either because the project is situated in several adjacent countries (an example would be a river valley project) or because it is individually financed by an international agency or another country.

Investment must be understood, from the start, to mean investment in both material assets and men, since the two are complementary in production. Investment and planning in education have lagged behind investment in material assets in development projects, but the field of education is now receiving more adequate treatment. As was pointed out in section 6–2, the financial factor is not as great in education requirements as it is in material requirements — the requisite investment in the former may be only some 20 or 30 per cent of that in the latter — but the human factor is relatively greater, both as to trainees and trainers. A special problem is the length of the training period, particularly for higher skills.

The decisions on a world investment program should be taken in a number of successive steps. The first decision must concern the size of the program. It should be based on the aim of replacing the present pattern of diverging standards of living or real incomes per head with a pattern of convergence. We interpret this to mean that the percentage rate of increase must be made larger for developing countries than for developed countries. The order of magnitude of the necessary increases in investment can be estimated with the aid of some crude coefficients. Since incomes per head in developing countries are now rising by 1.5 per cent per annum, increases in production must be at least 2 per cent per annum higher than they now are, and preferably 4 per cent higher.

Estimates made by the Netherlands Economic Institute[1] show that in order to achieve a 2 per cent increase in production, some $7 or $8 billion additional investment annually will be needed as a minimum. In view of the low incomes in the developing countries, a large part of the necessary increase will have to be provided from international sources. The minimum increment indicated repre-

1. *The European Community and the Underdeveloped Countries,* Netherlands Economic Institute and Documentation Centre of the Action Committee for the United States of Europe, May 1959 (mimeographed).

sents about 1 per cent of the income of the developed countries. Since the amount they now contribute is estimated to be somewhat more than $7 billion, their contribution will have to be at least doubled. Later a further increase might be desirable. In the last few years the experts of the main developed countries have come to feel that contributions of the order indicated are necessary to underwrite a new approach to international co-operation. Public opinion has not followed this lead; considerable doubt has been expressed whether:

(i) the developed countries can bear the burden; and
(ii) the developing countries can absorb the new investments contemplated.

In appraising the issue, the fundamental importance of stimulating growth in today's underdeveloped areas should not be overlooked. Once we are aware of the dimensions of the annual increase in income in the developed countries, the concern about our ability to bear the burden cannot be taken too seriously. The present population of the developed countries experiences on the average an annual increase in income of about 2 per cent, or some $15 billion. The increase — always in comparison with the same base year — is $30 billion after two years, $45 billion after three years, and so on. It should be possible, then, to increase the capital flow to the developing countries by some $7 to $8 billion in the first few years, bringing it thus to a level of about $15 billion annually, and later to increase it by an additional smaller amount to a still higher level. It goes without saying that the problem of financing this aid would be considerably simplified if an arms reduction could be agreed upon.

As for the absorptive capacity of the developing countries, this is a problem in the short run only. This means that the most desirable features of the program can be achieved in only a few years of intensive effort. In view of the dangers involved in allowing the gap in well-being between the developed and the underdeveloped countries to widen, it is wrong to conclude from the fact that present absorptive capacity is limited that our task is not as large as originally indicated; instead we must step up that absorptive capacity by all available means.

Some of the activities which can contribute to increasing the absorptive capacity of underdeveloped countries have not been given sufficient attention.

Contracting firms that do a large part of their business in developing countries could give the local citizens more instruction and training, at different levels. The cost of these additional business activities could be financed by development aid. We could take advantage of the presence of specialized personnel by extending knowledge in these countries, and after the termination of the job the trained persons could make use of their acquired skills elsewhere.

Similar advantages could be derived by establishing enterprises in which local as well as foreign capital and personnel participate. Some developing countries promote these "joint ventures" by investment laws and the activities of development banks. However, more initiative could be taken by authorities of the developed countries. One possibility would be a joint effort by countries at all stages of development to establish an international insurance system for investments abroad (see p. 134). Joint ventures not only facilitate the transfer of technical and managerial skill; they are also a means of mobilizing more local capital.

An appropriate measure to step up absorptive capacity may be to grant licenses conferring industrial property rights.

The favorable impact of investment aid on the balance of payments of the receiving countries deserves more attention than has so far been given to it. Many institutions are now engaged in dealing with exchange controls and trade restrictions; they will find their problems largely solved if more aid is given for development. This is particularly true of the activities of the International Monetary Fund.

7.2 BALANCED INTERNATIONAL GROWTH –
I: RESOURCES

Decisions must also be made regarding the composition of the program. Recently some writers have advocated an "unbalanced"

process of development rather than a balanced one.[2] Arguments advanced are that:

  (i) some strategic industries may be pushed so as to automatically induce other activities; and

  (ii) some industries or countries have a higher absorptive capacity than others and may therefore be used as levers.

Admittedly there are such industries and such countries; their existence is among the data of the problem. And it is proper to use the "handles" or instruments which are most effective in reaching the goals of development policy. But what we seek to attain is a balanced situation, not one of disequilibrium. Unbalance, almost by definition, is a pejorative term. Of course there is a question here of choice of words; "balance" should not mean a static condition, but a dynamic one.

The program must be balanced, first of all, with regard to contributions. As set out in section 6.2, the best basis for discussion of an equitable assessment is the proposal of Professor Rosenstein-Rodan.[3] In principle, contributions should be made by all countries, developed and less developed, as an expression of the fact

2. See Albert O. Hirschman, *The Strategy of Economic Development,* Yale University Press, New Haven, 1958, and Andrew Shonfield, *The Attack on World Poverty,* Random House, New York, 1960, p. 6.

3. See "International Aid for Underdeveloped Countries," *Review of Economics and Statistics,* May 1961, pp. 107–138. Rosenstein-Rodan proposes that the developed countries contribute to a program of capital assistance according to a progressive tax schedule applied to their income per family (of standardized size). He also suggests that it might be appropriate to base such a system of contributions on a country's real family income (corrected for price differences with, say, the United States) instead of on its nominal family income. Applying the United States income tax progression to the incomes per family, and multiplying the results by the number of families, he finds that the burden of capital assistance should be shared by the donor countries in the following way:

Contribution as Per Cent of Total Capital Assistance Program

	Based on "Nominal" Income	*Based on Real Income*
United States	71.3	58.6
Canada	4.1	3.4
United Kingdom	5.8	7.7
France	4.0	4.8
Germany (Fed. Rep.)	4.1	7.0
Other Western Europe	4.3	7.8
Oceania	1.1	1.7
USSR	5.3	9.0

that the program is a common effort; and, following the example of IBRD, no distinction should be made between receiving and contributing countries.[4] In Rosenstein-Rodan's proposal this principle is not fully applied: only the developed countries — in his example countries with an income per head above $600 — would contribute. A further refinement of his approach, and one worth further exploration, is to make a country's contribution dependent upon its internal distribution of income as well as its average income.

The question may be raised whether the contribution should also be dependent upon the balance of payments position of the participating countries. Generally speaking this is not a logical notion, although there may be "hardship" cases which must be accepted as exceptions. What matters is a country's real income. Balance of payments difficulties can only be overcome by adapting national expenditures to national income plus income transfers. Developed countries can always contrive to cut expenditures, while an expanded program of international assistance will automatically improve the balance of payments of underdeveloped countries.

The contributions may be made in different forms and in the framework of different schemes, as set out in sections 6.3 and 6.4. There must be one center where records are kept and where the supplementary contributions necessary to bring the total program and the contributions by each country to the appropriate level are paid in. The data collected by this center — preferably the United Nations Secretariat — should be the basis of the annual discussion in ECOSOC.

The contributions can take the form of loans or grants. Market loans, loans on easier terms (low interest rate, long amortization period, repayment in local currency), and medium-term credits are now used in various combinations.[5] Naturally, the type of contribu-

---

4. This applies more particularly to technical assistance programs, where less developed countries can often be better helped by developing than by developed countries.

5. In the period 1956–1959 the proportion of total public help given in the form of credits and loans was roughly 20 per cent for France, 40 per cent for the United States, 45 per cent for the United Kingdom, and 70 per cent for the German Federal Republic. (Calculated from OEEC, *The Flow of Financial Resources to Countries in Course of Economic Development 1956–1959*, Paris, 1961, Tables 2, 3, and 4.)

tion must be geared to the character of the project financed and to economic conditions, present and future, in the country seeking assistance.

Particular forms of restricted contributions are gifts in kind and tied loans. Contributions in kind such as supplies of surplus commodities are useful, since any development program will generate a need for increased food supplies for the workers previously unemployed. However, care must be taken not to disrupt markets in the receiving countries. Tied loans, or loans designated for specified countries, are less desirable, since they may force the receiving country to pay higher prices than necessary. But obviously if the choice is between a tied loan and no loan, there is some advantage in accepting the tied loan.

Several attitudes are possible vis-à-vis the inclusion of private investment. Since what matters to the developing countries is the total capital flow, it seems proper to include private investment in the statistics showing the total size of the program and the distribution between contributing countries; and this is the point of view adhered to in this study. It seems useful to seek the co-operation of private firms for the development of the "superstructure" — a topic which will be discussed in section 7.6.

7.3 BALANCED INTERNATIONAL GROWTH –
      II: USES

There must also be balanced growth if we compare the countries benefiting from the program. So far this aspect of development policy has been neglected, as is illustrated by the figures in Table 7–1 showing the aid received by different countries per head of population.

An attempt to devise a more systematic distribution of the available international funds has been made by Professor Rosenstein-Rodan and his staff at MIT using absorptive capacity as one of the main criteria. Rosenstein-Rodan's work would seem to provide a good starting point for programs in the immediate future. His figures center around an annual increase of 2 per cent in income per head. Countries with a relatively large absorptive capacity are sup-

Table 7–1

PUBLIC ECONOMIC ASSISTANCE RECEIVED BY VARIOUS COUNTRIES
IN DOLLARS PER HEAD OF POPULATION, 1953–1958

Country	1953–54 to 1955–56	1957–58 to 1958–59
Countries with Per Capita Income Below $100		
Jordan	$ 9.40	$36.30
Korea	13.32	14.13
Bolivia	4.85	8.52
Indonesia	0.14	1.24
India	0.24	0.74
Countries with Per Capita Income Between $100 and $200		
Libya	17.00	31.64
Taiwan (Formosa)	9.62	9.14
Brazil	1.58	1.05
Ghana	0.46	0.48
UAR (Egypt)	0.80	0.41
Countries with Per Capita Income above $200		
Israel	25.00	24.61
Costa Rica	3.60	11.20
Mexico	0.86	2.04
Cuba	0.27	1.20

Source: United Nations, *Statistical Yearbook,* recent years.

posed to grow on a per capita basis by around 2.5 per cent, while countries with a relatively small absorptive capacity are expected to grow at rates ranging from 0.6 to 1.9 per cent, and some are even given negative figures.

These projected rates can only be of temporary significance since the absorptive capacity of a number of countries can be increased. One must also ask what effect these growth rates would have on the pattern of real incomes. It is unlikely that Rosenstein-Rodan's distribution would lead to a reduction of the gap between per capita incomes in developed and developing countries.

We are not convinced that an attempt should be made to concentrate aid on a few countries having an exceptional development potential;[6] the political implications of such a move would in our opinion be unfortunate.

There are other relevant criteria in addition to those already mentioned — desirable growth of income and absorptive capacity. As will be made clear later, there is some point in giving additional investment aid to countries willing to give up some of the trade preferences they at present enjoy in the framework of the European Economic Community.

Countries soliciting aid should have detailed development plans since these would facilitate an appraisal of their absorptive capacity. Many countries have already worked out such plans, and the habit is rapidly spreading. In some cases, such as Turkey, a development plan has been considered a condition for foreign assistance. This seems a useful approach. A development plan may be and should be an aid also in designing efficient investment policies, including policies governing the use of the country's own savings. A plan, if it is to be of any use, must indicate not only the rate of growth of national product envisaged but also the rates of growth in the main sectors of the economy and the most important individual projects to be carried out. For large countries, estimates of the regional distribution of growth and investment are also desirable. Forecasting and planning techniques are developing rapidly[7] and a considerable volume of technical assistance is being given in this field.

The use of so-called shadow prices, defined as prices which would equate supply and demand, is an important technique in the appraisal of individual projects. For various reasons, the prices paid for goods and services (including labor and capital) in developing

6. See W. Krause, *Economic Development*, Wadsworth Publishing Co., San Francisco, 1961, p. 503.

7. A long list of publications bears witness to the excellent work done by ECLA in this field. Recently ECAFE has made useful contributions, among which may be mentioned a summary of techniques in *Programming Techniques for Economic Development*, Bangkok, 1960 (Sales No. 60. II.F.3). A standard work is H. B. Chenery and P. G. Clark, *Interindustry Economics*, Wiley, New York, 1959.

countries are often not an accurate measure of the intrinsic value of these commodities. The main reasons for this are to be found in some fundamental disequilibria characteristic of these countries,[8] such as the following: a disproportion between the amount of labor and capital available, which often leaves a considerable part of the labor force without a necessary minimum of capital; a compartmentalization of the capital market, which leads to subnormal interest rates in the favored compartments; commonly, a fundamental disequilibrium in the balance of payments; and the protection of industrial markets in the initial stage of development. Under these conditions the intrinsic value of a project may be better estimated with the aid of shadow prices than with market prices.

Another factor which must be considered in appraising individual projects is the possible need for complementary investments. Investments in "international industries," i.e., industries producing goods which can be imported or exported, can only contribute to the balanced growth of a country if capacity is correspondingly increased in "national industries," i.e., industries producing items which cannot be moved over the frontiers, such as inland transportation, energy, and residential building. By a particular use of input-output tables, these complementary investments can be estimated.[9]

As we stated in section 6.5, an efficient international economic policy requires planning activity "at the top." The task, therefore, is to co-ordinate the planning activities of the international community, and to check the consistency of the national plans. This is largely a problem of organization, and as such it has two aspects of sufficient practical and political importance to mention.

One question is whether an organization comprising about 100 planning countries with one control center can be effective. Most organization experts would agree that there is room here for an "intermediate level," i.e., a grouping of the countries so that the center deals only with continental (officially, "regional") organizations,

---

8. For a general treatment of the problem see A. Qayum, *Theory and Policy of Accounting Prices*, North-Holland Publishing Company, Amsterdam, 1960.

9. See J. Tinbergen and H. C. Bos, *Mathematical Models of Economic Growth*, McGraw-Hill, New York, 1962, section 5.2.

while the latter maintain contact with the individual countries.[10] This implies, then, the need for continental organizations, perhaps with the continents split up into a few very big countries and groups of smaller nations. The regional commissions of the United Nations in Latin America, in Asia and the Far East, and in Europe would certainly be able to assume such a task, and it is to be hoped that the Economic Commission for Africa will soon develop the capability. A country like the United States could be in direct contact with the center, and one wonders whether in Western Europe an organization such as OECD might not be of help (see, however, section 8.4).

Another question concerns the checking of national or regional plans with the aid of a cross-tabulation of plans according to countries and production sectors. Certainly, a condition for balanced world growth is a harmonious distribution of investment over the main production sectors, that is, a distribution corresponding to the distribution of the demand arising from increased incomes. For reasons of information and democracy, organized producers (including employers' associations as well as employees' unions) should advise on the expansion of their trades.[11] This idea has been applied in France with considerable success. Obviously, producers must be organized on a world scale — or something comparable — and must have arrived at a common opinion as to the most desirable development of their industry before such a contact can be made.

7.4 THE OPTIMUM PATTERN OF DIVISION OF LABOR

Planning on an international scale will make it possible to consider more explicitly than any single nation can consider the problem of the best international division of labor. The various products demanded by the world should in fact originate wherever they

---

10. Similar reasoning must have led the Soviet Union to follow the creation of about 100 *sovnarkhozy* — the geographic planning units — with the creation of 17 larger units.

11. This idea will be elaborated in a forthcoming volume on planning which is to be a joint publication of Yale University and the Netherlands Economic Institute.

can be produced most cheaply. The main factors at stake are those summed up by the theory of international trade, namely comparative advantages in production and transportation. The mechanism of free competition does help to bring about an optimum pattern for some types of products. Yet free competition is hindered in so many ways that some checking is desirable. Such checking may be attempted with the aid of estimates of the costs of producing a large number of items at a large number of different locations. Proposals have been made[12] to make available to planners — national and international — the vast amount of material scattered over government agencies, offices of consulting engineers, scientific institutions, and perhaps even private enterprises. What might be done first is to estimate the cost of making the material comparable and publishing it: possibly the cost would be prohibitive.

Planning the best division of labor between countries is a relatively simple problem for activities where the optimum-size enterprise is relatively small. Small enterprises can be apportioned in an almost continuous way, as is usually suggested by economic theory. One additional unit will not influence prices very much and the criterion for establishing an additional unit is that the unit cost of the marginal enterprise will not be higher than the world market price. Evidently, we must define cost as the figure to be expected after a learning period, calculated by using shadow prices. If trade policy and subsidies are optimal, the pattern emerging under free enterprise would not differ very much from such a planned optimal pattern of production. This is not true for activities subject to considerable economies of scale or long gestation periods. The development pattern of free enterprise has a tendency to show, in the first case, an overemphasis on diminutive units, leading to excessive costs; and, in the second case, an alternation between too much and too little total production. National governments should not be free to plan such development without consulting with neighboring governments. Good advice can be obtained from comprehensive studies by the continental planning agencies. These agencies

12. In the Advisory Committee on the Work Program on Industrialization of the United Nations and in the ECAFE publication *Programming Techniques for Economic Development,* Bangkok, 1960.

devote considerable attention to determining the appropriate location and size of the units needed for an optimal market supply. As a rule there will be alternative solutions to the problem. A guiding principle should be to distribute the big units evenly among the countries of the continent so that all of them have a chance to reap the benefits of large-scale industry.[13]

7.5 TRAINING OF QUALIFIED PERSONNEL

As already observed, development rests on two complementary types of investment: investment in equipment and investment in qualified manpower. Today this fact is generally understood, and a modern economic development policy implies a policy of training at all levels. The training process is a lengthy one. A university-trained technician goes through some eighteen years of learning before entering the phase of practical experience — which, for that matter, must be considered part of his training, and not the least important part. In a period when the West's need for trained personnel for internal purposes — especially for further research — is increasing, we are confronted by the added demand for technical assistance to developing countries. In view of the numerous kinds of trained manpower at different levels of responsibility, the process of training requires co-ordination as much as the process of production does. A further complication is created by the fact that increasing the number of trainees necessitates increasing the number of instructors, who themselves must first be trained to teach their specialty. We must make every effort to use simplified procedures wherever possible, and to help the developing countries by temporarily offering them foreign teachers within the limitations of language difficulties referred to in section 6.2.

A distinction can be made between general education and specialized education and training. Specialized education is in many fields more closely connected with economic development, and

13. See W. Isard, E. W. Schooler, and T. Vietorisz, *Industrial Complex Analysis and Regional Development: A Case Study of Refinery-Petrochemical-Synthetic-Fiber Complexes in Puerto Rico,* The Technology Press of the Massachusetts Institute of Technology and John Wiley and Sons, New York, 1959.

complements it most clearly. General education, no doubt, is of significance for economic development, but it is also desirable for its own sake. A similar distinction can be drawn between medical care, strictly speaking, and health education. Distribution of the available resources over these and other fields must take into account not only the costs and the material results to be obtained but also the period of "production" and social satisfaction to be derived.

A major problem of technical assistance in this area is the training site. At the higher levels of training — the specialized intellectual levels — it would be natural for the trainees to move to the training agencies, which would be mostly, though not entirely, Western universities and production units. Some alienation from home conditions might occur, but this danger is more serious at the lower levels of training. Then, too, at the lower levels the number of people to be trained is so large that it would not be economical to move the trainees to the trainers. A shift in the opposite direction is needed here. There is, however, a growing tendency to send trainees at different levels to countries not too far away. This has the advantage that living and working conditions are more similar to home conditions than they would be in the West. In this context, regional training institutes designed to serve groups of countries are important. Western teachers can make valuable contributions as part of the international staff of these institutes.

Training should not be restricted to official education or schooling; to a considerable extent it must also include training on the job. Clearly, business firms — or, more broadly, production units including, of course, public enterprises — can make important contributions in this respect.

7.6 THE ROLES OF THE PUBLIC AND PRIVATE SECTORS

Finally, growth must be balanced with regard to public and private activity. As we have stressed earlier (in section 5.5), the dividing line between the two should not be drawn in a dogmatic way.

The balance between the two sectors should be determined by circumstances with efficiency as the main criterion. Efficiency must be measured in social terms; thus it is necessary to compare benefits to the nation as a whole with the sacrifices required. Those who want to do everything by private initiative or want to eliminate private activity altogether are guilty of a doctrinaire approach to the problem.

There is some consensus about the need for public activity in the infrastructure (see section 6.3). The main reason for this is that many of the projects involved do not yield an income to the investor, because for technical or social reasons no price can be charged for the product (e.g., roads and education). In addition, the large capital sum often needed is not always available in the private sector.

The superstructure — comprising manufacturing, agricultural, and mining activities — may be efficiently built up by private enterprise, if the local business community is sufficiently enterprising or if there is some interest from abroad. Many countries now try to encourage outside interest by laws or regulations guaranteeing fair treatment to foreign investors, and sometimes joint ventures with local investors are specially privileged. But if private capital is not forthcoming, recourse must be had to public industrial activity. Today's public enterprises do not differ much from private enterprises as to management and efficiency, but — if necessary — modern business forms can be introduced with assistance from abroad.

Mixed enterprises are another possibility. To take but one example, co-operative ownership of agricultural processing plants by farmers has been a successful expedient in several countries. Finally, private activity may be stimulated by subventions and technical aid, especially to small units. These smaller manufacturing units may be concentrated in industrial estates, where various elements of the infrastructure and technical assistance are available simultaneously.[14]

Subventions should place a premium on the use of labor rather

14. See J. Tinbergen, *The Design of Development,* Johns Hopkins Press, Baltimore, 1958, Chapter 4.

than on the use of capital; any worthy new project should emphasize the abundant rather than the scarce factor of production. Of
course, the system of subventions has to be adapted to circumstances. In sparsely populated underdeveloped countries the use
of the labor factor should not be encouraged. Furthermore, natural
conditions and technical factors have to be taken into account;
sometimes there is little choice as to the production methods to be
used. As much as possible the administration of subventions should
be linked to existing tax or social insurance schemes in order to
facilitate supervision and keep costs down.

If waste is to be avoided, some interference by government seems
necessary in all cases; big private units should be created only with
the permission of the administration so that a check can be made
to see whether they fit into the general plan. It goes without saying
that if private enterprise develops in a way which complies with
the criteria for efficient investment, it should be accepted even
though it was not foreseen in the plan.

Private foreign investment — in which joint investment with local capital is of growing importance — will be facilitated if some of
the noneconomic risks can be insured. Schemes already exist in the
United States, Western Germany, and Japan to insure the risks of
exchange difficulties (delays in payments and, in the German system, devaluation), nationalization without satisfactory indemnification, and war damage. Risks can be insured if they arise from investments in countries that have concluded agreements with these
states in which stipulations are made for the treatment of capital;[15]
such agreements are not required in the Japanese system.

Although these national schemes have undoubtedly encouraged
the flow of private capital to the developing countries, a multilateral insurance scheme would seem preferable. Such a scheme
would place a common responsibility on all countries concerned,
capital-importing as well as capital-exporting. Developing coun-

15. In the German system insurance of an investment is possible even when an
agreement with the country concerned has not yet been concluded, if that country
has taken satisfactory measures to protect foreign capital. (See documents on "Gesell-
schaft zur Förderung des Schutzes von Auslandsinvestitionen e.V.")

tries thus could influence the setup and the implementation of the system and they could, together with the developed countries, share the burden of some form of guarantees. Capital-exporting countries could share the risks with many others, and so it may be expected that a large number of them would join such a scheme. The result might be a considerable expansion of the international flow of private capital.

Several proposals of this kind have been made recently. Of these we would like to call attention to the plan for a "Mutual Investment Insurance Corporation," which is designed to be an affiliate of IBRD. Recently this plan, together with some others, has been the object of study by the Bank.[16]

16. The idea for such a corporation was first discussed in a meeting of the CAFEA group of the International Chamber of Commerce in Karachi, December 1960. See the discussion paper by E. H. van Eeghen, *Memorandum on an International Guarantee Institution Covering Political and Calamity Risks of Private Capital in Development Countries.*

MYOPIA AND FARSIGHTEDNESS IN TRADE POLICY

8.1 THE CASE FOR LESS CHAOS

The second group of means and instruments of economic policy to be considered is trade policies. More perhaps than other issues of economic policy, changes in trade policies are a matter for detailed negotiations. The results of such negotiations depend on a formidable quantity of technical minutiae which change almost from day to day. This study cannot hope to formulate proposals for direct negotiation; it can, however, help in analyzing the problems and suggesting a few main lines of action. This is of some value even for practical decisions because of the unparalleled complexity of the subject. The number of political leaders with a thorough knowledge of trade policies is more restricted than the number in-

136

formed about other economic policy issues. Much is left to technical experts in numerous specialized fields and to the innumerable pressure groups operating in this field.

The subject is complicated by the large number of goods and countries involved and by the fact that trade always involves pairs of countries. In addition there is the time element: changes in policy must be properly timed. A minor complication is the number of instruments applied: duties, quantitative restrictions, combinations like tariff quotas, and in some countries exchange rates which differ for different commodities. Viewed in toto, trade policy is a monster with a multitude of dimensions or degrees of freedom; an exact description of its state would require thousands of figures at the least. Trade policy is in chaos. That it has become so is partly the inevitable result of its multidimensional quality — a characteristic it shares with, say, detailed planning in Communist countries or in wartime economies — and partly the fault of governments that have left too many decisions to pressure groups.

This situation is undesirable if for no other reason than that it enables pressure groups to operate in the dark: almost nobody else knows his way around the subject. If in the past, trade policy had been less opportunistic and more systematic, a greater degree of public control would have been possible. A more systematic policy might be followed with regard to the rate structure or, if that is asking too much, with regard to rate levels. Thus EEC has been able to institute proportional reductions for large numbers of tariff items. Because of the fear of commitment referred to in section 3.2, the American government has not been permitted by Congress to follow this procedure.

The current situation with regard to trade policy is also undesirable because it is doubtful, to say the least, whether highly differentiated tariffs are in accord with the optimum conditions for social welfare.

A case can be made, therefore, for some streamlining, or simplification, of rate structure as advocated by GATT.[1] This would not

1. In the November 1961 Meeting of Ministers held in connection with the 19th GATT Session this view was accepted (see *Conclusions of Meeting of Ministers,* Press

only widen the opportunities for democratic control but would also speed up the processes involved in reducing trade impediments. The present technique of item-by-item negotiation is highly inefficient.

Another requisite for a more systematic trade policy is official recognition of the fact that internal taxes on products are a trade impediment of the same nature as import duties, and subject to the same criticisms. So far there is only the GATT rule prohibiting internal taxes which privilege domestic producers (Article III, 1). Of course, we do not mean that indirect taxes such as general purchase or turnover taxes should be regarded as a major trade barrier; the argument applies to discriminating — and usually rather heavily discriminating — fiscal duties levied on specific products (coffee, cocoa, tea, sugar, etc.). Internal taxes of this kind should be internationally negotiable just as import duties are; they should be brought under the "jurisdiction" of GATT. This fact was recognized in the Havana Trade Charter and in the ITO Charter. The Haberler Report advocates extending the GATT rules so as to cover those internal duties which are comparable to import taxes, a recommendation fully endorsed here.[2]

Since changes in trade policy are bound to affect adversely some groups in the population, they always meet with some opposition. Proposed changes will be more acceptable if they are grouped so that each country will derive advantages as well as disadvantages. Of course, this is more of a problem in the short run; in the long run, interests are more parallel (see section 8.2). Although we are concentrating on the policy of the West as it affects underdeveloped countries, we are thinking in terms of proposals which will fit into a world pattern of changes in commercial policy.

Release GATT/651, Geneva, November 30, 1961). The recommendation of the ministers that machinery be established for considering new techniques, in particular some form of linear tariff reduction, was approved by the Contracting Parties on December 7, 1961. Also, recent proposals of the American government aim at enlarging the powers of the President of the United States in negotiating tariff reductions.

2. See *Trends in International Trade*, Report by a Panel of Experts, General Agreement on Tariffs and Trade, Geneva, 1958, pp. 107–108.

8.2 ETERNAL MYOPIA?

There is a clear difference between the short-term and the long-term effects of a reduction in trade impediments. In the short run a reduction in a tariff or a quota may force an industry into losses; workers may have to be dismissed and capital goods may stand idle. In the long run (that is, if the reduction is only applied after capital goods have been worn out and written off and the workers retrained), unemployed capital and labor can be used in another industry, to the advantage of everybody. Therefore, as a first approximation it can be maintained that in the long run a tariff reduction is in the interest of all concerned: importing countries, consumers, and the erstwhile producers. This is what the theory of international trade has always maintained — and rightly so, at least for industrial countries under the conditions enumerated in section 3.1.

A student of trade policy is soon depressed by the little attention given by politicians to the long-term aspect of economic events. Everyday policy is too much concerned with short-term consequences, and insufficiently aware of longer-term implications which may be favorable. There have of course been notable exceptions to this rule in countries where the free-trade doctrine was well understood. Thus Dutch agricultural policy around the nineties was such that the Netherlands exposed its farmers to the full consequences of cheap overseas grain; it gave them no protection but only support in the form of specialized schools and technical consultation services. It is not by chance that today agriculture is much more efficient in the Netherlands than in neighboring countries.

The tendency to emphasize short-term interests is a general human trait, but this is not to say that it is the course of wisdom. In the case of trade policy it is even less so, since it leads to undue concern for the short-term interests of certain producers; other interests are disregarded. Yet it is true that the idleness of factors of production works a hardship on the nation as a whole. For that reason protection for a transitional period makes sense; it may even

take the form of quantitative restrictions (especially tariff quotas) as a transitional measure.

Yet we cannot respect short-term interests forever. It is against the long-term interests of the population to protect an industry permanently — unless that industry produces vital supplies, as discussed in section 3.1. It is unwise to display myopia in designing trade policy. Protection should be temporary in principle, and be granted at a declining rate so that it will come to an end automatically. To cite an example, when the Netherlands instituted a scheme to promote new industries after World War II, protection was given for three years only, and then stopped. Out of some twenty industries given this protection, three emerged successful; protection to the others was stopped in the general interest. The same philosophy has been followed in the scheme for the Rome Treaty. Here the reductions in intramural protection originally scheduled were gradual, extending over some twelve years. It is a matter of satisfaction that it has been possible to shorten this period by the so-called accelerated execution of the treaty.

In cases where quick action on trade policy is necessary, measures such as the insurance scheme advocated in section 9.4 or increased financial aid may be used to compensate the groups or countries adversely affected. It does seem desirable to act quickly in some cases. Generally speaking the time pattern should be based on the doctrine "first things first." Instruments causing tensions and those least in accordance with the general aims of our policies should be removed first. This applies first of all to quantitative restrictions on industrial products of "low-wage countries," since these are in "flat contradiction to the formal obligations of the importing countries under GATT,"[3] particularly Articles XI and XIII. If imports from these countries cause or threaten serious injury to producers in other countries, the latter are authorized by Article XIX of GATT to take protective measures; this can be settled by agreements between importing and exporting countries. But the protection should not take the form of a long-lasting dis-

3. See E. Wyndham White, *Some Structural Problems of International Trade,* GATT, Geneva, 1961.

crimination, and it should be gradually reduced. ECE has made the constructive proposal[4] that each industrial Western European country "might agree . . . to abolish all tariffs and import restrictions on such exports of manufactures by individual underdeveloped countries as do not, in any year, exceed a certain proportion — say 3 to 5 per cent — of its total imports in the previous year in that commodity group."

8.3 ONE AIM AND SEVERAL ROADS

In order to devise the main lines of action we must further define the aims of commercial policy. To a considerable extent these can be scientifically derived. Our analysis of section 3.1, based on the theories of welfare economics, yields some optimum solutions, best and second best. Trade impediments should be minimal provided that there are sufficient income transfers between wealthier and less well-to-do countries, and that it is possible to organize subsidies for infant industries and industries supplying vital goods. Insofar as these conditions are not met, some kind of protection can be accepted, namely protection of developing countries in a general way, and particularly their infant industries, and protection of vital supplies everywhere. However, the level and duration of the protection applied must be related to the particular object in view. Thus young industries should not be protected by more than the margin that the learning process may be able to eliminate, and for a longer period than the learning process requires. Similarly, the protection of basic industries should be limited by the cost reductions to be expected from economies of scale and external effects once these industries are fully developed. In other words, protection should be reasonable; it should not be simply a type of featherbedding for industrialists.

As to the protection of vital supplies, the whole argument may require overhauling. In Europe it is gradually being recognized that the argument is no longer applicable to small countries, since

4. ECE, *Economic Survey of Europe 1960,* Geneva, 1961, Chapter 5, p. 50.

they will not be isolated in the event of war. What will matter then is only whether a continent as a whole commands sufficient supplies of agricultural products. This can be ensured with relatively lower import duties since there are unexploited productive areas in every continent.

The condition that subsidies be organized for infant and vital industries probably cannot be fully met, and protection will have to be accepted to some extent. The number of units involved and the type of administration necessary for a viable scheme of subsidies are arguments in favor of this point of view. The condition that income be sufficiently redistributed can be complied with, and general protection of underdeveloped countries on this score can therefore be avoided. The rise in income or capital transfers proposed for the future (see section 7.1) seems to meet reasonable standards in this respect. However, until this aid materializes the developing countries will have to take measures to protect their balances of payments. Such measures may include bilateral trade agreements, but they should be considered as a second-best solution only. We do not agree, therefore, with A. Shonfield when he advocates new trade rules for GATT.[5]

What we are left with, then, as a program for trade policy consists of temporary duties or quotas for infant industries in developing countries, perhaps some agricultural protection in industrial countries (to be verified by further research), and temporary protection in the event of sudden changes in competitive conditions.

The central aim of freer trade is not incompatible with controls on trade. It is a question of technique, and the relevant issue is whether or not trade which makes sense from the standpoint of comparative advantages is materializing. In centrally organized economies trade as well as production is the subject of detailed government decisions. Evidently the trade partners of such countries must also have regulations, and these regulations need not impede the development of optimum trade patterns. Whether centralized

5. Andrew Shonfield, *The Attack on World Poverty*, Random House, New York, 1960, p. 56.

decisions are useful even in Communist countries is still another matter.[6]

In addition, the question may be asked whether trade with the Communist countries can be expanded. We think it has been unduly restricted in a number of cases.

The aim of a sounder pattern of international trade can be reached by different roads. One of the conditions determining the choice of route may be — but need not be — that no new discriminations are introduced. This has been the British philosophy for the last ten years or so. The signatories to the Rome Treaty chose to eliminate impediments among themselves first, and then to try to enlarge their group. The establishment of EEC could stimulate the creation of other groups, which might finally merge. Some group arrangements have been accepted by GATT as "legal." The disadvantage of customs unions and free-trade zones is that they may divert trade[7] from more desirable channels. Their advantage is that countries with similar standards and experience in administration can co-operate more easily.

8.4 A WORLD OF AREAS?

There are further arguments in favor of a regional or continental grouping of countries for the purposes of economic policy in general and trade policy in particular. One argument lies on the plane of general organization. Thus the planning, execution, and supervision of a world economic policy could be streamlined and made more efficient by such grouping. Also, groups of neighboring countries often have common cultural elements, sometimes even a common language (as in Latin America and the Arab region). Finally, trade is more intensive as a rule between neighboring countries than between widely separated countries.

6. For some suggestions concerning the conditions which must be satisfied if a centrally planned economy is to comply with the principles of GATT, see E. Wyndham White, *Looking Outwards*, GATT, Geneva, 1960.

7. Jacob Viner, *The Customs Union Issue*, Carnegie Endowment for International Peace, New York, 1950; see also J. E. Meade, *The Theory of Customs Unions*, North-Holland Publishing Company, Amsterdam, 1955.

As a consequence of common cultural elements and regular trade relations, adjoining countries have in many cases a similar way of life, associated with comparable psychological and material needs. Further, they are, on the average, more interested in each other's situation than in the situations of remote countries. These factors can facilitate the conclusion of negotiations and — most important — the execution of common policies. It is true that the mutual interest of neighboring countries may be based in part on fear; historically there have been ardent enemies among neighboring states. The danger of a common frontier without any organizational tie has often led to a merger — frequently accomplished by conquest, but not always. Clearly if adjacent countries enter into communal arrangements, the danger of hostile acts by neighboring states will become weaker. This in turn will make feasible a further approach to co-operation.

The organization argument was discussed briefly in section 7.3 in the context of planning; it applies also to the use of instruments of economic policy. Integration between countries is resulting in the creation of supranational agencies, but their scope is not always world-wide. Continental institutions are being created to serve the ends of financial and monetary policy. Other policies should be co-ordinated at the continental level before world-wide co-ordination is considered. Regional co-operation may become increasingly important in the field of heavy industry. It is a well-known organizational principle that one agency can directly control only a limited number of groups. There are too many nations for them to co-operate efficiently in the world at large. An intermediate role may have to be played by "areas," roughly coextensive with the continents. It must be assumed that the Communist parts of Europe and Asia will act autonomously.

We have already stated that trade within continents is often larger than trade between continents. This will become increasingly true as the developing parts of the world industrialize. Of course, intercontinental trade will always remain. In terms of market areas, commodities can be divided into the following groups:

(i) world trade commodities, those which for the most part

cross continental frontiers (e.g., coffee, copper, oriental carpets);

(ii) semi-world trade commodities, those important in intercontinental trade as well as in trade within each continent (e.g., sugar, several kinds of fruits, cotton fabrics);

(iii) continental trade commodities, mostly traded within the continents (e.g., steel, coal, potatoes);

(iv) nationally traded commodities (e.g., building materials, vegetables); and

(v) locally traded commodities (e.g., bread, repair services).

Although in the course of time the pattern will change and commodities may move from one group to another, it is helpful to make this division for trade policy purposes.

For intercontinental trade it would seem advantageous to introduce an intermediate level of organization. One reason is that it would reduce the number of trade treaties and trade negotiations required. If 100 countries wanted to trade directly with each other on the basis of bilateral agreements, 4,950 trade treaties would have to be negotiated. If they traded directly with each other only within each of five areas of 20 countries and their trade with other areas was dealt with through area organizations, the number of treaties needed would be 1,060, i.e., 10 between areas, 100 between each country and its own area, and 950 between any two countries within the same area.[8]

Finally, important political reasons exist at present for further co-operation within continents or comparable regions. In the existing political situation, the newly independent countries of Asia

8. Of course in practice by no means all international trade is covered by trade treaties. But the argument also applies to trade contacts of other types. Moreover, many developing countries like to embody certain aspects of their trade relations in treaties: it imparts an element of security to their economic structure, and may facilitate their development planning and policy-making. If the principles mentioned above are observed in these treaties, and if they are adapted to changing circumstances at the proper time, they surely may be useful. Area agencies could facilitate this process because they could survey and appraise the economic developments and opportunities in an area better than national governments can. Also, they might reduce the danger of economically unjustified bilateral equilibria becoming a goal of trade policy.

and Africa would probably prefer to make arrangements with EEC as groups rather than individually. Certainly their bargaining power will be greater if they do so. Agreements between areas may then be concluded. Possibly the most far-reaching agreements of this kind could come into being between Latin America and North America, and among the areas of the Old World. In the present chaotic situation in Africa innumerable local political difficulties will have to be overcome before any streamlining is possible; even so, policies may be formulated with this end in view.

The decentralized system of world organization suggested implies an element of competition between areas of comparable strength. Competition of this sort will be sound and stimulating. The guidance of world institutions will be necessary to create and maintain the conditions for balanced area competition. The process will have to be gradual and piecemeal. As an example let us consider the Arab world. In section 3.4 the status of economic co-operation between the Arab League countries was described briefly (p. 54). On the one hand there is an urge to unity and an awareness of the advantages of economic co-operation; on the other, there are many political difficulties, based on differences in politico-economic structure and stage of development.

Because of these difficulties, it has often been suggested in these countries that a start must be made by the formation of smaller groups. These would co-operate with each other on an economic level and, possibly, eventually integrate. Suggestions concerning the size and composition of the smaller groups differ widely. Other people have advocated expansion of direct economic co-operation among all members, but only in a restricted number of economic fields. There is the further possibility that these two approaches could be combined (see Appendix II).

8.5 EUROPE IN THE WORLD

Europe, and more particularly EEC, will exert a considerable influence — for good or ill — by its own activity in the field of trade policies. It will have to show whether it understands its new responsibilities: whether it can be broadminded in designing its own new

pattern, and whether it can be farsighted. Even though the creation of EEC does almost no harm to the outside world at large (see section 3.3), some countries suffer by it. If developing countries feel that they are being unfairly treated, EEC must be careful in discussing with them the sources of tension; it must open up the prospect of better treatment or of compensatory measures.

The most important steps EEC can take are to lower the outer tariff further and to reduce some consumption taxes. We think it is particularly important that the duties or consumption taxes on coffee, tea, sugar, cocoa beans and products, and bananas be lowered, and we suggest schemes for some commodities in later sections of this chapter. Such reductions would have to be accompanied by small increases in the general turnover tax to compensate for the decline in fiscal revenue.[9]

The proposed reductions will effect a corresponding reduction in the privileges promised to associated countries in the form of higher prices for their products. Here we have a case in which compensation must be offered.[10] The most appropriate form which compensation can take seems to us to be an additional amount of financial assistance for development purposes. More precisely, this amount should correspond to the reduction in export values to be expected from the reduction in outer tariffs applied to outsiders. The case can be illustrated by hypothetical figures.

Suppose a reduction in the outer tariff on an important export article of an associated country is expected to diminish the total annual export proceeds of that country by $12 million. The tariff reduction will be put into effect in six equal steps in the course of six years; every year, then, a decrease in export value of $2 million will occur. Marginal producers of the commodity will have to cease operations and attempt to switch to other occupations. Development plans will have to be reconsidered and efforts may have to be made to introduce new branches of production. If after the

9. Some estimates of the order of magnitude of the decline in fiscal revenue and of other consequences of a lowering of tariffs and internal taxes are presented in the next section and in Appendix VII.

10. See *La politique de la CEE à l'égard des pays en voie de développement* (Colloque de Bari, October 1961), Comitato Nazionale per l'Energia Nucleare, Rome, 1961.

period of six years the export value of new articles is, say, $8 million and production for home consumption of commodities formerly imported amounts to $4 million, a new equilibrium will have been attained.

The following schedule of assistance for development purposes may be imagined:

Millions of Dollars

Year	Financial Assistance	Increase in Production as a Result of Assistance[a]	Decrease in Exports of Less Protected Commodity
1	6	—	—
2	6	2	2
3	6	4	4
4	6	6	6
5	6	8	8
6	6	10	10
7	—	12	12

a. Here a capital-output ratio of 3 years has been assumed, leading to an annual increase in production of $\dfrac{6}{3} = 2$.

This simple example may be made more complicated at will. The gestation period of newly invested capital can be figured at more than 1 year; if this is done the assistance must be higher in the early years to prevent balance of payments deficits. The total amount needed in the form of additional financial assistance will be three times the annual value of the privileged exports to be replaced, this ratio coinciding with the capital-output ratio for additional investments.

If an international scheme for insurance against the risks of declining exports — as mentioned in section 4.5 — could be effectuated, member countries might receive part of any compensation due them from the insurance fund.[11] In this connection, the establishment of a special EEC insurance fund which might later be integrated into a world-wide insurance scheme could be considered.

11. See also section 9.4.

A world body might act as an overseer for a number of area insurance systems.

If EEC were to reduce its outer tariff, as suggested above, the prices at which European industrial products are supplied to associated territories could be reduced at the same time. At present industrial products are supplied by France at higher than world market prices, but these products can be supplied by other member countries at world market prices.

EEC will also have to decide on its future policies of association. Association with Turkey is under way, and association with a number of African countries must be negotiated anew before the current association treaties expire on December 31, 1962. Association of individual countries seems a natural development when these countries are potential members, as is true more particularly of European countries. As we have said, for non-European countries area agreements are preferable in principle. But until such areas exist, the privilege of individual association must be continued. In these circumstances some of the preceding considerations regarding compensation for reduction in privileges apply.

Many details will take shape only after negotiations with the United Kingdom are further advanced. Two major sets of problems will have to be solved during these negotiations: relationships with the Commonwealth, and agricultural policy. With regard to the Commonwealth countries on the one hand and the associated territories of EEC on the other, it is natural to think that both groups of countries would be placed in the same position in relation to the joint market of EEC and the United Kingdom. Since the Commonwealth countries do not export the same class of goods as the EEC associated territories, different treatment of different commodities will have to be instituted to establish some sort of equilibrium.

8.6 SUGGESTIONS FOR A TRADE POLICY

We must bear in mind that the ultimate aim of international trade policy is the liberalization of world trade, except in the cases

mentioned in section 8.3. As explained above, there is a place for area co-operation in the context of world economic integration. However, developments in this respect have been out of balance: Western Europe is far ahead. For the present this means that special discriminations against outside countries are in force. Because of this situation it seems wise to consider the future integration process of the Western European countries (including their relations with the associated countries and the Commonwealth[12]) against the background of Western Europe's relations with the rest of the world. In other words, in studies and negotiations on the dismantling of trade impediments between Western countries, attention should constantly be given to the position of the outside countries. It would also help to bring about a balanced treatment of the problem if we distinguished groups of commodities according to their relative importance, not only to the EEC countries and their Associates, the United Kingdom and the Commonwealth, but to the outside countries as well.

With regard to import duties we suggest that as a rule they should be proportionally reduced for all commodities of one group. The agreed-upon EEC outer tariff for these commodities would be reduced by the same percentage, the reduction to be accomplished gradually, and the level aimed at in our provisional plan to be attained at the end of the transition period, December 31, 1967 (see Appendix VII). The result would be a common outer tariff for EEC and the United Kingdom. Exports from the Associates and the Commonwealth to EEC and the United Kingdom would be duty-free. The same would apply to any other European countries that might join the extended Common Market. Exports from EEC and the United Kingdom to the associated countries and the Commonwealth would be duty-free too, unless industrialization problems or balance of payments difficulties made protection imperative (these are the exceptions mentioned in the EEC treaty).

In other respects, however, the commodities of one group would

12. As used in this section, Commonwealth excludes the United Kingdom.

have to be dealt with in different ways. This applies, for instance, if a shift in the production pattern of a single commodity — due to the lower import duty — has to be compensated for by special aid to one or more exporting countries. Also, some regulations concerning tariff quotas might have to be made. It is conceivable too that, after being maintained for a short period, import quotas would be gradually enlarged. Where the system of selling contracts exists, it seems desirable that limited periods of maintenance and normal prices be indicated in the contracts. Finally, we think that in many cases internal taxes should be reduced in order to encourage consumption in developed countries and increase the export possibilities of developing countries.

There might be exceptions in each group, "special cases" in which the decrease in import duties could only be different from the general run. It is also to be expected that in some cases no agreement as to import duties will be reached by EEC and the United Kingdom, so that the commodities in question cannot be subject to the same procedure. In such cases we can only hope that the differences will eventually be smoothed out.

If a commodity is of especially great importance to outside countries it should be considered a candidate for the greatest decrease in European preferences. Striking differences between the protective duties on a commodity in its successive processing stages should be reduced. This must be done carefully in order to enable the industry concerned to switch to another line of production if necessary.

To illustrate our train of thought we will set down a tentative scheme of commodity groups, and then consider a representative commodity from each group. Thus we will try to arrive at proposals for tariff reductions which could be acceptable to all concerned, exporting as well as importing countries.

It goes without saying that if area association is speeded up in other parts of the world, European trade policy will have to adapt itself to the new constellations.

In accordance with the design of this book, we have included in

our proposals those commodities which are of great importance —
or at least of special interest — to developing countries. Our suggestions are in line with the developments we recommend in world
trade policy.

The groups to be distinguished are:

  I. Commodities very important to outside countries, impor-
     tant to the Associates, also produced in the Commonwealth
     (e.g., coffee). Because of the great importance of these com-
     modities to outside countries the decrease in the EEC outer
     tariff will have to be large. We propose 80 per cent.

 II. Commodities very important to outside countries, impor-
     tant to the Commonwealth, also produced in the Associates
     (e.g., bananas and beef). As in group I, and for the same
     reason, we propose a tariff reduction of 80 per cent.

III. Commodities very important to outside countries, and also
     important to EEC and Associates and to the United King-
     dom and Commonwealth (e.g., sugar). A number of these
     commodities are vital for Western Europe, so this area
     must continue to produce them to a certain extent. But as
     they are highly important to outside countries we propose
     a reduction of 70 per cent.

 IV. Commodities very important to the Commonwealth, also
     produced in outside countries, but of slight importance to
     the Associates (e.g., tea). Notwithstanding the great im-
     portance of these products to the Commonwealth, the
     United Kingdom general tariff — and the Commonwealth
     preference — is in many cases not very high. In order to
     reach an agreement with the United Kingdom, EEC must
     lower the planned outer tariff significantly. The fact that
     these products are more important to outside countries
     than to the Associates also makes such a reduction reason-
     able. We propose 70 per cent.

  V. Commodities very important to the Commonwealth, also
     produced in outside countries and in the Associates (e.g.,
     cocoa beans and palm oil). As in group IV, the great interest

of the Commonwealth argues for a considerable decrease in the outer tariff. But because these products are more important to the Associates than those in the preceding group, we propose to restrict the reduction to 60 per cent.

Groundnuts, which also belong to this group, will not be subject to an EEC import duty; therefore, if the United Kingdom joins the Common Market, the Commonwealth preference of 10 per cent will disappear.

VI. Commodities important to outside countries, to the Commonwealth, and to the Associates, and of some importance to the United Kingdom and EEC (e.g., dried fruits). A certain degree of self-sufficiency in these products is often useful to Western Europe. In most cases the planned EEC outer tariff is not extremely high. A decrease of 60 per cent would therefore bring the outer tariff to a reasonable level, and give outside countries a fair chance to compete in the European market.

VII. Commodities important to outside countries, to the United Kingdom and the Commonwealth, and to EEC and the Associates (e.g., cotton fabrics). Since on the one hand the EEC countries frequently seem to have overprotected their own producers and on the other hand products of this group often have the character of vital supplies, a decrease of the outer tariff by 50 per cent might be justified.

The reductions in the EEC outer tariff suggested for the various groups of commodities are listed in Table 8–1. A detailed discussion of the market situation and the import duties at present levied on these commodities will be presented in the next section. First, however, we will examine briefly the consequences of such a program of tariff reductions for the economy of the country lowering or abolishing duties.

Table 8–2 summarizes the results of a calculation of the consequences of a complete abolition of all the taxes and duties that are levied on the import and consumption of a few commodities. The method of calculation is set out in detail in Appendix VII. The

Table 8–1

PROPOSED PERCENTAGE REDUCTIONS IN EEC OUTER TARIFF FOR
SEVEN GROUPS OF COMMODITIES, WITH EXAMPLES
(to be realized by December 31, 1967)

		Commonwealth, excl. United Kingdom			
		Less Important	Important		Very Important
		EEC Associates			
		Important	Less Important	Important	Less Important
Outside Countries	Very Important	I 80 (coffee)	II 80 (bananas)	IIIa 70 (sugar)	
	Important			VIb 60 (dried fruits) VII 50 (cotton fabrics)	
	Less Important				IVc 70 (tea) V 60 (cocoa beans)

a. Also important to the United Kingdom and EEC.
b. Of minor importance to the United Kingdom and EEC.
c. Of hardly any importance to EEC Associates.

Table 8–2

ESTIMATED EFFECTS OF ABOLISHING ALL IMPORT AND
CONSUMPTION CHARGES ON SELECTED COMMODITIES (1959 data)

	INCREASE IN IMPORTS AS A PERCENTAGE OF TOTAL IMPORTS			LOSS OF GOVT. REVENUE AS A PERCENTAGE OF TOTAL INDIRECT TAXES		PERCENTAGE DECREASE IN PRODUCTION AND EMPLOYMENT IN INDUSTRY CONCERNED (UPPER AND LOWER ESTIMATES)	
	Coffee, Tea, Bananas	Sugar	Cotton Grey Goods	Coffee, Tea, Bananas	Sugar	Sugar Production and Refining	Cotton Textile Industry
BLEU	—	0.4	0.6	0.2	1.2	72–100	8–11
France	0.2	2.3	1.8	0.7	0.9	80–100	11–15
Germany (F. R.)	0.3	n.a.	0.7	2.5	0.5	n.a.	4–6
Italy	0.4	3.2	n.a.	2.1	3.5	82–100	n.a.
Netherlands	—	0.8	0.5	0.3	6.4	72–100	7–9
Austria	—	2.5	0.9	0.4	1.8	66–100	13–17
Denmark	0.1	0.6	0.1	1.5	—	40–60	4–5
Finland	0.1	0.1	n.a.	7.3	3.8	96–100	n.a.
Norway	—	—	0.1	0.1	0.3	—	6–8
Sweden	0.1	n.a.	0.3	0.9	1.5	n.a.	6–8
Switzerland	0.1	0.1	n.a.	1.4	2.3	47–70	7–9
UK	—	n.a.	0.6	0.9	2.3	n.a.	7–10
Canada	—	0.1	n.a.	0.1	0.5	37–55	n.a.
USA	—	0.5	n.a.	—	0.3	15–22	n.a.
Australia	—	—	n.a.	0.1	n.a.	—	n.a.
New Zealand	—	—	n.a.	0.3	1.0	—	n.a.
Japan	—	0.5	n.a.	1.6	5.4	70–100	n.a.

—: nil or negligible.
n.a.: not available, i.e., impossible to estimate.
Sources: See Appendix VII.

commodities chosen are all important export products of several developing countries. They fall into three categories:

(i) agricultural products not directly competing with production in developed countries (e.g., coffee, tea, bananas);

(ii) agricultural products competing with production in developed countries (e.g., sugar); and

(iii) industrial products competing — almost by definition — with production in developed countries (e.g., cotton grey goods).

The consequences of abolishing all import and consumption charges cannot easily be assessed; a crude estimate was the most that could be arrived at in the present study. An attempt has been made to quantify, for a number of countries, three different effects of an abolition of charges, namely:

(i) the increase in imports;

(ii) the loss of government revenue; and

(iii) the decrease in production and employment.

Obviously these effects will be regarded unfavorably by the country concerned, albeit to a varying degree. The loss of government revenue will not be taken too seriously in most countries, as this loss can easily be compensated for by a modest increase in other tax rates. The decrease in employment (which is, to be sure, only a short-term effect) will probably be regarded as a more serious threat of the increased competition of foreign goods in the domestic market.

It should not be overlooked, however, that there are consequences of a positive nature as well. These positive consequences have not been estimated quantitatively here, but they are tangible. To mention only the most immediate beneficial effect, consumer prices of the commodities involved will be lowered, which means of course a higher income and consumption level in terms of goods.

The following conclusions may be drawn from the figures in Table 8–2. It appears that a simultaneous abolition of all duties and taxes on coffee, tea, and bananas would have little effect on the balance of payments of the importing countries. But if similar

measures were taken with respect to sugar, the increase in imports would be more pronounced in several countries. In the case of cotton grey goods the import increase to be expected is fairly modest for most countries.

The impact on government income is unimportant. Even if a loss of receipts of 10 per cent of total indirect taxes were to result, this could be offset by raising the general turnover tax rate from, say, 4.0 to 4.5 or 5.0 per cent (depending on the importance of the turnover tax relative to total indirect taxes).

The estimated decrease in production and hence in employment would be much greater in the sugar industry than in the cotton textile industry. A complete abolition of import duties on sugar might result in the cessation of all production in Western Europe and Japan. To the extent that some domestic production is considered essential, less drastic measures than a full abolition would be called for. In the next section we propose that import duties be lowered by 70 per cent only; this reduction should be put into effect gradually, and measures should be taken to ease the adaptation process.

The consequences of an abolition of duties on cotton grey goods would be less serious. The resulting decline in production and employment would be around 10 per cent in most countries, and only modestly higher in countries with relatively high tariffs. As this decline would be spread over a period of at least six years, the annual incidence would not exceed 2 or 3 per cent. Particularly in a period of general economic expansion and full (or even over-full) employment, the adaptation process would not be a very painful one.

It should be borne in mind that the effects set forth in Table 8–2 would follow only from the most ambitious and drastic measures that could be taken — that is, a complete abolition of both import duties and internal taxes. The program of tariff reductions outlined in Table 8–1 and to be discussed in detail in the next section would have more limited consequences. The present analysis has shown that, except for sugar, these consequences are such

that they can certainly be borne by the economies of the developed countries, especially if measures are taken to overcome temporary difficulties in the industries that are affected.

8.7 ILLUSTRATION OF A TRADE POLICY FOR GROUPED PRODUCTS[13]

GROUP I *Proposed reduction of EEC outer tariff: 80 per cent Example: coffee*

In many respects the position of coffee is serious; overproduction exists and moreover the economies of a number of developing countries that produce this commodity are threatened with stagnation. The success of the International Coffee Agreement has been demonstrated by the virtual cessation of price deterioration since 1958 for the varieties produced by the member countries. However, the situation requires permanent attention; coffee producers must intensify their co-operation. Production must be kept within reasonable limits, and consumption will have to increase.

The United Kingdom levies a general import duty on unroasted coffee with an incidence of about 4.5 per cent, and a preferential tariff for the Commonwealth with a 1.5 per cent incidence. The future EEC outer tariff will be 16 per cent. In several Western European countries — Germany and Italy for instance — fiscal duties on coffee are extremely high.

A cut of 80 per cent in the EEC outer tariff — resulting in a tariff of 3 per cent — would give significant impetus to consumption. So would a considerable reduction in European internal taxes. The latter measure would be important to all exporters; the former would be advantageous to outside countries, the largest coffee producers, especially Brazil. The African Associates, also important producers, would be less protected. Where necessary they might be given compensatory development aid. For a limited period of time, for instance two years, France could be allowed to buy fixed quantities of coffee from the Associates; later these quantities would have to be reduced. Prices would have to be lowered to a normal level, as would the prices of certain French industrial goods exported to the African Associates. The French quantitative restrictions on outside coffee would have to be gradually abolished.

Together these measures are expected to encourage coffee consump-

13. Main sources: *The Commonwealth and Europe,* The Economist Intelligence Unit, London, 1960; and *Trends in International Trade,* cited in footnote 2.

tion. Without a successful agreement between producing countries, however, they could only lead to undesirably intense competition between producers all over the world. Therefore, efforts to promote regulation of production and trade, price stability, and increasing coffee consumption, together with investment aid when needed, should be effectively co-ordinated. This will require close contact between the members of the Coffee Agreement, the EEC countries, including the United Kingdom, and the United Nations agencies concerned.

GROUP II   *Proposed reduction of EEC outer tariff: 80 per cent*
            Example: bananas

The incidence of the United Kingdom tariff on bananas is 12 per cent, the same as the Commonwealth preference. The future EEC outer tariff is fixed at 20 per cent. Germany has tariff-free quotas at least during the transitional period of EEC. France buys African bananas at prices above the world level. The Italian state monopoly gives special privileges to Somalian producers.

Central America, Colombia, Ecuador, and the Canary Islands are the chief producing countries. Of secondary importance are the Commonwealth countries, followed by the Associates.

Production is expanding rather fast; new production schemes are under consideration. Demand in importing countries is increasing, but whether it will be able to keep pace with production is questionable.

If the EEC outer tariff of 20 per cent should become a reality, there would be a strong incentive to expand production in the Associates, a development which might strengthen the tendency to world overproduction. This would work a hardship on the outside countries which have no preference at all.

An 80 per cent reduction would bring the outer tariff to 4 per cent. The banana-producing countries among the Commonwealth and associated countries could be awarded compensatory development aid. Discrimination against the Latin American producing countries, which constitute by far the biggest production region, would be substantially diminished. Although there would remain a European tariff of 4 per cent, this does not seem an unsurmountable trade barrier. The Latin American producers, moreover, have easy access to the United States, which levies no duties at all. It is hoped that when Latin American integration has made further progress the high Brazilian import duty of 80 per cent will soon be reduced.

It has been suggested that France and Italy be permitted to continue buying fixed quantities from the Associates during a certain period, for

instance two years; thereafter, however, these quantities would have to be reduced. Prices should be dealt with as in the case of coffee.

It might be useful to consider the possibility of an international agreement which would prevent an excessive extension of production and promote a more even distribution of production.

GROUP III   *Proposed reduction of EEC outer tariff: 70 per cent Example: sugar*

Sugar, too, belongs to the semi-world trade commodities. Western Europe and the United States are important producers, ranking next to the West Indies (mainly Cuba) and Central and South America. Other main producing areas are India, Australia, and the Philippines. In Africa, the Union of South Africa and some of the African EEC Associates deserve mention.

The EEC countries have a large domestic sugar production. Western Germany and the Netherlands are net importers; France, Italy, Belgium, and Luxembourg net exporters. Together the Six have a bare net import balance. The main suppliers are the Latin American export centers, though France imports mainly from the Associates. Consumption in the Six is severely hampered by the high level of taxes and by government price fixing. If these impediments were substantially diminished or abolished, consumption could be expected to increase significantly; domestic production would not be able to keep pace.

The future EEC outer tariff on sugar will be 80 per cent. The general incidence of the United Kingdom tariff can be roughly calculated at 30 per cent and the preferential duty on Commonwealth sugar at 9 per cent. Of the United Kingdom's imports 60 per cent originate in the Commonwealth; other important suppliers are Cuba and the Dominican Republic. Trade between the United Kingdom and the Commonwealth is covered by the Commonwealth Sugar Agreement, according to which the United Kingdom imports large quantities of sugar at prices substantially above the prevailing world market level. To date the Commonwealth has not sold in the EEC market.

The world sugar market is permanently threatened by export surpluses. But free-market prices have been reasonably stable since the International Sugar Agreement came into force. This agreement covers the "free market," which is that part of the international sugar market not covered by special arrangements, excluding among others the large trade covered by the Commonwealth Sugar Agreement and all imports into the United States. Even within the free market, a considerable amount of trade takes place on a bilateral basis (private or govern-

mental). We think that an extension of the field of action of the International Sugar Agreement is very desirable from the standpoint of the world sugar trade.

On the consumption side, material reductions in duties and taxes are essential conditions for increasing demand.

In summarizing, we would like to make the following recommendations:

(i) Sugar should not be excluded from the negotiations between the EEC countries and the United Kingdom, as is sometimes suggested. Instead the Commonwealth should be given free access to the market of the Six, and the common outer tariff of 24 per cent (the result of a 70 per cent reduction in the planned EEC outer tariff of 80 per cent) for the United Kingdom and EEC should be accepted. This would be favorable to outside countries but would not bear down too heavily on European domestic production.

(ii) Domestic fiscal charges should be drastically reduced.

(iii) The United Kingdom should submit to the regulations of the Sugar Agreement. If necessary for purposes of agreement, provision must be made for the protection of Commonwealth interests — for example, by special quota restrictions on non-Commonwealth imports into the United Kingdom.

(iv) In special cases provision of compensatory aid should be considered.

A more balanced pattern of world production and trade may be expected in this way.

GROUP IV *Proposed reduction of EEC outer tariff: 70 per cent
Example: tea*

The United Kingdom levies a general import duty on tea with an incidence of about 4 per cent, but imposes no duty on tea imported from Commonwealth countries. The future EEC outer tariff will be 18 per cent, which is considerably below the arithmetic average of the duties of the member countries. Fiscal charges in Germany are very high, with an incidence of 74 per cent; in the other EEC countries they vary from zero to 12 per cent.

In general the world market shows a tendency toward oversupply. Up to now, however, no steps have been taken to renew the International Tea Agreement, though the International Tea Committee has a permanent character. By far the largest producers are located in the Commonwealth, especially India and Ceylon, but fairly important pro-

ducers are found among the outside countries, e.g., Indonesia, China, and Japan; little production comes from the Associates.

The effect of EEC will be to stimulate production in the Associates, and this does not seem advisable in view of the general market situation. A considerable improvement could be effected by reducing the outer tariff by about 70 per cent to 5 per cent, which is about 1 per cent higher than the incidence of the United Kingdom specific duty. This outer tariff of the extended Common Market would be equal to the Commonwealth and Associates preference. Discrimination against the outside countries would be substantially reduced. If the economies of certain Associates should be unfavorably affected, there might be room for counterbalancing development aid.

The reduction of the EEC outer tariff to the level proposed should be accompanied by the elimination of fiscal duties in the European countries. This would be of special importance with regard to Western Germany (which has a duty of 74 per cent), the biggest tea-consuming country in Western Europe after the United Kingdom and the Netherlands.

GROUP V   *Proposed reduction of EEC outer tariff: 60 per cent*
            Example: cocoa beans

Cocoa beans are produced in tropical countries, and consumed mainly in countries in the temperate zone of the Northern Hemisphere. The principal producing countries are, first, the Commonwealth members Ghana (about one-third of world production) and Nigeria, and second, the Latin American countries Brazil, Ecuador, and Venezuela. West African Associates are also important producers.

The planned EEC outer tariff on cocoa beans is 9 per cent. The United Kingdom specific duty has an incidence of about 5.6 per cent,[14] and the Commonwealth preference amounts to about 1.1 per cent. Several European countries levy high internal taxes on cocoa products, especially finished chocolate. After a postwar shortage which strongly stimulated production, the present market position of cocoa is not encouraging, unless consumption can be stepped up. There is more scope for a rise in consumption per head in continental Western Europe than in the United Kingdom and the United States, which are nearer to the saturation level.

A reduction of 60 per cent in the future EEC outer tariff would

14. Incidences are approximate since they are based on import values of selected years, in general 1957–58 or 1958–59. The import duties used in this section are those fixed formally by the governments concerned; actual duties may be somewhat different. This may explain why our figures do not always coincide with those of EEC as shown in Appendix I, p. 207.

bring it to 3.5 per cent. If EEC and the United Kingdom merge, the most important producers, the Commonwealth countries, would be accorded more preference in the United Kingdom market because they would have no more duty to pay on entering the United Kingdom. Specifically, the preference would go from 1.1 to 3.5 per cent. In the EEC market they would be on an equal footing with the Associates, with a preference of 3.5 per cent. Discrimination by EEC against Latin American producers would be diminished significantly. The big consumer in the Western Hemisphere, the United States, levies no import duties at all.

The position of the Associates, on the other hand, would deteriorate as they would be expecting a preference of 9 per cent. Free entry into the United Kingdom market would not be of much importance to them, but if other European countries joined the extended Common Market this might provide new opportunities. It would be wholly justified to give compensatory development aid to those Associates that met with difficulties.

A second measure we suggest is a substantial decrease in the high internal taxes on cocoa products. This would encourage consumption and thus benefit all the producing countries.

Finally, we hope that the international discussions with regard to an international agreement for cocoa will meet with success. Because of the long time it takes to grow a tree and its long productive life, there is danger of serious error in estimates of future supply. Events since 1945 may be a reflection of this.

GROUP VI　*Proposed reduction of EEC outer tariff: 60 per cent Example: dried fruits*

Dried fruits — raisins, currants, dates, and others — belong to the group of semi-world trade commodities (see section 8.4). In all continental areas there is room somewhere to produce dried fruits under more or less favorable conditions. The importing continents will have to consider to what extent they wish to rely on their own production, and to what extent the interests of underdeveloped exporting countries must be respected.

The EEC countries import dried fruits from Greece, Turkey (a probable future EEC Associate), North African countries, Iraq, Iran, and the United States; Afghanistan is a potential supplier. United Kingdom imports come for the most part from Australia and South Africa.

The EEC outer tariff will range from 9 per cent (for raisins, currants, etc.) to 12 per cent (dates, etc.), the only exceptions being the 18 per

cent tariff on prunes and the tariff ranging from 8 to 20 per cent on dried citrus fruits (most of the citrus fruit is imported fresh, however). The United Kingdom general tariff varies from nil (for, among others, pitted dates and the cheaper kinds of unpitted dates, and prunes) to 15 per cent (among others, figs and citrus fruit), the tariffs on the more expensive unpitted dates being 10 per cent. The incidence of the specific duty on raisins amounts to nearly 7 per cent, on currants to about 2 per cent. Commonwealth dried fruits enter duty-free.

A reduction of 60 per cent in the EEC outer tariff would result in a tariff generally ranging between 3.5 and 5 per cent. This would mean that a small margin of preference would be left to Greece and the future Associate, Turkey. The exports of these two countries together with some local production in the other EEC member countries would be a guarantee that Western Europe would to a certain extent be self-supporting. (In times of scarcity dried fruits may be a welcome and easily obtained food.) Exports of South Africa and Australia would be most exposed to the increased competition. On the other hand, the less developed North African and Southwest Asian countries would benefit. The fact that the United States export position would also improve might stimulate these underdeveloped countries to improve the quality of these export products.

There are cases in which a 60 per cent reduction in the EEC outer tariff for the extended Common Market would result in an increase as compared with the present United Kingdom tariff. The most striking case would be prunes; a 7 per cent tariff would be instituted whereas now they are duty-free. In the case of pitted and the cheaper unpitted dates, the difference between the EEC outer tariff and the United Kingdom tariff amounts to 5 per cent (the United Kingdom tariff incidence being 2 per cent, and the reduced EEC outer tariff 3.5 per cent). These might be cases in which exceptions to the rule of proportional reductions in the EEC outer tariff for all the commodities of a group could be considered. It might be advisable to reduce the tariffs on these products by more than the proposed 60 per cent since strengthening of the preferences given by one of the two negotiating parties should be avoided as much as possible.

GROUP VII   *Proposed reduction of EEC outer tariff: 50 per cent
                Example: cotton fabrics*

The main producers of raw cotton are the United States (responsible for nearly 50 per cent of all non-Communist world production in 1959), India, Pakistan, the United Arab Republic, and Brazil. Together they

account for about 75 per cent of the raw cotton produced in the non-Communist world. Cotton fabrics are produced mainly in the United States, Western Europe, India, Pakistan, Japan, and Hong Kong, which together represented about 80 per cent of world production in 1959. Both the production and the processing of cotton are gradually spreading over a wider geographic area.

As to international trade in cotton fabrics, Western Europe represents about two-fifths of the imports and exports of the non-Communist world; its export surplus is small, a remnant of an impressive surplus at the time of the First World War. The United States share in the international cotton trade is rather small. The main exporting areas besides Europe are, since the thirties, Japan (about 25 per cent of total exports in 1959), and since the end of the forties, India (nearly one-sixth of total exports), Pakistan and Hong Kong.

Cotton fabrics are a striking illustration of the problem of future coexistence between the Eastern and the Western world in the sphere of industrial development. With regard to cotton fabrics a dynamic adaptation process is in full flower. There is a tendency in Western Europe to reduce productive capacity, and at the same time to concentrate on quality production. The industry meanwhile is concentrating ever more on the European market, and a reorientation is taking place with regard to outside markets. On the other hand, the cotton industry in Asia is expanding and there are shifts in production and export relations, occasioned by such factors as the growing importance of mainland China. Recently the United States, too, has experienced greatly increased imports of cheap cotton fabrics from the East, in spite of its relatively high import duties. This world-wide adaptation process could be furthered by a well-balanced Western trade policy. We think that a merger between EEC and the United Kingdom, and probably other European countries, is of primary importance, for it would free the Western European cotton industry from the worst ravages of outside competition and enable it to find its optimal structure. This in itself would permit a more tolerant attitude toward the liberalization of trade policy.

The projected EEC outer tariff on cotton yarn is 10 per cent. The United Kingdom tariff is 7.5 per cent, while imports from Commonwealth countries are duty-free. For cotton cloth these figures are 17 per cent for EEC, and 17.5 per cent for the United Kingdom, equal to the Commonwealth preference. It would appear that the United Kingdom is exposed to the unlimited competition of Hong Kong, India, and Pakistan; so far, however, this competition has been limited by voluntary export restrictions by these three countries.

We noted in Chapter 3 that in 1961 a "short-term agreement" was concluded by a number of importing and exporting countries in the context of GATT (see p. 49). This agreement was recently followed by a longer-term agreement which provides for a doubling of the EEC quota in the next five years. Some comments on the situation may be appropriate.

To begin with, trade in cotton fabrics is becoming more and more a matter of East-West trade, for which special lines of conduct may be needed, though here too an increase in nonstrategic commodity trade seems desirable. Trade between non-Communist developing countries and developed countries should be expanded in any case, however, and the expansion planned in the agreement is disappointingly modest. To be sure, total trade in cotton fabrics is larger than the quotas indicate, since some items are not regulated by quotas. It is also apparent that some European countries, like Great Britain, have had a considerable reduction in exports and so have played their part in accepting structural changes advantageous to Asian countries. Countries like the United States, which never had large exports, and France and Italy, which are particularly restrictive at the moment, should also make a contribution to a more economic pattern of trade.

European textile producers fear that their product is the focal point of the export drive by the developing countries and hold that this justifies the rather strict regulation of their market. The history of Japan shows, however, that the industrialization process tends to spread to other industries, thus automatically distributing the pressure. Moreover, textile markets do not exhibit the typical features of unstable markets which require regulation (see section 4.2). We do not think, therefore, that such regulations deserve further application. Some attempt at international planning of investments should be made, based on studies of comparative advantages and on the notion of diversifying production in developing countries, following the example of Japan.

While provision must be made for temporary disruptions, these protective measures should be short-lived, and the general trend should be toward a lowering of trade barriers. Reduction of the EEC outer tariff by 50 per cent would result in a tariff of 5 per cent on cotton yarn and 8.5 per cent on cotton cloth. This would mean a substantial decrease in the Commonwealth preferences and at the same time a closer approach between the tariffs on yarn and cloth.

FINANCIAL AND MONETARY SYSTEMS AND STABILITY

9.1 ROLE OF FINANCIAL AND MONETARY POLICIES

Each country has a financial and monetary system which plays an important part in its economic order. The system has two poles, the central bank and the treasury. The central bank mainly carries out monetary policy and the treasury conducts financial policy. In modern terminology we may characterize these two institutions as dealing respectively with the stock of money and the flow of money. Responsibility for the quantity and quality of the monetary circulation was felt much earlier than responsibility for the maintenance of a certain flow of money transactions. In most countries central banks were given charters enabling them to assume this responsi-

167

bility. In a period when competition was highly valued as an efficient mechanism, these charters gave central banks a *de facto* monopoly on the emission of notes. Originally central banks were to be mainly "lenders of last resort," a source of help in emergencies. Later they were more permanently engaged in maintaining a specified relation between their gold stock and monetary circulation, i.e., the quantity of money in circulation.

Much later, after the depression of the thirties, it came to be understood that the treasury could exert a considerable influence on the money flow — that is, on the total demand for goods and services — by manipulating total public expenditure and taxes. In fact, the most important lesson learned during the great depression was that total demand cannot be influenced very much by indirect instruments such as interest rates and other credit conditions.

Today if we want to rethink the operation and organization of our financial and monetary system, the first point to be made is that the flow of money is more important than the stock of money. It is the flow which determines the volume of production and is the source of material well-being. We can observe that the relation between money flow and money stock is a loose one, especially in the short run. Only severe restrictions on new credits have any direct influence on the flow of total demand; other instruments of monetary policy are of secondary importance, as already observed.

The main aim of financial and monetary policy must be to attain a steady growth of demand with a stable price level, that is, to avoid either inflation or deflation. The classical ideas about the best operation of the monetary system overemphasized the importance of maintaining a fixed ratio between money stock and gold stock, for the sake of creating confidence in the monetary unit. The classical "rules of the game" — which prescribed that international payments be made as much as possible in gold and that money circulation be adapted to gold stock — would, however, work unfavorably in certain circumstances. In fact, a country with a balance of payments deficit had to cure itself — according to these rules — by contracting activity rather than by reducing prices, which is the proc-

ess actually needed. The maintenance of a rigid ratio between money and gold cannot therefore be considered a wise policy for treating short-term disturbances.

In the longer run a certain ratio between gold stock and money stock is desirable, as a basis for confidence. But the ratio cannot be constant if we wish to keep the average price level constant. Gold stocks have increased over the centuries less than production. Monetary systems have adapted themselves by letting the same stock of gold "cover" an ever increasing quantity of money. This was done partly by increasing the share of bank deposits in the total monetary circulation. Today the gold stock normally serves as "cover" in two ways. In the balance sheet of the central bank it "covers" a certain percentage of central bank notes circulating with consumers, plus deposits held by private banks at the central bank. In the balance sheet of the private banks, deposits at the central bank "cover" a certain percentage of private deposits, which therefore are only indirectly and to a much lesser extent covered by the central bank's gold. It is in part this system of a "second floor" which makes it possible for the same gold stock to cover a much larger circulation of notes plus private deposits than formerly. While the monetary system must, in the longer run, try to maintain a certain ratio between gold and money stock, the optimum ratio is not a constant one. So far it is because of incidental changes in structure that no shortage in liquidity has developed.

The maintenance of healthy conditions in the monetary sphere remains one of the basic tasks of our financial-monetary authorities. But, as was already noted, regulation of the money flow is more important than regulation of the money stock. Thus a correct financial policy is more vital than a proper monetary policy, and the role played — for good or ill — by the treasury is of the utmost significance.

It follows that genuine and wholehearted co-operation between the "two poles" is necessary: contradictory policies are intolerable. That being the case, the government must have the last word in any conflict between the central bank and the treasury: there can-

not be two captains on one ship. At the same time, this final responsibility puts a heavy obligation on the government. Not all
governments have been sufficiently aware of the role they should
play, and this explains why central bank experts and others tend to
favor an independent central bank.

9.2 THE NEED FOR FINANCIAL AND MONETARY
WORLD AGENCIES

The complex of financial and monetary policies adopted by any
single country is of primary importance not only for the well-being
of that country but also for the well-being of other countries. This
is why a considerable degree of centralization in the world's (or at
least the non-Communist world's) financial and monetary policies
is indispensable. National autonomy in this matter cannot be accepted as a healthy condition, for mistakes made in national policies will inevitably have consequences extending beyond national
frontiers. Some forms of consultation between governments, with
which we have had experience, have been useful. Conferences
should be carried out at the ministerial level rather than by their
aides, in order to strengthen the commitments made. But a weak
form of centralization, such as simple consultation, is not enough.
The reason we have not made more progress is the undue respect
our world has for national autonomy — at least in the developed
countries. A much stronger policy will be possible if central agencies are created with responsibilities in this field.

So far it is mainly at the central banking "pole" of financial-
monetary policy that some international centralization has come
into existence. Historically, a tendency toward centralization appeared first in what Professor François Perroux has called the
"dominant countries." For a long time the United Kingdom, as the
richest and most powerful country in the world and a very important capital exporter, acted as the world's banking center. Later this
task was partly taken over by the United States. After World War
II the International Monetary Fund started operation. It has some

resemblance to a world central bank, but is not really one. Perhaps we may say that it is a central bank in its early stage of lender of last resort.

The present international monetary system, if we may call it that, was not based on a deliberate attempt to create an optimum system; rather it was the outcome of contact between national systems. With regard to the other "pole" of the world's financial-monetary order — the one handling the more efficient policy instruments — centralization hardly exists at all.

Again we must press for the application of the principles used inside our own countries to a wider area and the establishment of the necessary bi-polar set of institutions: a world treasury and a world central bank. It is only through such agencies that an efficient financial and monetary policy can be carried out. As an example we may consider the situation where a major country follows an inflationary or deflationary policy which harms the rest of the world. Consultation alone is not an effective method for correcting the situation. A world treasury would be able to give substance to a corrective policy by its own financial activity. A world central bank could give support by its credit policy. A central government has the means to correct an ill-advised gesture by provincial or local authorities; if our recommendations are carried out, similar means would exist in the international field.

In the monetary sector, it should be possible to build a system which would supply the international economy with the best quantity and quality of money and help to prevent crises of confidence. The systems demonstrated to be the most appropriate could be applied. But it should no longer be the dominant country system, with its inherent threat to confidence.

The case for a world budget was made in sections 6.2 and 6.3, in the context of development policies. From early remarks in the present section, it should be apparent that such a budget could also be used for anticyclical purposes. One possibility consists in the operation of the insurance scheme discussed in section 4.5. It is conceivable that gradually other tasks might be added. The world

budget may be put partly in the hands of IDA or OECD, but it should be, at least in part, a true world budget, handled by the United Nations.

9.3 LIQUIDITY PROBLEMS AND KEY CURRENCIES

As already briefly stated, monetary policies have grown out of national preoccupations, and have hardly been considered the task of a world agency. They have dealt more with the question of the qualitative conditions for sound money than with the question of a sufficient supply of the means of payment. Not that this latter problem has been unrecognized by experts; measures have indeed been taken, but in an incidental way. By chance, the ratio of gold to money has been decreased, as it should have been. We have mentioned the development of bank deposits as a means of extending the coverage of gold. Another measure taken by a number of the smaller countries was to use certain key currencies — sterling or dollars mostly, and other currencies in certain political areas — as substitutes for gold in the so-called "gold exchange standard."

In a recent book Professor Robert Triffin exposed the dangers of this key-currency system.[1] He showed that liquidities are not created systematically and for their own sake; they develop as a by-product of decisions of a completely different character. Thus in the last few years reserves of Western European countries have increased substantially because of (i) gold payments by the USSR, depending to a considerable extent on political decisions, and (ii) current deficits in the American balance of payments, considered an evil in themselves. Under the key-currency system, the danger exists — and by no means only in theory — that a key country will so mismanage its over-all financial policies that its currency will weaken and suddenly become the object of speculation. This makes for unrest, movements of "hot capital," and shifts from one currency to another, rather than confidence in the money supply. If the balance of payments position of the key country then improves, as a con-

1. See R. Triffin, *Gold and the Dollar Crisis — Future of Convertibility*, Yale University Press, New Haven, 1960.

sequence of, say, a stronger anti-inflationary policy, the outside world may be confronted by a liquidity crisis.

Professor Triffin has proposed another system which may be viewed as an application of sound national monetary ideas to the international community. His idea is to add another "level" to the monetary system, in the form of a truly international central bank. In principle, this bank would hold the world's gold stock — or most of it — and issue world paper money which would constitute the material for national central bank reserves. The central banks would base their notes and bankers' deposits on this world paper money — rather than on sterling, dollar, or gold holdings — and the private banks would cover their private deposits with the balances they maintain at the central banks. In all there would be three levels. Actually Professor Triffin later suggested a fourth level, to be created by inserting a continental central bank between the world central bank and the national central banks.

His system avoids the dangers of instability characteristic of the key-currency system. It also opens up new possibilities for conserving gold, and in a way therefore contributes to the problem of a future lack of liquidity. However, it is no better than the preceding system, as long as it would prescribe fixed reserve ratios throughout the banking community. The problem of having the correct liquidity volume cannot be solved if fixed reserve ratios are used. The idea of flexible reserve ratios, already accepted for short-term anti-cyclical policies, needs to be applied to long-term policies.

Two main problems must be considered in choosing between Professor Triffin's proposal and some other, less radical proposals to be mentioned below.[2]

One of them can be called the problem of management. Most central bankers today are afraid to accept Professor Triffin's ideas since they see implied in them a shift in management from the national central banks to the world central bank, presumably the International Monetary Fund. They seem to fear that the Fund, under pressure from the less developed member governments, would

2. See also *The Economist*, May 6, 1961, pp. 528–530, for a brief discussion of several proposals.

yield to more inflationary policies than are at present being pursued by the world at large. This fear is not shared by Mr. Edward M. Bernstein, who proposes that the present quotas of the member countries be integrated with their working reserves so that they can be freely drawn upon. Mr. Bernstein proposes further that creditor countries be asked to lend additional amounts to IMF.

Mr. Bernstein's proposal would solve the liquidity problem but it would leave the key-currency system intact. In his opinion this system is intimately connected with the role the United States and the United Kingdom play as international bankers and he places a high value on this role.

The other problem involved is one of transition. On the basis of the figures applying to today's situation, Mr. Bernstein fears that the shifts involved in switching from the present system to Triffin's would have a deflationary effect. But this problem of transition — with several others — can be a point for separate negotiation.

It is obvious that the change-over from national reserves to deposits with IMF should only occur gradually. It has been suggested that each country's initial IMF deposit be equal to at least 20 per cent of its central bank reserves. These deposits would enable the Fund to begin creating international credit, just as, on the national level, increased deposits enable banks to expand their operations. In order to avoid inflationary developments, Professor Triffin proposes that a ceiling be put on the annual increase in IMF's net lending in such a way that total world reserves would not be augmented by more than, say, 3 per cent a year. A smooth transition also requires that changes in the nature of the investments taken over by the Fund from the central banks be made very gradually, not surpassing, say, 5 per cent of these assets annually.

To some, Triffin's proposals appear too complicated. A shortcut method of increasing world liquidity has been proposed by Mr. Maxwell Stamp. Mr. Stamp suggests that IMF be authorized to issue Fund certificates up to a certain amount, say $3 billion for the first year. These certificates would be distributed among the newly developing countries, which could use them as an international means of payment of equal standing with gold or a key currency; a developed country willing to accept these certificates could use

them as part of its reserves, or sell them to other countries. A drawback of this system is that it would not solve the basic problem of the ambivalent role played by key currencies like the dollar and the pound.

Many other plans have recently been developed in this field, notably those of R. F. Harrod, M. Heilperin, A. Lamfalussy, J. Rueff, and X. Zolotas. A proposal to be mentioned explicitly is that of Professor James Meade.[3] Meade's ideas are similar to Triffin's, except that Meade proposes to transfer both the monetary gold stocks and the key-currency reserves to IMF so that national reserves would consist wholly of certificates issued by the Fund. Also, Meade wants to introduce a system of fluctuating exchange rates with IMF acting as an international equalization agency, whereas Triffin's plan calls for fixed exchange rates.

It is our conviction that the world's financial and monetary system would be better served by the Triffin system than by the simpler proposals. This does not mean that the simple proposals are not useful and would not work. In the end, however, something more would have to be done. Triffin's proposal fits very well into what we feel is a natural progression: to introduce a world policy and to apply internationally the principles tried out in the most advanced countries.

Professor Meade's proposal to introduce floating exchange rates would not be accepted by today's central bank managers. They intuitively feel that fixed rates would make a greater contribution to economic stability than fluctuating rates. The heart of the question is not always set out clearly or explicitly; it is whether adjustments with fixed rates are preferable to adjustments with flexible exchange rates. The most important adjustments possible within a system of fixed exchange rates are those concerning wage rates. Adjustments in items such as credit terms affect the economy in only a very superficial way.[4] Adjustments in wage rates without adjustments in exchange rates are not very satisfactory, however — an

3. J. E. Meade, "The Future of International Trade and Payments," *The Three Banks Review*, June 1961.

4. See J. Tinbergen, *Economic Policy: Principles and Design*, North-Holland Publishing Company, Amsterdam, 1956, especially pp. 113 and 114.

argument which appears to support Professor Meade's view. It is to be hoped that future discussions will bear more explicitly on this crucial aspect of the problem, and that in the end Meade's proposal will become acceptable to central bank managers.

9.4 WORLD STABILITY, NATIONAL STABILITY, OR COMMODITY STABILITY?

In this section we will take up once more the question of price stability, the importance of which has already been stressed (sections 1.6, 4.2 to 4.5, and 6.1). We do so because some of the instruments proposed as alternatives to price stabilization schemes for individual commodities are instruments of either financial or monetary policy. In fact, the choice before us may be formulated as in the title of this section.

Theoretically, the simplest scheme proposed is the commodity standard (see section 4.5). This constitutes a special type of central banking regime, in which not only gold but also a package of raw materials would be accepted as cover. The anticipated effect would be the stabilization of one thing only, namely the weighted price index of the commodities included in the package. This means that the average world price index would probably be stabilized too. The components of such an index, however, would not be stabilized.

The next simplest proposal is the scheme to insure countries against reductions in their export receipts (see section 4.5). As noted earlier, this is mainly a financial scheme, comparable to schemes of unemployment insurance, implying a system of money flows which will tend to stabilize the foreign exchange receipts of individual countries. The number of possible effects is much larger than in the case of the commodity standard. Stabilization of an element of income will help, in all probability, to stabilize total demand inside each country. Again, this scheme does not promise to stabilize the prices of individual primary commodities; the factors making for variations on the supply side will not disappear, though their effects will be weakened because the economic situation of the

producing countries will be less strongly dependent upon market conditions. The scheme under discussion is relatively simple and is confined to the relations between the insuring institution and member governments.

The third alternative is to increase the number of commodity agreements. The effect would be to more or less stabilize prices, and probably quantities sold. We might also hope that the incomes of a large number of producers would become more stable. Countries whose products were in large part covered by the scheme would also be less prone to fluctuations. Against this more refined set of results must be set the more cumbersome set of activities required to negotiate and supervise the schemes. In addition, we may ask to what extent natural equilibrating forces would be unnecessarily ruled out. The answer to this question has to be that free-market forces have not proved very helpful in restoring and maintaining equilibrium in these markets, and that there are a number of irremovable disequilibrating factors, such as crop variations and long production lags.

Of the two general schemes mentioned — the commodity standard and the scheme to insure against export declines — we consider the second preferable. It does not require the acceptance of any new monetary techniques, as the first system does — if only by some large central banks — and it can stabilize the economies of member countries. It represents another example of the application to world affairs of a principle that has shown its usefulness inside the developed countries: the principle of unemployment insurance. Moreover, the scheme has a large degree of flexibility in that the percentage decline in export income which warrants compensation can be chosen freely and may even be gradually increased if no unfavorable effects are experienced.

In addition, there are good reasons to conclude more commodity agreements. Most important is the fact that in some cases free competition does not have the generally favorable effects it is claimed to have. This applies to products with a long production period and low elasticities of demand and supply. Irrespective of other measures, such as the insurance scheme just discussed, there is al-

ways room for regulations where markets are inherently unstable. In our opinion, serious efforts should be made to extend the number of commodity agreements, and to improve their functioning.

With regard to the International *Wheat* Agreement, we note that too small a part of world wheat trade comes under the terms of the agreement, and that too much bilateral trade persists. We think it is gratifying that the USSR has recently shown its readiness to join the agreement. Finally, we point out that the International Wheat Agreement is suffering from a disturbed price structure because of government interference in wheat-producing countries. The chief offenders are the United States and Canada, the main exporters. These countries give support to domestic agricultural producers, a move which weakens the export position of the commodity. They also handle their marketing problems in such a way that world prices are constantly between the limits set by the agreement. This means that they are in a position to force relatively high prices upon importing countries with a lower standard of living. This seems contrary to the general principle applied in international integration treaties, namely that national regulations should — gradually — be adapted to international regulations and not international regulations adapted to one or more national schemes. We suggest that a transition period be agreed upon during which agricultural policies would have to be harmonized.

The same applies to *cotton*. As we have seen, the United States is by far the largest cotton-exporting country, and by its domestic support policy it imposes relatively high prices on the importing countries. United States agricultural policy has so far been one of the main obstacles to an international cotton agreement. Nevertheless, we think that, as with wheat, an agreement providing for the adaptation of national policies should be strongly promoted.

One of the characteristics of the International *Sugar* Agreement is that its "free market" sector covers less than half the world sugar market, the preferential blocs being subject to special regulations. In view of the increasing disequilibrium between world sugar production and consumption, the agreement's structure should be strengthened by simplification; in other words, the preferential

blocs should be included in the agreement's "free market" sector and made subject to its rules.

The International *Tin* Agreement has so far been successful. Although granting that the agreement, based on the buffer stock principle, is workable, we think it would function more efficiently if the United States and Germany joined (see page 79).

With regard to *nonferrous metals* we conclude that international commodity agreements are desirable. As production and consumption of the various nonferrous metals are often closely related, it has been suggested that these products be combined in a single commodity agreement, in order "to avoid some of the negotiations and economic disadvantages involved in tackling only one product at a time."[5] We fully endorse this suggestion.

The International *Coffee* Agreement is at present only a short-term agreement, and a long-term agreement is needed. To cope with present and future market problems, consuming as well as producing countries must be included. The same applies to *cocoa*. Insufficient attention has been given to the problem of long-term market stability. For both commodities, long-term agreements have been drafted and are being studied by interested governments.

In our opinion the discontinuation in 1954 of the International *Tea* Agreement was regrettable. Although the international tea market has since been stable, market conditions may change. Insiders admit that re-establishment of the agreement may be desirable sooner or later. We are in favor of its revival in the near future.

It is generally felt that international co-ordination is needed with regard to *bananas, citrus fruit,* and *olive oil.* So far a study of an international price stabilization scheme has been started only for the olive oil trade. We would strongly recommend the introduction of such schemes for each of these commodities.

5. See *Trends in International Trade*, Report by a Panel of Experts, General Agreement on Tariffs and Trade, Geneva, 1958, pp. 78–79.

C H A P T E R   1 0

CONCLUSIONS AND RECOMMENDATIONS

10.1 TODAY'S CHALLENGES

In this concluding chapter an attempt will be made to summarize, in simple language, the ideas guiding this study and the suggestions for action resulting from them. In today's world we are faced with three great challenges. The first and greatest is the threat of nuclear war. The second is the misery in developing countries. The third one is the challenge of the Communist political and economic system. These three challenges are interconnected. The war threat is directly linked with the contrast between Communist and non-Communist systems. The Communist challenge, itself a result of the marked inequalities which existed in 19th century European societies, is considerably strengthened by the persistent inequalities in the low-income continents. The possible solutions to these challenging problems are also intimately linked. West and East

180

are competing doctors for the world's misery lands. A stronger West is one possible contribution to peace, but an even greater one is solidarity with the low-income countries.

This study deals mainly with the economic aspects of the world problems mentioned, but since the political and social aspects cannot be neglected, a few remarks going beyond the economic realm will be included in the final pages of this chapter (sections 10.8 through 10.11).

10.2 UNDOCTRINAIRE APPROACH NEEDED

In the present serious circumstances, when a maximum effort must be made, doctrinaire paths must be avoided at all costs. They are not compatible with an open-minded approach to world problems, and they imply a loss of effectiveness. In our opinion the West has been doctrinaire in two ways: with regard to economic systems and with regard to national autonomy. Even so, economists have shed light on both issues.

Neither of the *economic systems* defended today by doctrinaire extremists is particularly effective in creating well-being and development. A pure free-enterprise economy is not optimum; neither is a completely regimented economy. *Mixed* systems are better; the nature of the mixture depends on circumstances and must be the subject of careful engineering.

Autonomous national policy-making is not necessarily the best way to guide the affairs of the international economic community. More centralization is needed with regard to some instruments of economic policy. Either the use of these instruments could be coordinated at the international level or, better still, the instruments themselves could be handled by *supranational agencies*. The main reason is that these instruments will not be used with maximum efficiency if decisions are taken at the national level.

Careful research in the last ten to thirty years has pinpointed the *optimum instruments* of economic policy (discussed in Chapters 5 through 9), and indicated the *degree of centralization*, i.e., the level of governmental authority — local, state, continental, or world —

necessary for their optimum use. In the light of this knowledge it can be stated, among other things, that excessive national autonomy in economic policy aggravated the great depression; that the increasing role played by the federal government in the United States is fully justified; and that several functions of national governments may have to be partly transferred to a "higher level."

10.3 EFFICIENCY AND SOLIDARITY

Mixed social systems as they now exist in most countries function on the basis of efficiency and solidarity. These principles must not be confined to national units; they must be applied to the international economic order. As applied to economic policy *efficiency* means that an effort is made to determine the best means of reaching clearly defined goals; an efficient policy requires systematic planning, partly at a world level.

Solidarity means an element of common responsibility, and a regard for the well-being of groups, as contrasted to individual members. "Team spirit" is a typical expression of this notion; "the strong for the weak" is another expression of it. Social insurance and progressive taxes are instruments for its realization. So far, however, they have not generally been applied beyond national frontiers.

More intensive international co-ordination or integration may be said to mean the *application of our own principles* — i.e., those applied at home — *to the world at large,* or at least to the world of non-Communist countries. Only a timid beginning has so far been made. The spirit of the *Marshall Plan* is what is needed; and other countries along with the United States should display this spirit.

10.4 LACUNAE IN OUR INTERNATIONAL MACHINERY

Present-day agencies handling international economic policy must be judged against the background of the optimal system just indicated. Many of the instruments needed are already in existence,

but there are some clear lacunae. The most conspicuous are those in financial policy, in the realm of stabilizing the revenues of countries producing primary commodities, and in the field of insurance against noneconomic investment risks.

There is a need, first of all, for *centralized expenditure for development purposes*. The present level of such expenditure, international and national together, is insufficient, perhaps half of what it should be; and its geographic distribution is unsatisfactory. Existing national and international institutions are not able to correct these two defects; a larger portion of this expenditure must be guided by an agency with wider-than-national responsibilities. There must be an *international financial authority* of considerable strength, and it seems natural that this authority should be able to make *current expenditures* as well as provide loans, just as any central government makes a considerable portion of its development expenditure on a current basis.

The authority would have to finance its expenditures through *current contributions* from member countries. Apart from its role in development, its existence would strengthen considerably the influence that can be exerted on the *business cycle* and induce a more co-operative attitude on the part of national governments: by its policy the authority could *create incentives* for intergovernmental co-operation.

Secondly, there is a need for more agencies to deal with the problem of stabilizing the revenues of countries producing primary commodities. This may be accomplished by the conclusion of more commodity agreements or by the introduction of an insurance scheme against declines in export revenues.

Thirdly, private foreign investment in developing countries may be substantially furthered by the establishment of an international insurance scheme against noneconomic risks (see Chapter 7).

10.5 IMPROPER USE OF EXISTING INSTITUTIONS

In other cases the necessary institutions exist, but are not being used in the best interest of the world community. Usually this is

so when the form of centralization is one of the weaker types. Thus it may be said that some *trade policies* do not comply with the rules set by GATT and formally accepted by numerous governments. *Unjustified quantitative restrictions* on Asian industrial products and *excessive protection of European agriculture* are important examples. Also, trade with Communist countries is unduly restricted.

In addition, the *technical methods* used to bring about a reduction of impediments on trade are inefficient, especially item-by-item negotiations.

There is need for a *regional approach* to the ideal of GATT; Europe's example might be followed in Asia and in Africa, where a beginning has been made by groups of neighboring countries. Latin America has made progress in this direction. At the same time, the European Economic Community should be careful to reduce the level of its agricultural protection and discrimination against nonassociated areas. In this study we have made detailed suggestions concerning the *import duties and consumption taxes* on a number of primary commodities (see Chapter 8).

Some of the principles of GATT require revision; thus certain tariffs should be considered legal only if applied temporarily (see Chapter 8).

Finally, international balances with IMF might well replace key currencies as the cover for national circulation (see Chapter 9).

10.6 AN OPTIMUM POLICY FOR THE NON-COMMUNIST WORLD

Since the Communist world cannot be directly influenced by Western countries, the responsibilities set out in the preceding sections charge us to organize the best conceivable policy for the non-Communist part of the world. Thus the financial authority recommended may be organized within *IDA,* or possibly *OECD* if it could extend its membership to developing countries. More *commodity agreements* must be concluded at least between the non-Communist countries. This is particularly important in the case of cocoa, some nonferrous metals, bananas, and cotton. The scheme to

provide insurance against export declines may also be organized among these countries.

Western European integration is the aim of a group of non-Communist countries, and attempts at closer co-operation are being made in the Arab region, Asia, and Africa. A number of *ad hoc* organizations such as the Colombo Plan and many forms of bilateral co-operation are serving a useful purpose at "lower levels"; this is all to the good, provided that the organs at the highest levels are sufficiently endowed with supplementary means to carry through a program of optimal intensity and optimal geographic distribution.

10.7 THE ROLE OF THE UNITED NATIONS

It would be a mistake, however, to confine ourselves to the non-Communist world. The ideas set out must be applied to the whole world. They must be used to give strength and perspective to the idea of a truly *international order,* that is, they must be used to strengthen the United Nations. The Charter of the United Nations is couched in general terms only. With our present knowledge of how international economic and social affairs can best be conducted, we can give more precise and more efficient content to the tasks of the United Nations. We can define the instruments and organs to be used, and in so doing we can give real meaning to the idea of "peaceful coexistence."

Some will point out that the Communist countries may not want to co-operate and may even try to frustrate such activities as may be entrusted to the United Nations family of agencies. Our answer is, first of all, that the aim of increasing world stability and peace is worth some risk; and secondly, that the risks seem to be small in the case of some of the tasks to be given to the United Nations.

We see three new sets of tasks for the United Nations in executing the policies advocated.

   (i) The United Nations could formulate the *main aims* of world economic policy and prepare, at regular intervals, five- or ten-year forecasts of economic development. More precise suggestions are offered in Chapters 5 and 6. On the

basis of these studies, the *annual discussion* in the Economic and Social Council of the United Nations could be given more operative importance. Following the example of OEEC, *national policies* may be discussed with a view to convincing governments of the overriding importance of world aims. Depending on the preparation and organization of this discussion, ECOSOC might be more instrumental in creating an international order than it has been so far.

(ii) If more development funds were given to it, the United Nations could correct some of the undesirable features of to-day's geographic distribution of aid and private investment. The financial resources needed to accomplish such a *supplementary task* do not necessarily have to be concentrated at the United Nations: the better some "lower" organs, including those discussed in section 10.6, carry out their tasks, the smaller the sum needed at the center. But the funds available for this purpose must total considerably more than the amount now in the United Nations' hands.

(iii) Important tasks could be carried out by some of the *Regional Commissions* of the United Nations, both in the field of *planning and forecasting* and in the field of *regional co-operation and integration*. More precise suggestions will be found in Chapter 7. In a region where co-operation is in its first stages, the Regional Commission could be especially helpful in spreading objective information about the advantages to be obtained from regional co-operation and integration, and in taking steps to bring such co-operation about.

10.8   OTHER ASPECTS OF THE INTERNATIONAL ORDER

The contribution of the Western world to strengthening the international order cannot be solely an economic one. We have already noted the intimate links between the problems of *security, political organization,* and *economic policy.* To be sure, the economic contribution is the one which seems most promising, regardless of the

response from the Communist world. A stronger international economic order, along the lines indicated, would contribute to peace in several ways. It would remove some of the tensions existing today; it would also counter the Communist belief that the West is unable to survive. Yet the overriding problem of security cannot be solved by economic measures alone.

One disequilibrating aspect of today's world is the two-pole system of thought and action. It is comparable to the internal political structure in Germany around 1932, where the extremists at the right and the left were strong and the center grew weaker and weaker. (This is not to say that the ideologies involved then bear much relationship to the ideologies at stake in the world today.) There must always be a stable center if there is to be a stable world.

Because of the conflicting views and the mutual distrust existing between the Communist and the Western world, it will be necessary — in light of world interests — for the uncommitted countries to take over more and more tasks of crucial importance in the international field — not only tasks of an executive nature, like heading international agencies, but also tasks in the sphere of decision-taking. In other words, in future years it will be the voice or the vote of the uncommitted countries that will tell the world what to do when the opposed blocs of East (used here to designate the Communist countries) and West cannot agree on a policy. If such an arrangement or constellation is to operate effectively, the uncommitted countries must of course be truly uncommitted — in the fullest sense of the word — to either bloc, and in addition they must be capable of developing clear policies.

For this reason, it seems to be in the interest of world peace that the uncommitted countries remain or become as independent of both East and West as it is conceivable for them to be. This, however, would require a reorientation of the international policy of the two blocs. The Western countries would have to abandon policies designed to "induce" the developing countries to choose to join the West's ranks, and adopt instead policies based on the assumption that the developing world will follow an independent path.

It might be argued that such a turnabout would be unwise because the Communist part of the world is not likely to follow suit,

and with the lack of counteracting Western forces, Communist attempts to make friends among the newly developing countries would be more successful than at present. The answer to this is that many — if not all — countries not directly associated with either West or East are eager to retain, and even reinforce, their uncommitted status. If one of the two blocs competing for their friendship and favors withdraws voluntarily for the sake of strengthening the independent position of the developing countries, it is very likely that the other bloc's overtures will be rejected. Many developing countries that now have rather close ties with the Communist bloc have established these relations for fear of Western dominance of their international contacts.

10.9   SOME SUGGESTIONS ON SECURITY

The political considerations just discussed may even be of some relevance to the most important problem of today, which is without doubt that of security. In the final analysis this problem may be said to be one of devising institutions and procedures which will help to achieve and maintain a stable equilibrium of forces. That the lack of trust between the two major powers is a major obstacle to the establishment of such institutions and procedures goes without saying. Any suggestion must take this distrust into account. An equilibrium of forces might be said to exist at present, but if so, it is far from stable. The elaborate studies made by Schelling and Halperin[1] show the multitudinous aspects of the equilibrium, and the many different unstable and stable movements which may occur depending on the random disturbance that starts them. Their analysis is bewildering because it shows how many unknown risks there are and because many people in responsible positions will probably never fully understand the mechanism.

Some comfort may perhaps be found in a remark made by Professor J. Goudriaan with regard to business cycle policy but applying equally well here: "We do not need to know the dynamics of the present unstable equilibrium just as an engineer does not need

1. Thomas C. Schelling and Morton H. Halperin, *Strategy and Arms Control*, Twentieth Century Fund, New York, 1961.

to know the dynamics of a collapsing bridge. What we need to know is the statics of a stable equilibrium, just as the engineer must know the statics of a bridge that will not collapse." Let us therefore look for a stable equilibrium, or at least for a more stable one.

The well-known solution, which is stable indeed, is the establishment of a world government with a world armed force while all national governments are disarmed. This solution has been on the minds of all those interested in world security; it was the idea at the basis of the creation of the League of Nations and the United Nations, and it still is the idea basic to world federalism. It demonstrates at the same time the interdependence of security, political, and socio-economic conditions which we reminded the reader of in section 10.2. World government presupposes the acceptance of a duly elected authority by all concerned.

That a satisfactory voting system can at the moment be devised is highly doubtful. We must explore that side of the problem nevertheless, and some suggestions will be made in section 10.10. In this section we will discuss what the position is in the absence of a common voting system. The machinery for a stable solution does not presently exist. Are there power configurations with a higher degree of stability than the present system of two more or less equal power centers?

The reason why neither West nor East is willing at the moment to accept a world force is simply the fear that in the event of conflict between them the world force might side with the other party. To mitigate this risk a system might be tried whereby both camps would be only partly disarmed; as one possible example we can imagine a situation with three forces of, say, comparable strength. Such a system would indeed be stabler than the two-pole system in a number of circumstances. This would be true in cases where an aggressor could be defined, assuming that the world force would take the other side. It would also be true in a class of cases where criteria could be devised to determine the legitimacy of one or the other stand and the world force would back the legal side. There might be other cases where stability would not be increased.

The risk characteristic of the one-force case would remain, but on a smaller scale. The action of the world force would again have

to depend upon a voting system and the outcome of the vote might be unacceptable to one of the parties. But this risk would now apply to only one-third of the total force. One can also imagine an extremely controversial case where the unity of action of the world force was broken; this would bring us back to the present situation of two poles.

The process of exploration can be taken one step further. If the main risk involved in the three-power configuration is that the world force might choose the "wrong" side — whatever that might mean and whatever motivation might be involved — we can think of a four-power system, the fourth power being a neutralist force, one organized by the "South," the uncommitted countries. To be sure, the uncommitted countries are militarily weak at present, but they need not remain so. If co-operation between groups of developing countries in the economic, social, and political field should indeed develop further, it might lead to area-wide co-operation in the security field also; and collaboration of these "area defense systems" could facilitate the organization of a Southern force. The merit of such a four-power system is that if the world power chose the "wrong" side, there would be a tendency for the Southern force to choose the opposite side.

These schemes are suggestions only. They are presented here for two reasons. They are intended as examples of a static analysis of security systems which seem to us to make sense even if they are much simpler than the dynamic analysis favored by some other authors. And they are intended as examples of the sort of specifications one might hope to obtain from more highly qualified experts on both sides of the iron curtain.

10.10 REVISION OF VOTING SYSTEMS

Another issue to be resolved by anyone speaking about coexistence or about revision of the United Nations Charter concerns, as we observed earlier, voting rights in the United Nations. These rights become the more important the larger are the tasks entrusted to the United Nations. As we said in section 6.4, we attach signifi-

cance to efforts to construct a better international order despite the risk that the Communist countries may, from the West's viewpoint, abuse them. Such efforts are important not only for their own sake but also for the sake of clarifying our intentions, including our willingness to do positive work with the Communist countries.

There are two main difficulties with the present voting system of the United Nations. First, it gives to a number of member countries an influence which, by all democratic standards, is not in conformity with their importance. Secondly, it does not sufficiently reflect the contrast which at present divides the world.

Less than proportional representation is found in many representative bodies, e.g., the legislative branches in many countries. It is essentially undemocratic for India to have the same influence on a United Nations decision as the Netherlands. Considerable weight must be given to country size, in terms of either population or contribution to UN activities. The latter way of measuring a country's role is an old democratic principle; it is realistic in that it is indicative of the economic effort a country is making. It has, however, a less attractive side in that it discriminates between the rich and the poor. It might be possible to compromise by giving equal weight to numbers and to contributions to UN work. This procedure would also facilitate the solution of a possible future problem: how many representatives should be apportioned to a new country that emerges through the integration of a group of former members?

The second issue should be dealt with along the lines followed repeatedly nowadays in social matters in democratic countries. Even democratic countries do not always have democratic institutions for all their important economic decisions. In business, decisions are often taken autocratically by management, with no influence from the workers. Some types of decisions have been democratized, however, and the principle applied is to give an equal number of votes to each "class" involved, e.g., to employers and employees. Sometimes three groups are distinguished and given equal influence, the third being either representatives of all other social groups or government representatives or experts appointed because of their personal knowledge of the subject. The latter principle,

somewhat modified, was applied in the organization of the oldest
international agency, that is, in the composition of the General
Conference and the Governing Body of the International Labor
Organization. Each national delegation is composed of one dele-
gate representing management, one representing labor, and two
government delegates. Various applications of these techniques
would seem possible with regard to the question of voting rights in
special United Nations bodies. One might be to give equal numbers of votes to the "West," the "East," and the "South." Another
possibility — not necessarily combined with the foregoing — is to
give voting rights to experts in the United Nations. These experts
have played their part on several occasions in the past.

Again our remarks are meant mainly to suggest that explicit
studies should be made and published so as to give more precise
content to coexistence possibilities as viewed from both camps.

10.11 DEFINITION OF LEGAL SOCIAL CHANGE

A new international order must also be explicit about economic
and social matters. If an armed force of some size is available to the
international government, there must be rules and procedures for
its use; certainly it cannot be used in cases where changes are
brought about legally. Legal changes may include all internal revo-
lutions, or they may include only some types. The broader concept
seems to be implied in the present United Nations Charter, except
in cases where international peace is endangered by the situation
within the country. Other specifications may be desirable, but
agreement must first be reached as to what social changes are acceptable. Agreement does not seem to be impossible with regard to
changes such as the elimination of feudal and colonial regimes or
the nationalization of industrial enterprises, provided satisfactory
compensation is offered.

This problem, and others mentioned in the last four sections of
this chapter, may be said to reflect the full difficulties of the present
conflict between Communist and non-Communist ideas. The importance of these problems is such that unprecedented efforts must

be made to solve them. It is amazing, and highly unsatisfactory, that so relatively small a part of the vast intellectual resources now directed at solving scientific problems is being devoted to the problems touched on in the preceding pages. A modest beginning has recently been made by some institutions.[2] The few groups that are operating in this field urgently need our attention and firm support.

2. See Schelling and Halperin, *op. cit.*, and D. H. Frisch (ed.), *Arms Reduction: Program and Issues*, Twentieth Century Fund, New York, 1961.

Economic Development and Co-operation in Africa

by Floor Hartog

I.1 BASIC FACTORS INFLUENCING ECONOMIC DEVELOPMENT

Natural Resources. On the whole Africa is not richly endowed with natural resources. The soil generally is not fertile, the climate is too dry in most regions, there are relatively few minerals, the coast is in general difficult of access, and the rivers are mostly unnavigable. In addition, stock raising, which is valuable among other things in manuring the soil, is often not feasible because of the tsetse fly.

Population. Some of the traditions and attitudes of the African population hamper economic development. In the first place, individualism is not very strong; the family (in a broad sense) is the natural unit. Since any advantages acquired have to be shared by a great many relatives, economic incentives exert only a weak influence on the individual. Secondly, the instinct of acquisition, insofar as it is present, often works in an unfortunate fashion. There is a desire to get rich quickly, rather than by sustained exertion.

These factors and the opportunities for large illicit gains probably explain to some extent why native intellectuals are strongly attracted by politics. The possibility of corruption has greatly increased in the last few years with the large amounts of money made available from abroad to carry out development projects. For officials who decide or advise on the award of contracts to (nearly always) non-African contractors, graft is in many cases a rich source of revenue. For the country concerned this works a double disadvantage: development capital disappears into the

consumption sphere (as contractors increase their prices by the gratuities demanded of them) and intellectuals are absorbed in sterile activities.

It is difficult to say whether the African population shows little aptitude for sustained economic activity as we know it because of in-born characteristics or because of exogenous factors such as those mentioned in Chapter 1 — climate, low standards of nutrition, etc. Against the climate hypothesis it may be observed that the Ethiopians, who live in a country with a largely temperate climate, are in general more passive than the rest of the African population. The one thing that can be said with certainty is that education and the development of individual initiative as a basis for satisfactory economic growth will take decades.

The level of nutrition is generally sufficient, but the diet is often one-sided. The Economic Commission for Africa is trying to get more accurate information on this point, in order to formulate a program for stimulating internal trade. An unbalanced diet is one of the factors contributing to a bad state of health in many places. In some regions alcoholism also exerts a negative influence.

In view of all the drawbacks to African industry, it is not very surprising that in nearly all countries most activities which go beyond the traditional economy are in non-African hands. Even the internal trade of the continent is largely controlled by West Europeans, Greeks, Arabs, and Indians.

Population Density.   Although the population is rapidly increasing, there are as yet few regions where population density is a serious problem. This is not to say that the present distribution conforms to the requirements of economic balance. Especially in West Africa over- and underpopulation occur side by side. This may be explained by the historical growth of cash crops in this area. Before the period of export crops, the coastal regions were densely forested and consequently not well suited for habitation. The savannahs farther inland had a much greater density of population. But the typical export crops can only be grown on the coast whereas the climate of the interior is generally too dry. The labor force of the savannah regions can therefore be profitably occupied in the coastal regions, especially in the growing season. To this end different systems of recruitment have been in use. The political disruption of West Africa has not yet seriously interfered with this symbiosis.

I.2 INSTITUTIONAL FACTORS AND INFRASTRUCTURE

Land Tenure System. With a few exceptions (Union of South Africa, Kenya), land in Africa is predominantly owned by the native population. This means that there are few plantation crops. The way in which land is treated in law and used does not meet the requirements of modern development. Therefore, in several countries land reform is considered an essential condition for economic growth. There is little chance of its being achieved, however.

In black Africa land is family-owned. This works against individual initiative and prevents or hampers the sale, mortgaging, and improvement of land. In regions where individual ownership exists (as in North Africa) the extreme fragmentation of holdings renders impossible the use of modern techniques. Where landlordism is characteristic (especially in Ethiopia), the leaseholder generally has to pay the landlord so large a part of the harvest (often 50 to 75 per cent) that he has little incentive to increase his output.

Communications. Adequate means of communication are lacking; existing facilities are largely confined to linkages with the former mother country. The transportation system is often a bottleneck, especially for export crops. The construction and maintenance of roads and railways is generally difficult and expensive in the African climate. Transportation facilities for internal African trade are lacking in many cases. Moreover, the secondary roads, so important for the conveyance of crops of small producers, are often more neglected than the primary roads they should complement. In many regions the principal means of transport is by foot. No developed economy can be built on this basis.

Administration. There is a big difference between the newly independent and the traditionally independent countries. In general, the countries of the first group have inherited a relatively efficient administration which the second group lacks. The ex-colonies are now making a determined effort to "Africanize" their administrations. In several cases this has led to a lower level of efficiency and reliability. However, the countries concerned hope that a well-functioning African administration will be obtained in some five to ten years. This optimism is based on the large increase in the number of African students at African and foreign universities.

In several countries it is not so much the top organizational layer that is lacking as the intermediate layer. A native intelligentsia, thin though it may be, exists in all countries, and is available to fill top-echelon government jobs; it is also possible to attract foreign advisers at this level. But there is often a shortage of specialists on the performance level. This is a common experience in business life also.

This is one of the reasons why there is often a big gap between knowing and doing. There are several leading Africans who have a clear insight into the problems of their country. However, improvement is often slow because of an insufficiency of people to execute plans, obstruction by vested interests, and immobility.

I.3 DEVELOPMENT POLICY

Primary Products.   Until now most development schemes have centered on increased production of those primary products in which the countries already specialize. More production means more cotton or more coffee, depending on the structure of the economy. What exists is well known, from the technical as well as the commercial standpoint, and usually there is little imagination or initiative in trying new products. A typical example is provided by the Sudan, where a huge irrigation scheme (the Gezira project) is being carried out to increase the production of cotton, though cotton already accounts for two-thirds of the national exports.

Accentuation of the already existing onesidedness often leads to disappointment. Africa's share in the world production of some primary products is large. An increase of the rate of growth can therefore easily lead to lower prices. For products where the African share is smaller (e.g., long-staple cotton, robusta coffee), there are nevertheless often particular markets where the African supply is dominant, so that in these cases too prices react perceptibly to an increase in African production.

In many cases it is more advantageous for these countries to increase quality rather than quantity. This may lead to higher instead of lower prices. Sometimes products can be improved merely by better grading or cleaning. In some countries there is a conscious development in this direction; a popular policy is to differentiate prices paid to farmers in such a way as to create an incentive for improving quality.

Industrialization.   Africa, with the exception of the Union of South Africa, is at the very beginning of its industrial development. Most in-

dustry above the handicraft level is non-African. There are two focal points for industrialization: light consumer goods industries (textiles, furniture, shoes, food, etc.) and industries processing native raw materials (e.g., vegetable oils). The first group of industries is to some extent represented in nearly every country, and in a few cases there is a surplus to export to neighboring countries. Senegal, for example, is relatively industrialized. The opportunities for processing industries depend on the technical complexity and the capital intensity of the production process, on the difference between the import duties on raw and on processed goods in the countries of destination, and on the resistance of vested industry in the (previous) mother country. All this industrial enterprise is more or less grafted upon the African economy.

There are some cases of heavy industry settling in Africa (oil refining, motor car assembling). In general, attractive fiscal facilities are offered; in some cases the government is willing to participate financially, while the African sales market is being developed. However, at bottom there is often antagonism between the governments and the industries. The governments want primarily to create a harmonious industrial structure, and industries which get their raw materials, spare parts, and higher personnel from outside and transfer their profits outside are viewed and treated with suspicion. On the other hand, the foreign enterprises want a free hand in their commercial activities. Consequently they are often not integrated into the respective national economies. Interest on the part of private investors is not very active on account of real or supposed political uncertainty.

Marketing Boards and "Caisses de Stabilisation." Rarely are the producers of indigenous products directly confronted with world market fluctuations. There are Marketing Boards in the former British territories and *Caisses de Stabilisation* in the former French territories. These government agencies guarantee the farmers a fixed price before the crop is under way and take care of the sale of the product on the world market. Use is made of the services of private traders, who also handle the payment of advances to farmers. The important difference between the French and the British system is that under the French system not only the price to farmers is guaranteed but also, for the principal products, the sales price in France, which is usually higher than the world market price. The latter guarantee holds for limited quantities, which are based on the absorptive capacity of the French market. Any surpluses have

to be sold on the world market, and this condition poses an especially acute problem for coffee interests. Thus French consumers are subsidizing both producers and middlemen.

The Marketing Boards are interesting organizations from the standpoint of development policy. They export at world market prices. For the first ten years after World War II these were generally favorable. The prices guaranteed to farmers reflected this situation only partially, with the result that large reserves were built up (the sterling balances of the previous colonies). These reserves have been used in large part to finance economic development, especially to build up the infrastructure in the various countries concerned. Export taxes (partly on sliding scales) also served to channel large amounts into the public treasury. All this may explain why the previous British territories until recently had little need to import capital.

As a consequence of the recent weakness in the market for primary products, the reserves have been largely used up. In most cases, when current balances of the Marketing Boards are added to the proceeds from export taxes, some profits still result, but they are insufficient to cover expenditures. In this connection it is worth noting that the European Economic Commission is considering instituting the Marketing Board system in the associated countries when the French-guaranteed prices are abolished. In view of the downward trend of prices on world markets this seems an unfavorable moment to start the system. With overproduction threatening, there is the risk that it would turn into a subsidy arrangement.

In some African countries a move is under way to eliminate middlemen and replace them by producer co-operatives. In Ghana and Senegal the government is engaged in changing the existing marketing organizations into monopolistic government agencies, which will take over the conduct of trade as well as the system of advance payments. The producer co-operatives, which are the cells of these bodies, are compulsory organizations dominated by their secretaries, who are government functionaries. This development is still too recent to warrant an empirical judgment. What experience is available seems to show that intermediaries can be eliminated only gradually because of the lack of competent successors. Policy-makers are often deceived by the large margin between the world market price and the price received by farmers, and the temptation is great to try to channel this into the

treasury. But the costs of organizing the trade are so high that if it is not done efficiently, socialization results in the complete disappearance of profit.

Capital Aid and Technical Assistance. Insofar as it is possible to formulate general priorities for those development factors for which foreign contributions are important, the rank order seems to be the following: (i) initiative, (ii) technical ability, and (iii) capital. The governments themselves generally stress education and training. Education has to start from the beginning since in several countries the labor reserve is illiterate and thus hardly capable of being trained.

The volume of internal savings is influenced by several factors which pull in different directions. In the first place savings institutes are being created to take the place of saving in the form of nonmonetary valuables. Against this favorable development there are, however, two countertendencies. As already noted, the possibility of skimming export profits is constantly decreasing. Also, the rapid Africanization of the leading government posts implies that people with a relatively high propensity to save are being replaced by people who are much more inclined to consume. In connection with this development it is significant that the import of consumption goods has strongly increased in the last few years. This does not unduly burden the balance of payments because most Europeans are repatriating a large part of their savings, in the expectation of being replaced as soon as African successors are found.

The capital attracted from abroad is almost exclusively government aid, directed at the financing of infrastructural investments. The transport sector especially takes a big share. The former British and French territories are still largely provided for by their previous mother countries. The other countries take capital where they can get it: from multilateral and bilateral sources, from East and West; and the same applies to technical assistance. The Development Fund of EEC is beginning to assume significance in the associated countries. The general complaint is that it works slowly and is cumbersome. Here, too, stress is being laid on transport projects.

To the extent that a greater number of countries and organizations are supplying capital aid, problems are created for the receiving countries. All aid leads to some tutoring, because the supplier wants a say

in the spending of his funds. The more tutors there are, often with divergent views, the more difficult it is for the receiving country to co-ordinate its development program. In many cases the underdeveloped countries themselves contribute to a state of confusion by holding out their hands to all sides, in some cases deliberately in order to create or maintain a certain political equilibrium. It would help if the supplying countries and organizations would try to co-operate and specialize in local operations. Such co-ordination is beginning to take shape in some cases.

Until now there has been little inclination to force development by inflationary measures. The number of projects is usually no larger than the available capital permits, for the simple reason that the supplier of the capital in many cases also draws up the project. The recipient government often tries to set up as large a project as possible, for reasons of prestige. But the maximum size is not always the optimum size. The management of the Central Banks is still in European hands in most countries, and monetary policy is generally conservative.

Planning.   In several countries unco-ordinated foreign aid is the main challenge to the drawing up of economic plans. These plans are largely long-term and restricted to development projects in the government sphere. Officials either try to obtain new foreign contributions for the projects proposed or try to channel existing foreign aid in the desired directions. The goals relating to the national economy are largely dictated by the impulse to develop domestic resources as fully as possible. Attention is mainly focused on the supply side, and it is trusted that surpluses can always be exportable.

This schematization of development policy is typically European-American. In several cases a plan existed before a planning agency was established, implying that foreign experts had been attracted to set up a plan. As yet planning is still mostly in non-African hands. As a result there is often a considerable difference between the formation of a plan and its execution. The average African has only a limited time horizon and is too impulsive to hold himself to a fixed line of action. Also, the personal regime which characterizes some countries is difficult to reconcile with the impersonal regime of planned development. Senegal in West Africa and Morocco in North Africa are countries where the administration is most characterized by Western ways of thinking and organizing.

I.4 INTRA-AFRICAN ECONOMIC CO-OPERATION

The Great Disintegration. In the colonial period Africa consisted mainly of a British and a French sector. These sectors are now divided into a large number of states. Thus, French North, French West, and French Equatorial Africa have disintegrated into seventeen countries (including Algeria). Several of these still have a common currency, but in general they want to get rid of this relic of colonial times. Independence requires that coins and bank notes bear the national insignia and (less irrationally) that there be some monetary autonomy. Some customs unions are still in existence between former colonies from the same political system, but in general they function only partially. So customs and currency barriers are rising, while economic development requires exactly the reverse. The creation of separate currencies is especially disadvantageous for intra-African trade. These new currencies have a restricted circulation; consequently in commercial treaties there is a tendency to aim at bilateral equilibrium, with restricted fluctuations. In this respect Africa is in the same situation as Europe immediately after the last war, except that matters are deteriorating instead of improving. Dakar, formerly the administrative, commercial, educational, and to some extent the industrial center of French West Africa, is now reduced to being the capital of a small country. While all countries are trying to build up their infrastructure, Senegal's has become partially idle.

A legacy from the colonial period is the strict economic separation between former British and former French territories. The means of communication are almost exclusively directed at the ex-mother countries; transportation facilities and telecommunications between neighboring countries are often lacking. This makes an economic regrouping extremely difficult.

Groupings and Regroupings. We will start our discussion with the former French territories, because they form the core of existing groups, or at any rate have one or more representatives in each group.

The most inclusive group of the previous French territories is the Organization of African States and Madagascar for Economic Co-operation, usually called the Brazzaville Group. This comprises all countries of French origin associated with EEC, except Mali. Guinea, which broke out of the French system, is not associated with EEC and

therefore does not belong to this group. The member states form a preferential area. The group must be considered a counterweight to EEC especially in deliberations on association problems. In those cases Mali co-operates *ad hoc* (as at the parliamentary conference in Strasbourg in June 1961). Within this group there are two smaller clubs, each of which forms a customs union. The most important is the so-called Entente, embracing the Ivory Coast, Upper Volta, Niger, and Dahomey. The equatorial customs union consists of Congo (Brazzaville), Gabon, the Central African Republic, and Chad.

Some non-French countries (Nigeria, Liberia, the Sudan, and Ethiopia) have joined the Brazzaville Group in the last few years. These states together form the so-called Monrovia Group, which can be considered the more moderate bloc in black Africa. Among other things these countries are discussing the problem of communications.[1]

Along with the Monrovia Group there exists the Casablanca Group, which comprises the radical states of Ghana, the United Arab Republic, Morocco, Guinea, and Mali. These countries emphasize political co-operation and regard economic unification as a by-product of political unity. Within this group there is also a smaller club with closer economic co-operation: Ghana, Guinea, and Mali together form the Union of African States with a customs union as its economic core. Ghana, the leading country, is at present trying to detach other states from the French system; a customs union has already been concluded with Upper Volta and attention is being paid to Dahomey. Upper Volta is geographically the missing link between Ghana and Guinea.

The countries associated with EEC are called the lackeys of Western imperialism and the opposition in these countries is encouraged by the Casablanca Group. The latter tolerates Europeans as advisers only until they can be dismissed. It will be difficult to encourage the moderate Monrovia Group without compromising the countries belonging to it.

To complete the picture it may be mentioned that there are customs unions between the United Arab Republic and the Sudan and among the former British East African territories. A Commission for Technical

1. At the conference of twenty African states held at Lagos in January 1962 it was decided to create a customs union which should ultimately lead to an African common market. Appropriate steps will have to be taken to this effect by the Organization of African States and Malagasy that is to be established. The countries participating in this conference were mainly those of the Monrovia Group; the total population of the represented countries is estimated at 130 million.

Co-operation in Africa South of the Sahara is engaged in co-ordinating activities in the field of technical assistance.

For the future, the Consultative Assembly of the Council of Europe advocates the creation of an African Development Bank. If such an institution could channel the greater part of development aid, this would be an important advance in the ordering of African affairs. However, it must be said that an arrangement of this sort will be difficult to achieve.

Measured by results, African movements toward economic integration are still insignificant. There are many resolutions and treaties, but few concrete measures. It is symptomatic of the disorganized state of trade policy that Upper Volta at present belongs to two different customs unions. Much needs still to be unraveled before proper work can begin. African commercial treaties are in many cases no more than declarations of intent. There are three types of such treaties:

   (i) those with quotas for separate products;
  (ii) those where an over-all amount is specified but the products have
       no separate quotas; and
 (iii) those where only products are mentioned.

Loose forms of the second and third type are the most frequent.

The sharp political differences between the Casablanca Group and the Monrovia Group are impediments to an economic rapprochement. Mali, which is the natural hinterland of Senegal, has disrupted all economic connections with that country. Ghana is trying to route the trade of Upper Volta through its own territory instead of via the Ivory Coast. On the other hand, Togo is boycotted as much as possible because of political antagonisms.

It is also significant that there exists in several of the moderate countries an opposition, or at any rate an undercurrent, which tends to admire Ghana's anticolonial attitude. Rationality is often a thin veneer over emotional political attachments. This undercurrent could become dominant in the event of a further fall in world market prices or difficulties in transition from the French system of protection to the preferential system of EEC. Because of this, private capital is hesitant, even in the states with a Western orientation. Also, it is as yet difficult to say how far Ghana's state socialism will spread.

Motives and Possibilities for Economic Co-operation. The African states have no extensive mutual trade. They are not complementary;

nearly all are self-sufficient in foodstuffs, and raw materials exports are directed at the European industrial countries. An increase in mutual trade will have to be based on the desirability of diversifying the contents of the food basket. As for industrialization, the restricted size of the national markets requires consciously arranged specialization, and consequently investment co-ordination, preferably on a regional basis (e.g., North Africa, West Africa). The few existing export industries, but for protection, would not be able to cope with the competition of the established industrial countries. The loosening of ties with the metropolitan countries leaves the governments more instruments of economic policy. A pre-condition for the tightening of economic connections between the African states is the improvement of communications.

The dream of an African common market cannot be realized within the foreseeable future. Smaller regional groups make more sense. However, on this point also no great optimism seems to be justified. Political factors are dominant; economic relationships are cemented or disrupted in order to give force to political rapprochement or estrangement. The personal sympathies and antipathies of the leading statesmen play an important role and render the whole process of intra-African co-operation impulsive and unstable.

In this situation the Economic Commission for Africa does not want to burn its fingers by propagating solutions. It tends to remain aloof and to restrict itself to documentation and analysis. A study on the development of economic co-operation in Latin America concludes that political cohesion in that part of the world is much greater, so that economic integration is largely an economic problem for which the Economic Commission of Latin America is well equipped. In accordance with this point of view the Economic Commission for Africa does not play a leading role in the process of intra-African economic co-operation.

I.5 ECONOMIC CO-OPERATION WITH INDUSTRIAL COUNTRIES

The British System. Apart from capital aid, preferences in the British market are of special importance. These are still in force for Nigeria and Ghana. Table I–1 shows tariff preferences for African products on the United Kingdom and the EEC markets. Even where

Table I–1

TARIFF PREFERENCES FOR AFRICAN PRODUCTS (per cent of import prices)

	On UK Market[a]	On EEC Market[b]
Bananas	11	20
Unroasted coffee	2.5	16
Black tea	3.6	18
Green tea	1.4	18
Pepper	2.2	20
Groundnuts	10	—
Palm nuts and palm kernels	10	—
Raw groundnut oil	15	10
Raw palm oil	10	9
Cocoa beans	1.1	9
Cocoa butter	0.5	22
Raw tobacco	30	30
Timber	10	10

a. General tariff minus Commonwealth tariff.
b. Outer tariff.

there are no preferences, certain products, e.g., raw cotton, are traditionally marketed in the United Kingdom. On the other hand, British products hardly enjoy a preferential position in the African Commonwealth countries. The concentration on imports from Great Britain is again largely a traditional phenomenon.

The French System. This system also embodies preferential tariffs, but more important is the fact that some African products are granted guaranteed prices for limited quantities on the French market while the African territories place strong quantitative restrictions on non-French imports. This arrangement has not changed since colonial days; it remains a closed system, in which both sides trade goods at prices above the world level. The influence of EEC is still difficult to ascertain. The countries concerned all belong to the franc system, with currency reserves centralized at the Banque de France and drawing rights used in consultation with it. The hothouse atmosphere is strongest in the Ivory Coast, a coffee country, since coffee receives substantial protection on the French market.

These relationships cannot be terminated without causing a basic economic (and perhaps also political) upheaval in the countries concerned. The problem is most urgent with regard to coffee. For cocoa there is no guaranteed price; for bananas the guaranteed price is of little practical importance because the principal exporter, Guinea, broke out of the system; and for groundnuts the preference is relatively moderate.

Association with EEC. The present French system is to be replaced by the preferential treatment of the EEC treaty. Paragraph 132 of this treaty states that member countries should apply their system of trade benefits to associated countries. This means that in the final analysis the associated countries will enjoy a preference which is equal to the outer tariff. For the principal products this preference is shown in Table I–1.

There has been consideration of the possibility that the process of association might be stepped up in order to match the accelerated development of the European Common Market. However, it is felt that while deliberations with the United Kingdom are in progress it would be unwise to widen the gap between former British and former French territories. On January 1, 1963 the associative system is to be renewed, and there is good reason to put it on an entirely new footing. The political basis of the association arrangement disappeared when the associated countries gained their independence. The continuance of the existing relationships is only provisional. There is no longer any reason to discriminate between associated and other African states, or even between Africa and other raw material producing parts of the world.

On the other hand, any new arrangement will have to pay heed to the fact that in the present situation several African countries enjoy protection or preference on the European market and that their economic activity is based on this privilege. Such ties cannot be disrupted suddenly.

The European Economic Commission has suggested that markets be regulated with some guarantees for producers' prices. The problem with this is that the principal African products are strongly competitive with non-African supplies, so that a partial African arrangement would not be sufficient to stabilize the market. Such a system could easily deteriorate into a scheme to subsidize producers. If financial aid is to

be given, it is preferable to choose the form of investment. If EEC development financing could be co-ordinated with the British system, and if perhaps contributions could be asked from the United States in exchange for Africa's giving up discrimination against Latin America, a way could be found to get rid of the preferential system.

The associated African territories are clinging to their preferences, if only to have a favorable bargaining position in the deliberations on the renewal of association. To date they have experienced little advantage from the preferences; the relationship with the former mother country still prevails. The extent of protection which EEC will grant is in general less than the favored treatment extended by the mother country. On the other hand, the EEC market is much larger and expansive. Coffee will probably present the greatest difficulties of transition. The high excise taxes on coffee in some EEC countries should be abolished or drastically lowered. The associated African countries hope to retain many of the existing price guarantees by extending them to EEC as a whole, though possibly with a smaller margin of protection. The United Kingdom's joining is anxiously viewed, because it might lead to the inclusion of other countries, with consequent reduced protection and lower prices.

Among the Commonwealth countries Nigeria is watching the deliberations between the United Kingdom and EEC with confidence, but Ghana has made itself the leading exponent of the outsiders. These outsiders consider the economic relationship between the associated countries and EEC to be unjust. The term often used in this connection is neocolonialism. It is argued that the support given to the associated countries is aimed at keeping them raw material producers, that it prevents their industrialization and guarantees that they will remain importers of industrial products. This view is not wholly wrong, as the associated countries are restricted in their use of instruments of protection. On the other hand, it holds much less for the relationship of association than for the bilateral connections still existing with the former mother countries. Moreover, in a certain respect association with EEC favors industrialization, because no tariffs will be levied on semifinished products (processed goods from the associated countries).

It must also be borne in mind that some African countries, because of their political convictions, do not want to be involved in an association for the whole of Africa. If such an association appeared imminent, they might be tempted to turn to the Communist countries for consola-

tion for the discrimination. In this connection the Casablanca Group may be mentioned.

Finally, the EEC policy toward temperate zone products deserves some attention. The autarkic tendency which seems apparent in the framing of a common agricultural policy is feared most of all. However, it is not important for African countries as they mostly specialize in tropical products. Only for meat and sugar may some disadvantage thus be created for African suppliers.

Relations with the Communist Bloc. In the matter of trade Communist penetration is as yet of rather small importance. There are an increasing number of commercial treaties with Communist countries, but most are of the nonobligatory type. The United Arab Republic, Ghana, and Guinea are the most obvious examples of African countries having important trade relationships with Communist countries.

Communist influence is much more significant in the field of technical assistance. This is especially directed at spectacular objects. Significant also is the fact that in Ghana the educational system is used more and more for indoctrination with the state ideology.

The neutralist states in many cases are very much interested in Communist help as a counterbalance to their former Western orientation. The colonial past often continues to have a traumatic effect, so that the West in several respects is at a psychological disadvantage. Where Western influence is still dominant, it is to a large extent connected with the continuance of the hothouse system.

There is no reason to regard Africa as an appendage of Europe, and still less to treat it so. We shall have to canvass in sharp competition with the Communist countries for satisfactory relationships with the African countries. Like us, the Communists make mistakes in their approach to African problems, but theirs are more readily forgiven.

For the moment, Africa is still predominantly oriented to Europe in the economic field, so some time is left to formulate a constructive African policy. Such a policy will have to be based on full recognition of the independence of the African countries, and it will have to reckon with and be ready to learn from Communist approaches.

Economic Development and Co-operation in Middle East Countries

by Aleida van Oven

II.1 INTRODUCTION

When preparing for a trip to Afghanistan, Iran, Iraq, Lebanon, and Libya, I accustomed myself not to use the expression "Middle East." I thought it a vague term. Just as some people include Libya in the West and others do not, so some include Afghanistan in the East — and sometimes even India and Pakistan. Moreover, I had been told the expression was not much liked in these countries. So I spoke of Southwest Asia and Northeast Africa.

But once in these countries I found that the term "Middle East" was frequently used and that many inhabitants had a feeling of communication with the other nationals of this — rather ill-defined — group. So the unofficial term could be used freely. Most Afghans I met did not consider their country part of the Middle East, though they conceded that they had important historical, religious, and other cultural ties with this neighboring region.

The purpose of my visits to the different countries was to gather opinions on the special subject of this book. For the greater part I will confine my notes to this field, although I had the pleasure of receiving information on other topics too. Nearly everyone I met was quite ready to give me the information I asked for, to make things as clear as possible to me, and to co-operate in the accomplishment of our study objectives. I would like to express my sincere gratitude to all who helped me.

II.2 ATTITUDES TOWARD REGIONAL ECONOMIC CO-OPERATION

As the book deals with the actualities and potentialities of international economic co-operation, on a regional as well as a world-wide basis,

opinions on regional co-operation in the countries concerned will be cited first.

The idea of economic co-operation within and among groups of neighboring countries as such generally meets with approval. There are, however, critics — mostly economists — who fear that every grouping with an economic aim will eventuate in a strongly protectionist bloc. Because European economic co-operation is most intensive, we shall start with the attitudes toward this integration.

Judgments on European Integration.   The need of European countries to co-operate more closely is well understood, and so also the foundation of the European Economic Community (EEC). But it is often feared that EEC's trade policy will be protective. Serious objections are raised too against the association of the former French and Belgian African territories. Even with regard to commodities (e.g., raw cotton, exported by Afghanistan and Iran) on which the Common Market outer tariff will be zero, the Six are expected to privilege the associated countries, in the first instance, by buying from them. As is pointed out in Iran and Iraq, Saharan oil will no doubt be subject to similar preferential treatment. The association of Greece and, possibly, Turkey is not appreciated in Afghanistan and Iran because it will hamper their exports of dried fruits and carpets.

The attempts to merge EEC and all — or part of — the European Free Trade Area (EFTA) also give rise to some uneasiness because the aforementioned disadvantages could be extended to a larger area. On the other hand, the negotiations could result in a reduction in the outer tariffs planned by EEC — possibly as a result of pressure by the United Kingdom — and in a decrease in the preferences within the Commonwealth — possibly through EEC pressure — and in consequence a decrease in the preferences accorded the EEC Associates. In that case, the merger would be welcomed.

Hopes are set on a lowering of the prices of European industrial goods — regularly imported by the countries concerned — following from higher productivity brought about by European integration. For the Middle East countries[1] this could result in a better ratio between export and import prices. It is also hoped that EEC, as a well-organized

1. For the sake of simplicity I will use the term "Middle East" as including all the countries I visited.

economic community, will provide a relatively stable market for primary products.

There is a rather widespread feeling that the emergence of EEC has given an incentive to further co-operation in the Middle East. Co-operation is often felt to be an advantage, and sometimes a dire necessity. An organized group of Middle Eastern countries would be in a position to conduct trade negotiations with EEC, and probably with other groups as well. This, again, could improve the ratio between the Middle East's import and export prices. Consultation between the groups concerning capital transfers might also be fruitful, and possibly result in a more co-ordinated investment policy.

Co-operation among the Arab Countries. The Arab League was founded in 1945. In the course of time all of the independent Arab states, including the North African states and the Sudan, became members. It was originally conceived of as a political and defensive alliance, designed to prevent foreign interference in the internal affairs of the Arab states. But attempts at economic co-operation were increasingly made, and some results have been obtained.

Import duties on agricultural products have been abolished among the members, excluding the North African countries west of Egypt, and import duties on a number of industrial goods have been reduced so that they are from 25 per cent to 60 per cent below the general tariff. But so far, the effect of these measures has been significantly reduced because of import licensing systems. The ultimate goal is an Arab customs union. One of the difficult issues which will have to be resolved is the level of outside tariffs. For instance, Lebanon as a trading country wants the level as low as possible, whereas the United Arab Republic and several other members want rather high protective duties.

Agreement has been obtained on the creation of an Arab Development Bank, to be known as the "Arab Financial Institution for Economic Development." The capital will be £25 million, and bonds can be issued for the same amount. Like the World Bank, it will make loans for development purposes to governments, or to private companies if the government concerned is prepared to give the necessary guarantees. Sometimes the remark is heard that a subsequent bank similar to the International Finance Corporation, which grants loans and participates with private companies without government guarantees, may be desirable. It is hoped that the Development Bank will promote more

saving, particularly in the oil-producing countries, that would find its way to investments for the development of the region.[2]

The League organizes yearly Arab Oil Conferences where the oil problems of the region are discussed. Representatives of non-Arab oil-producing countries and oil companies are invited to attend these meetings.

Plans for an Arab tanker fleet and an aviation company have been in existence for several years, but the members have been unable to agree to their implementation.

It cannot be denied that serious difficulties stand in the way of Arab economic co-operation. These arise from:

    (i) political discord, *viz.*, frequent political disputes among the members and fear of domination;

   (ii) differences in politico-economic structure of the various countries, especially in the degree of government influence on economic life (strongest in the UAR) and in the emphasis placed on self-sufficiency in essential goods (strong in the UAR and Iraq);

  (iii) differences in economic and social environment.

On the other hand it is certain that:

    (i) despite the political difficulties, a feeling of Arab unity exists — *"On se dispute toujours entre frères,"* as they put it in Lebanon;

   (ii) it is generally realized that co-operation has great economic advantages, especially for industrialization;

  (iii) the emergence of EEC has given a new stimulus to Arab economic co-operation; everywhere studies on the possible expansion of this co-operation are under way.

Because of the difficulties mentioned, there are many different opinions about the time it will take to achieve significant economic co-operation. In many Arab countries, it is felt that priority should be given to the formation of smaller groups, which might later integrate. Suggestions concerning the make-up of these smaller groups vary widely. Two quite different proposals are as follows:

  1. Five groups consisting of:

    (i) Iraq, Jordan, and Syria;

---

2. According to recent information (December 1961), there seems to be some uncertainty with regard to how promptly the plans for this bank can be realized. Meanwhile, the Kuwait government has announced the establishment of the "Kuwait Fund for the Economic Development of the Arab Countries." Its lending budget for a five-year period is said to amount to £50 million.

   (ii) Lebanon;

   (iii) Saudi Arabia and the smaller Arab countries of the Arabian Peninsula;

   (iv) the UAR and Libya;

   (v) Morocco, Algeria, and Tunisia (the Maghreb).

2. Two groups consisting of:

   (i) the African Arab countries;

   (ii) the other Arab countries.

There is also the possibility that all the Arab countries can co-operate directly on a limited number of issues, i.e., those where agreement is possible. Economic policy would then have to take due account of the differences in the stage of development reached by the various countries (e.g., in investment policy, transfers of know-how, and trade policy). In the context of this possibility we may refer to the plans for the foundation of the Arab Development Bank, which have met with general approval. Also to be borne in mind is the existence of several Arab institutes, such as the Industry Institute in Beirut,[3] which is investigating the possibility of a division of labor in industrial development within the Arab region.

It is also possible, of course, that a middle way will be followed. Some problems could be dealt with by one or more subgroups only, and others by the full complement of countries.

Libya is in a somewhat different position from the other Arab countries visited, namely, Iraq and Lebanon. She has concluded bilateral trade agreements with Italy and Egypt involving mutual preferential treatment. The Western countries, especially Italy, are her most important trade partners (especially as regards imports); her trade with Arab countries other than the United Arab Republic is small. It is true that Iraq and Lebanon trade more with the West than with the Arab countries, but for Lebanon in particular Arabian trade is important. Iraq, as an oil-exporting country, finds her most important markets outside the Arab region, but she hopes — as a consequence of further industrialization — to expand her trade with the Arab countries. Libya and the other North African countries, being convinced members of the Arab League, are thinking of intensifying their economic relations with the countries of black Africa, though they are separated from them by the

3. This is a purely Lebanese independent nonprofit institution operating in the field of economic and technological research.

Sahara and have only minor trade with them at the moment. Prospective supplies of oil and petrochemical products play a part in these considerations. The economic grouping of Arab countries may therefore tend to pave the way to better economic relations between the Arab group(s) and Africa south of the Sahara. Possibly this in turn might stimulate the black African countries to joint efforts in the economic sphere (see the discussion of African co-operation in Appendix I, pp. 203–206).

Israel is part of the Middle East. Needless to say, the Arab states do not wish Israel to participate in arrangements for regional economic co-operation. The tragedies connected with the emergence of the state of Israel seriously affected the Arabs as well as the Jews, and created painful and strained relations. After my visits to some Arab countries I think there are other aspects of the situation worthy of consideration.

It is often emphasized that the Western powers encouraged the foundation of the state of Israel in order to gain for themselves a strategic foothold in the Arab area. Therefore, it is claimed, Western policy should be regarded as the indirect cause of the injury done the Arab refugees. The West is said to continue its strong economic aid to Israel in order to strengthen and maintain its strategic position in the Middle East. Moreover I was struck by the fact that the feelings of the Arabs toward the Jews were not always wholly negative. For instance, mention was made of a certain religious relationship: as Christianity emerged from Judaism, so did Islam.

Statements like these leave us with some hope. Perhaps the West could eradicate the impression that it regards Israel as a strategic point for itself. The Arab states have started an accelerated program of economic development, and Western co-operation could be helpful. The environment for such development is becoming more favorable as co-operation between the Arab states gathers momentum. Perhaps in time contact may be made with Israel, possibly in the first instance by a subgroup of the Arab region, in the sector where contacts are least difficult, namely the economic sector. If so, it is the author's sincere hope that this first contact may be extended to other countries and to other fields of human activity.

Co-operation in South and East Asia. The tendencies toward regional co-operation in South and East Asia are dealt with in Appendix III. There it is stated that economic co-operation in Europe and in

Latin America stimulated the attempts at Asian co-operation. Up to now a few practical results have been attained within smaller groups of countries. In the United Nations Economic Commission for Asia and the Far East (ECAFE), the possibility of collaboration in a larger region is being considered; the consequences for technical assistance, planning methods, transport, and other sectors are outlined in Appendix III (pp. 238–242). Here I will only comment on the attitudes toward Asian co-operation in the two ECAFE member countries I visited, Afghanistan and Iran.

While the leading personalities in Afghanistan generally look with favor on Asian economic co-operation, they see the intensive participation of their country as a dream of the future. Afghanistan is still preoccupied with the basic requirements of economic development. Also, political difficulties with neighboring Pakistan — concerning the Afghan claim for an independent state of Pashtunistan — give rise to pressures, of uncertain degree, for economic self-sufficiency. Because of these political difficulties Afghanistan's rights of access to Pakistan's sea coast are always uncertain. However, in the setup of educational institutes, technical assistance, roadbuilding, statistical methods, and some other fields, consultation with other Asian countries is recognized as useful. With respect to industrialization, Afghanistan is thinking of giving preference, for some time to come, to rather small projects in various sectors, in order to determine the kind of activities that are most suitable for native labor and resources. In a later stage of development there will be more room for industrial specialization between Afghanistan and other Asian countries.

Iran is willing to take part in Asian economic co-operation, but she is careful to avoid committing herself too much. If, for instance, an Asian financial institution should be founded — and this is under study in the ECAFE Secretariat — she would probably participate. But with respect to trade policy agreements, she is reserved, and apparently willing to accept only very flexible arrangements. Iran is afraid of damaging her trade relations with other parts of the world. Moreover, many Persians would like to see an expansion of Iran's trade with the Arab countries of the Middle East, which is small at present. While Iran trades chiefly with the West and the Soviet Union, she has important trade relations with some South and East Asian countries as well. She feels herself to be in the position of a *trait d'union,* a link or bridge. If the Arab countries come to a further economic agreement, and if plans for

a broader Asian economic community materialize, Iran may induce the two areas to realize, at an early stage, the potentialities of mutual relations.

II.3 INFRASTRUCTURE, AGRICULTURE, AND INDUSTRY

Planning. Since the beginning of the fifties Iran, Iraq, and Libya, and since 1956 Afghanistan have had long-term plans for development. All of these countries have met with great difficulties in carrying out their plans, and the results have often been disappointing. However, experience is the best teacher.

Lebanon drew up a five-year plan in 1958, but because of political difficulties in that year the plan was never instituted as such. Not until 1961 was a five-year plan accepted.

In Iran, a revamped planning organization will come into operation for the execution of the third plan — a five-year plan whereas the first two covered seven-year periods. After the revolution of 1958 in Iraq, a provisional plan, partly a continuation of the previous government's plan, was made; this is just now being superseded by a permanent plan. In Libya, despite strenuous efforts of the Development Council (1956) the programs and activities of the various development agencies — financed largely by foreign means — and those of the federal and provincial governments could not be sufficiently co-ordinated to make planning workable. A Development Council of a new character has now started to draft an over-all plan and supervise its implementation. Afghanistan is at the beginning of her second five-year plan.

Infrastructure. Much attention is paid to the infrastructure in these countries. Expansion and improvement of all modes of transportation, of energy sources, of irrigation, and of buildings for many different purposes are an important feature of all plans and development activities. In several sectors there is a tendency to initiate projects smaller than those of the previous period. For example, it is realized that besides big dams for energy, irrigation, and flood control, there is a need for small dams dispersed over the country. An emphasis on less ambitious projects will lead to quicker results and to a better geographic distribution of productive capacity. This may be beneficial from a psychological as well as an economic standpoint.

Education is everywhere an important subject, but lack of teaching

staff hampers the implementation of plans in this field. The same applies to the expansion of health services.

Agriculture. The larger part of the labor force is engaged in agriculture, and agriculture therefore occupies an important place in development plans everywhere. In Iraq and Lebanon, however, there has been a shift in favor of industry. In Afghanistan's new five-year plan a larger amount has been set aside for industry than for agriculture, but it is continually pointed out that the projects for increasing agricultural produce have priority; they are simply less costly than the industrial projects.

Development of agricultural industries is on the agenda of all the countries. More attention is being paid to the geographic distribution of these industries. One advantage may be that migration to the big cities will diminish.

In Iraq, land reform right after the revolution took place at too rapid a rate. The new landowners lacked the required knowledge, equipment, and materials, and consequently the results were disappointing. Now the pace has been slowed and more government assistance is being given to farmers. The government is also helping to set up co-operatives. In Iran most of the lands so far distributed to farmers have been Crown lands. Lands in the public domain have been distributed to a certain extent, but large private estates have hardly been touched. A law restricting holdings in the form of landed property was accepted in 1960.[4] Iran now plans to found co-operatives first, and then to distribute the lands concerned. Land reform is being considered in Afghanistan too. But it is generally agreed that large landed estates do not pose as serious a problem there as in Iraq and Iran; they do not give rise to the same critical social situations. Some suppose that the property in question is no longer very extensive, because much of it has already been divided; but this will only be known when an agricultural census is taken. There is no thought of expropriating the land. There is, however, talk of regulations implying new relations between owners and tenants, and also of a progressive income tax.

Industry. Differences in the appraisal of individual freedom are likely to be revealed in the ownership of industry. Belief in liberty of the subject seems to be strongest in Iran and Lebanon. A Persian with a

4. In January 1962 the law of 1960 was replaced by a new one which limits private holdings of land to one village.

fine sense of humor told me that sometimes his desires for freedom, and those of his compatriots, grew into an urge to anarchy. A Lebanese complained that while it was indeed possible to draw up an economic plan and to set up an administration for industrialization and social security, for the time being it would be extremely difficult for Lebanon to put the system into practice. One of his more optimistic compatriots, however, stated that it was encouraging that everybody *talked* of planning and organizing nowadays.

In Iran the majority of the manufacturing industries are private. A number of big factories are state-owned but the government is trying to sell most of these to private persons (apart from the oil industry). All of the industries in Lebanon, except the public utilities, are privately owned.

In Iraq big industries are mostly state-owned and smaller industries are in private hands. Mixed industries, partly state and partly private, are encouraged, especially by means of the Industrial Bank, a state bank. The government is trying to further the establishment of smaller private industries by, among other ways, fiscal legislation.

A substantial part of the existing industry in Afghanistan is under mixed ownership. Apart from the public utilities there are some state-owned factories. Serious efforts are being made to encourage private investors to put their money into industry. There is a very sizable cotton factory which is largely privately owned, although the government exerts a certain influence on its affairs.

In Libya most industries are small-scale private operations. Some medium-size industries, e.g., tobacco and salt, are government-owned. Here, too, special facilities are offered to investors in new industries. Meanwhile, the government has started a few industries which it will — if possible — transfer to private owners.

Some notes may be added on a few specific industries.

Cement, as a building material, is considered an essential product in all countries, and efforts to achieve self-sufficiency are widespread. This end has been attained in Iraq and Lebanon, where there is even some export. Libya is still in the exploratory stage. The desire for self-sufficiency in this important commodity seems reasonable, but if the prices of home-produced cement are considerably higher than those of imported cement, partial self-sufficiency may be preferable, especially if supplies can be obtained from markets which are likely to remain open during periods of emergency.

The fertilizer industry — petrochemical or other — is also a popular subject for development planning. But there is no consensus of opinion as to whether various other petrochemical industries should be started shortly (see section II.5).

One or more big textile factories — besides small ones — exist in all countries, except Libya. Expansion of the textile industry is aimed at everywhere, although in Lebanon, where so far the factories are able to compete only if protected by high import duties, there are divergent views in this respect.

In Iraq a modest steel plant will be set up, which for the time being will work scrap and imported materials. It is hoped that eventually iron ore will be available locally; a geological survey is now in process. Iran has provisionally canceled her plan for a huge integrated steel plant. She is first going to investigate thoroughly the factors which will determine the viability of a steel industry — costs, possible site or sites, size, etc. In Afghanistan a small steel plant is programmed which will work up Afghan ore. In Lebanon some domestic ore is smelted and there is a plan to work scrap metal. It is quite understandable that these countries want to have some steel-making capacity, especially if materials are available locally. However, all the elements of cost must be carefully assessed, including the costs of transporting the heavy materials and finished products. Iran has set a good example. Besides, for developing a steel industry it seems advisable to keep in touch with neighboring countries to see whether a certain specialization of effort can be achieved.

In Lebanon much attention has been paid to the development of tourism. This is logical because the country has numerous attractions to offer, such as a beautiful situation, an alternation of lowland and snow-capped mountains, and splendid remains of ancient culture.

II.4 EXPORT-IMPORT PRICE RELATIONS

There is a general fear that the prices of agricultural and mining products will decline or fluctuate widely in relation to the prices of industrial commodities.

Attempts are made everywhere to improve the typical export products (dates, raisins, and other fruits, cotton, tobacco, wool, and hides, among others), or to improve their packing. In Iran special care is taken to keep the quality of carpets for export up to standard. It is recognized that a diversification of production, including a certain degree of in-

dustrialization, would be beneficial. It is hoped, however, that such a change-over can be financed in part out of increased income from exports.

It is often argued in these countries that trade treaties are a source of strength. This view does not stem from a preference for bilateral equilibria. In general, barter agreements with the Communist countries are not considered to be a particularly desirable type of agreement. But it is felt that trade treaties give a measure of stability to economic affairs.

Iraq has entered into a number of "proportional trade agreements," according to which imports from a certain country have to be counterbalanced by a fixed percentage of Iraqi exports, varying from 25 to 100 per cent. Such agreements have been concluded with Communist countries and with India, Ceylon, Denmark, and Finland. The annexed commodity lists do not give quantities or values.

As mentioned above, it is felt that further area association could channel international trade so as to minimize or even avert the danger of an adverse movement in the terms of trade. Such a goal might be realized assuming that there were regular consultations not only within but also among areas.

II.5 OIL

Oil occupies a special place in the economy of the Middle East. It is an important product of all the countries visited, though Lebanon has no crude production and Afghanistan's oil industry is still in the stage of advanced exploration.

In Iran and Iraq the general feeling is that the oil companies' profits on crude oil are excessive. As a consequence studies of the price structure of oil are being made by OPEC, the Organization of Petroleum Exporting Countries. Member countries are Iran, Iraq, Kuwait, Qatar, Saudi Arabia, and Venezuela. Headquarters are in Geneva. The next step will be to try to conclude new agreements with the oil companies which will give a larger share of the proceeds to the producing countries.

Other questions, such as the possibility of "pro rationing" — a device by which supply is controlled at the source — are also being studied by OPEC.

The USSR low-price competition is not seen as dangerous, at least for the time being, because exports from that country are still relatively small. The representatives of the big oil companies think that the im-

pact of cheap Russian oil exports on Middle East crude prices is quite noticeable. But to their minds, the growing diversification of productive capacity and the increasing number of competitors are even more important developments.

Sometimes the high fiscal charges on oil products in consuming countries are criticized because of their ultimately depressing effect on crude oil demand.

As indicated above (section II.2), Iran and Iraq are concerned about the privileges that may be granted Saharan oil by EEC.

Libya considers that she has an advantage over other Middle East countries because she is nearer to Europe in terms of transport costs. The possibility that Africa will some day provide a market, first for crude oil and later for oil products and petrochemicals, is also kept in mind.

Although Libya is just beginning to develop her oil economy, a pick-up of activity is already apparent in some other sectors, for instance, in trade, handicraft, transport, and building (Tripoli even has a surplus of large houses). There is, however, the danger that oil revenues will not be spent on the general development of the country. It is a good thing that many Libyans, especially the younger people, are fully aware of this problem. The government has learned that it may be subject to severe criticism if its activities appear to be not entirely justified.

As noted before, there is a divergence of opinion with regard to the desirability of developing petrochemical industries (see section II.3). Many people would like to see the full range of such industries come into being, but it is often argued that there should be a geographic complementarity in the distribution of the different sectors of this industry, among the Arab states, among the Middle East countries, or among the OPEC countries. Others would like to have the petrochemical industry reserved for the oil-producing countries; there are, for instance, Lebanese who are not in favor of a Lebanese petrochemical industry. Finally, it is sometimes argued that petrochemical processing is so complicated that developing countries are not yet in a position to cope with its problems.

II.6 THE POPULATION PROBLEM

Density of Population and Natural Resources. None of the countries visited has a population problem in the sense of having more inhabitants than its resources can adequately support, although Iraq,

Lebanon, and Iran have a rapidly growing population (yearly increases amount to 3.1, 2.8, and 2.4 per cent, respectively; Libya records 1.5 per cent; figures for Afghanistan are not available).

As for Lebanon, possibly a certain pressure is exerted by the population. It is the most densely populated country (about 385 inhabitants per square mile) of the group but it also has the highest income per head (about $300). There have always been many emigrants; emigration was especially noticeable during the period of Turkish domination, but it continues today, notably to Africa and the Western Hemisphere. Many Lebanese work in the neighboring countries and are welcomed there as good labor. But these people are not emigrants as they return home in the course of time. Emigration is, however, furthered by the fact that Lebanon is traditionally a commercial country. Apart from being a center of trade it is also a cultural and a tourist center. The highest incomes originate from these activities, and from the money transfers made by emigrants. As there is a growing feeling of uncertainty with regard to the continuance of these sources of income, more attention is being paid to the extension of industry and the improvement of agriculture.

In the other countries the density of population lies between 2 and 50 inhabitants per square mile (Libya 2, Iraq 30, Iran 41, Afghanistan 50). Owing to a lack of knowledge — in the broad sense — and of capital, the standard of living is low. There are, of course, large territories that, at the present stage of scientific development, are scarcely exploitable; this applies most to Libya with her extensive desert area. But on the other hand there are many regions which could certainly be productive — in agriculture and mining — if they were professionally exploited and if sufficient doses of capital were applied. As this situation is partly due to a lack of transport facilities, large amounts of capital are being invested in transport.

In some places, especially in the big cities, labor is available in adequate quantities; but elsewhere there is a shortage. This may be a latent shortage, in the sense that there is an insufficient local capital supply because of the supposition that it will be impossible to attract labor.

Employment. An oversupply of labor, implying underemployment rather than unemployment, is often apparent in the government sphere and in certain rural districts. The development of industries in coun-

try districts is therefore an important goal. Moreover, by subsidizing the peasants the Iraqi government tries to prevent a migration of labor to the cities in times of drought.

Underemployment seems preferable to unemployment. We shall take the government services as a case in point. In a situation of under-employment more people are engaged and have at least some earnings; in other words, "poverty is more fairly spread." Then, too, workers get experience and some insight into government activities, although this may not be the specific know-how which could be most useful to them later on. But there are disadvantages too. As wages are low, civil servants often take side jobs, which are sometimes more interesting to them than their professional work. They may also be tempted to accept extra-contractual payments. The bribery of officials makes impossible an ob-jective selection of contractors who have skills or goods to offer the government or the country. Moreover, because there are too many peo-ple available for the total quantity of work, activities are unnecessarily repeated and complicated. Underemployment in the government sector appeared serious, especially in Afghanistan and Iran. If some govern-ment officials could be transferred to industry, banking, or certain branches of agriculture and mining by means of additional capital and know-how, this would probably be most advantageous to the social and economic development of the countries concerned.

II.7 CAPITAL TRANSFER

A large part of the funds which Iraq needs for development purposes can be supplied by the oil industry. Besides, since the 1958 revolution big loans have been received from the Soviet Union.

Iran's development projects rely to a smaller extent on oil revenues. She has received large sums from the United States and some other Western countries and has obtained several World Bank loans. There are an increasing number of Iranian enterprises in which foreign pri-vate capital participates.

Afghanistan's development is strongly dependent on foreign capital. Until now the larger part of her investment fund has been supplied by the Soviet Union, with the United States ranking second.

In recent years Lebanon has borrowed a considerable amount from the United States. She has also contracted a loan with the World Bank for a "multi-purpose project." Other Arab countries, particularly Saudi

Arabia and Kuwait, have made large investments in Lebanon, but these are mostly investments in buildings. French, Swiss, and other private capital participates in a number of industries.

Libya has benefited from oil exploration since 1954, and exploitation activities have recently started at two points. So far, however, the most important Libyan income items are payments made by the United States and the United Kingdom for their military bases, and loans and grants given by these and other Western countries.

In Afghanistan and Iraq it is occasionally objected that the World Bank is not impartial and that it is unwilling to grant loans if the country soliciting funds harbors Communist influences. However, it is recognized that this situation is gradually improving. Further, the Bank is sometimes said to be too conscientious about collecting data and too occupied with details, which are not available in many of the developing countries because of lack of statistical services. This attitude on the part of the Bank leads to prolonged preliminary investigations.

Joint participation by foreign and domestic private capital in home industries is appreciated everywhere, particularly if combined with the transfer of know-how. It is also pointed out that this can pave the way for the mobilization of domestic savings.

In the Middle East countries there are laws protecting foreign capital and these laws often indicate a preference for "joint ventures." This preference is still more apparent in the countries' economic policy. In Iraq, planned private industries with up to 40 per cent foreign capital have the same facilities as new private industries with exclusively Iraqi capital. If foreign participation exceeds 40 per cent, these facilities are not available. However, the Iraqi authorities are being rather selective with regard to applications for companies in which foreign and domestic private capital will participate. Afghanistan would welcome more foreign private capital participation in her industry, but up to now she has not been very successful in attracting outside investors. This may be due to the fact that since the country was long isolated from the rest of the world by the United Kingdom, other countries had practically no opportunity to get acquainted with its needs and resources. Western reluctance to invest in Afghanistan because of the Soviet Union's foothold in the country is rightly considered by the Afghans to be shortsighted policy. Foreign private investment may also be hampered because the Afghans themselves have so far invested relatively little private capital in domestic industrial projects.

In all these countries industrial development banks are either in operation or in the process of being set up, as in Afghanistan and Libya. Whether government-owned, privately owned, or mixed, their aims always include channeling domestic private savings to industry and inducing foreign investors to participate in industrial expansion.

The plan to found an institution for multilateral investment guarantees (the "Mutual Investment Insurance Corporation") has met with great interest everywhere (see Chapter 7, section 6).

II.8 KNOW-HOW

Transfers of know-how, in various forms, play an important role in the relations between the developed countries and the Middle East countries.

Since 1958 Iraq has received more financial aid from the Soviet Union than from the West, but technical assistance is again increasingly coming from North America and Europe.

Afghanistan is receiving technical assistance from many countries in the East and West. A large number of United Nations experts are on the spot. The United Nations teams are sometimes composed of experts from developing, Communist, and Western countries. To my repeated question as to how East-West co-operation developed within such teams, all concerned answered that contacts were restricted in the beginning to purely formal matters. But beyond that the answers varied: some merely noted that gradually other subjects were discussed, while others stated that at present there is extensive contact between all team members. (It was observed that the experts' wives formed friendships among themselves and thus paved the way to a better mutual understanding.)

In Iraq and Afghanistan it is said repeatedly that financial or technical assistance is welcome from any source if no political conditions are attached to it.

In Iran and Libya a great deal of technical assistance is given by United Nations organizations. These two countries and Lebanon also receive assistance from various Western countries. In Libya experts from other Middle East countries, above all the UAR, contribute their services.

Leading personalities in each country emphasize the lack of managerial as well as technical skill.

It is often pointed out that those who received training in a foreign

country should have an opportunity to bring their knowledge up to date by further study abroad. This is not now possible because of the shortage of qualified manpower in the Middle East, and because not enough attention has been paid to this kind of assistance by the developed countries. However, an exchange of personnel between developing and developed countries might be a solution. This has the advantage of involving an exchange of knowledge, which would be very beneficial to both parties.

It is also felt that there are not enough opportunities for students to obtain practical experience after studying abroad. Such experience might be gotten in the country of study or possibly, and preferably, in a nearer country, with more comparable living and working conditions. Here, too, it may be useful to think in terms of an exchange of manpower, which would permit students in foreign countries to prolong their stay.

Lebanon is the least in need of foreign technical assistance, having by far the smallest percentage of illiterates (10 to 20 per cent of the population). The three universities in Lebanon — the American, the French, and the Lebanese, in order of age — have both Lebanese and foreign teachers, and there are many students from other countries in the Middle East and North Africa. In this way, and also through other channels, knowledge is conveyed throughout the area by the Lebanese. However, there is a need for foreign know-how in Lebanon, for instance, in some sectors of the handicraft and agricultural industries and in industrial planning generally.

As a rule, the leading figures in government and private business are working very hard in all of the countries visited. But they are repeatedly confronted with the problem of how to make the lower-level people understand the nature of the job at hand. Admittedly, many people are extremely eager to learn; this is apparent at all levels of teaching. Although the governments are aware that the general spread of knowledge is a long-term problem, much work is being done to extend education in all its ramifications. In this field, co-operation with neighboring as well as with remote countries is considered by everyone to be very beneficial.

Economic Development and Co-operation in Southeast Asia

by Hans Linnemann

III.1 CHARACTERISTICS OF THE REGION

In general discussions and writings on international economic affairs the countries of Southern and Eastern Asia are frequently grouped together and denoted as the Southeast Asian region. This terminology requires some further explanation if more precise statements are aimed at, and if confusion is to be avoided. In the present context, Southeast Asia comprises all the Asian member countries of the Economic Commission for Asia and the Far East (ECAFE) — except Iran and Afghanistan, which are included in Western Asia or in the Middle East region — plus the Asian Communist countries (except Asian USSR). The region thus forms a triangle with Pakistan in the West, Japan in the Northeast and Indonesia in the Southeast.

The economic characteristics of Southeast Asia are to a large extent the same as those of the other underdeveloped regions of the world. We shall pay little heed to these general characteristics, preferring to concentrate on those features which are uniquely Southeast Asian. Certain special features of the region's economic situation stand out clearly:

(i) Measured in terms of national income per head, Southeast Asia is in all probability the poorest of all the underdeveloped areas in the world. In no other region are living standards as low as they are in this part of the world; nowhere does poverty reign with such power as it does in Southeast Asia. This is not to deny that there are some remarkable islands of relative prosperity in the region, nor that there are some very poor areas outside Southeast Asia. However, in comparison with Latin America, the

229

Middle East, or Africa, the Asian region has the sad honor of topping the list of poverty-stricken areas.

(ii) In this region we find two giants (in terms of population) among the developing countries struggling to attain, among other things, a higher level of material well-being. Mainland China and India together house more than half of the people living in underdeveloped countries: their 1961 populations are estimated at 700 and 430 million, respectively. As these two countries — or rather subcontinents — follow different systems in their development policies, it is even more understandable that many developing countries, both inside and outside the region, look very attentively at the efforts made and the results obtained by these two big brothers.

(iii) The population problem is more pressing in Southeast Asia than in any other part of the world. Though a few pockets of low population density exist, the region as a whole has the burden of carrying, on an area smaller than that of Africa or somewhat larger than that of Latin America, an awesome number of people. Notwithstanding the attempts made by various governments to slow down the rate of population increase, the rate of growth is still high enough that India reproduces an "Australia" each year and China a "Canada."

(iv) Many countries in Southeast Asia have been very active in the field of national economic planning. Not only do almost all of these countries have development plans today, but several of them have had skillfully designed plans for a decade or so. It seems, moreover, that the national planning mechanism is on the whole more sophisticated here than in other regions. Attention is given not only to the preparation of plans but to their implementation as well. Other areas have tended to lag behind in this respect, although there are individual exceptions.

(v) If the Asian region seems to be leading in national economic planning, it is certainly not in the forefront in regional cooperation. The poor performance recorded in this field is mainly due to political factors. Apart from Communist countries and countries adhering to definitely Western ideas and principles, there are many nations that want to be — to a varying degree — politically and economically uncommitted. These contrasts are, generally speaking, more pronounced in Southeast Asia than in

other underdeveloped parts of the world; they make for a certain immobility, or at least sluggishness, in matters of regional cooperation.

It is tempting, on the basis of the above general statements — particularly those mentioned under (i), (iii), and (v) — to make an even more sweeping assertion, namely that the problem of developing the less developed part of the world is to a large extent the problem of developing Southeast Asia. In a sense this is true. If the development problems of Southeast Asia can be solved, those of other areas are also capable of solution. This does not imply that there are not specific difficulties to be overcome in every country or region, or that no serious problems exist outside the Asian region. Unfortunately, great misery exists in all of the less developed countries.

III.2 ECONOMIC RELATIONS WITH THE
OUTSIDE WORLD

It is not intended to enumerate in this section the economic ties that exist between Southeast Asia and the rest of the world, particularly the developed countries. Their general characteristics are familiar to everyone interested in world economic development. The comments which follow were inspired by a visit to a number of Southeast Asian states. They are grouped together under the headings Trade, Financial Assistance, and Technical Assistance.

Trade. The geographic pattern of the foreign trade of Southeast Asia[1] is such that one-third of all trade is intraregional, one-fourth is with Western Europe, and one-fifth is with the United States. This holds for both exports and imports, except that the region has a deficit in its balance of trade with the United States. The Communist countries of the region have only a small volume of external trade; their main trade relations are with the other centrally planned economies.

The export products of Southeast Asia fall into two distinct categories: manufactured goods (accounting for something like 90 per cent of the exports of Japan and Hong Kong, 45 per cent of those of India, and 25 to 30 per cent of those of Pakistan and Taiwan) and primary commodities (constituting about 60 per cent of Southeast Asian exports, or

1. The data on trade are mainly taken from the *Economic Bulletin for Asia and the Far East,* ECAFE, Bangkok, June 1961, pp. 20–26.

85 per cent if Japan and Hong Kong are excluded from the region). The bulk of the manufactured goods exported consists of light manufactured products, with textiles and textile products ranking first. Japan has a more diversified export list; ships and machinery are substantial items. As to primary commodities, the region is the greatest supplier of the world markets for natural rubber, tea, rice (traded mainly inside the region), copra, tin, and jute. Next to rubber, petroleum is the region's greatest source of foreign exchange, but Southeast Asia accounts for not more than 5 to 6 per cent of world petroleum production. These products constitute over 70 per cent of the region's primary exports.

On the whole, the growth of Southeast Asian exports has lagged noticeably behind the growth of world exports. If petroleum is excluded, the commodity composition of the region's exports is even more unfortunate than that of other primary producing regions. Many countries in Southeast Asia — and among them the largest — have serious balance of payments problems continuously. The developed countries could, of course, help matters by lowering or abolishing import duties, quantitative restrictions, and internal taxes on the region's export commodities. It should be noted, however, that for Southeast Asia the quantitative effect of an abolition of all duties on primary products would not be very large; it would not in any event solve the whole problem. More important would be a reduction in the protection afforded industrial consumer goods, especially textiles.

The creation of the European Common Market probably will not much affect the exports of Southeast Asia, at least in the short run. There may be adverse effects in the long run, if preferential treatment of the associated (African) territories continues. If the United Kingdom joins the Common Market, these preferences might either be reduced or extended to the Asian Commonwealth countries. These countries — India, Pakistan, Ceylon, the Federation of Malaya, and some smaller territories — are on the whole not opposed to a merger of the United Kingdom and EEC, provided that their special interests (tea, rubber, and to some extent textiles) are taken care of. Many of the non-Commonwealth Asian countries have only a limited interest in the Western European market; only 10 to 15 per cent of the exports of Burma, Japan, the Philippines, Taiwan, and Thailand go to Western Europe. (For Indonesia the percentage is as high as 30.)

This is not to say that Asian economists and political leaders have no objections to the European Common Market. They note several dan-

gers, or at least potential dangers. The European textile industry might well strengthen its position, and co-operate to prevent a lowering of protection. The synthetic rubber industry might, because of increased efficiency, expand its output to the detriment of producers of natural rubber. Co-operation rather than competition among the producers in a European industry might lead — and according to some has already led — to higher prices, particularly on foreign markets.

Also, in a broader context than that of the European Common Market, there is considerable ill feeling about some of the attitudes displayed by international private enterprise. The monopsonistic behavior of large concerns buying raw materials is a case in point. Monopolistic price setting by regional Transport or Freight Conferences is another example; it should be borne in mind in this connection that for several raw materials transport costs are as important a part of the selling price in the United States or Europe as local costs of production. It is feared, moreover, that these Freight Conferences sometimes collaborate with vested industrial interests in the developed countries by charging high rates for shipping manufactured or processed goods exported by newly industrializing countries. There is a general desire in Southeast Asia to break these monopolies by founding national (or regional) shipping companies.

For reasons of national autonomy and political independence, many Asian countries are opposed to too intimate economic links with the developed countries. It is unlikely that India would accept the status of an associated country of the enlarged European Common Market if the United Kingdom joins the Six. The Philippines have reached agreement with the United States about the special trade links between the two countries; these are to be completely eliminated by 1974. For somewhat different political reasons, some countries affiliated with the Western world (especially those having at present close ties with the United States) have embargoes on trade with the Communist world, particularly mainland China. India and other neutralist countries, on the other hand, count on the possibility of a substantial expansion of their trade with the centrally planned economies.

Any measures designed to give greater stability to commodity markets would be welcomed in Southeast Asia. The instability of primary product prices is one of the most pressing problems confronting some of the smaller countries that have no chronic balance of payments difficulties (like the Federation of Malaya, and Thailand). The point is

stressed that the co-operation of consuming countries — especially those having large stocks, as the United States does of many products — is essential. It is also argued in this connection that the substitution of synthetic for natural products — if it has to happen at all — should take place very gradually so as to allow producers of the natural materials to shift to other activities. As to the surplus-disposal program of the United States, some Asian economists suggest that the United States buy up the exportable quantities of the product concerned (or of close substitutes) which are produced by underdeveloped countries, in order to avoid a market disruption which would deprive the latter of their traditional export markets (e.g., the rice exports of Burma and Thailand).

The main contribution which the developed countries can make to the trade (and development) problems of Southeast Asia is to open their markets to the region's manufactured goods. Many industrialized countries are not applying the most-favored-nation treatment under GATT rules to imports from Japan. "Voluntary quotas" have been imposed by Japan on its exports to the United States. Similarly, several export products from Hong Kong, India, and Pakistan are subject to "voluntary restrictions" when entering the United Kingdom. Quotas are applied by several other countries. If the developed countries abolished their quantitative restrictions, lowered their duties, and concluded three- to five-year import contracts for manufactured goods, it would indeed be a major demonstration of their willingness to co-operate with the developing countries in building a sound world economy.

Financial Assistance.   There is no need to argue here the necessity for continued (and increased) financial assistance to Southeast Asia. In this region capital is still the scarcest factor of production. In recent years there has been much talk about the great shortage of entrepreneurial and technical skill in newly developing countries, and about the limit that this shortage imposes on the amount of capital which can be fruitfully invested. It is true that there is a limit to the capacity to absorb capital, but this limit has certainly not been reached in most Asian countries, including the most important ones (India, Pakistan, Indonesia; also mainland China). The argument of a limited absorptive capacity cannot in all honesty be used to justify turning down the region's demand for more capital aid.

To be sure, this statement does not imply that there is no need to

foster the training of technical manpower and the creation of more organizational skill. These things are important — as is, for that matter,
the development of capable and honest public administrations. More
training facilities in this field are required, and the United Nations
Special Fund — which devotes a substantial part of its funds to this
purpose — could well spend its entire budget in the Asian region.

Another pre-investment activity should also be given attention,
namely the search for the most promising individual investment opportunities. Despite relatively good over-all performance in economic planning, microplanning (i.e., planning on the project level) has been neglected in comparison to macroplanning. Agencies which give capital
assistance mostly on the basis of individual projects — like the International Bank for Reconstruction and Development and the (former) International Co-operation Administration — have recently been urging
the governments of several Asian countries to go more deeply into planning on the project level.

In many countries of the region the geographic distribution of
capital aid has been sharply criticized. The bilateral aid given by the
United States, which has frequently been used as an instrument of anti-
Communist policy, with little or no consideration for the real economic
needs and possibilities of the area, has especially come under fire. In
general, the countries more or less attached to either the Western or the
Communist bloc are in favor of continuing the granting of economic
assistance on a bilateral basis, whereas the more neutralist nations
would prefer the channeling of aid through multilateral institutions.
The uncommitted countries will accept bilateral assistance because
multilateral aid is far from sufficient. In some countries of the region,
however, it is feared that the economic aid given by the Communist
bloc may have undesirable consequences because of

   (i) the many technicians sent by the donor country, some of whom
       might be engaged in intelligence activities; and
  (ii) lasting dependency on the donor country for replacement and
       spare parts.

There are some general complaints about the conditions on which
loans are provided. The greatest objections are made to the short periods for which loans and credits, both public and private, are frequently
given. High interest rates and the fact that many loans are to some
extent tied to products of the lender also inspire complaints. Special
loans or grants should be given in cases of emergency; emergencies may

easily arise in a region where the well-being of the bulk of the population depends on agricultural production and hence, to a great extent, on uncontrollable weather conditions.[2]

Except, of course, for the Communist countries, private foreign capital is welcome in Southeast Asia. Government attitudes toward private capital differ, however, in different countries. In some countries, private foreign investors are virtually free of restraints, but in most countries there are laws and regulations limiting the freedom of international private capital, and guiding it in directions most beneficial from the national point of view. Co-operation of foreign with local private capital in joint ventures is promoted, although it is sometimes difficult to find the necessary domestic funds. Owing to a shortage of local capital, policies designed to reserve certain branches of production to national citizens — e.g., the Filipino-first policy of the Philippines — have often had little or no result other than to discourage foreign private enterprise.

On the whole, the role played by private entrepreneurs in the process of economic growth seems to be appreciated more today than it was ten years ago. This change in attitude may be due partly to the accomplishments of private capital in India during the first two five-year plans. In several Southeast Asian countries, however, there is some distrust of private capital (especially foreign capital) if it operates under some sort of government guarantee, as in the case of most medium-term suppliers' credits or a legal monopoly. Sometimes the technical merits of the projects financed or the quality of the goods produced are less than they might have been had there been no guarantee.

Technical Assistance.   The experience of Southeast Asia (excluding here the Communist countries) with technical assistance received from the developed countries on a bilateral or a multilateral basis has been fairly satisfactory. Nevertheless, there are a number of objections and desiderata for the future. These can be summarized as follows:

  (i) There should be more continuity in technical assistance activities. This is true of the advisory work as well as of the people giving the advice.

  (ii) Technical assistance work should be better planned and integrated. In part this is a task for the receiving country, but the

2. The reader may be reminded of the great impact of natural calamities on the level of production and consumption in mainland China.

multitude of agencies and organizations providing assistance must be willing to accept guidance in this matter. They must also be willing to co-operate, instead of competing with each other.

(iii) More attention should be given to the training of local people. Foreign advisers should make a serious effort to train the nationals with whom they are working.

(iv) In many fields experts are needed who are willing (and entitled) to accept operational and executive responsibilities instead of merely advisory ones. This requires a further extension of the OPEX scheme already in operation.

(v) Technical assistance has been fairly expensive in relation to the results obtained, both for the donor countries or organizations and for the receiving countries (which usually bear part of the costs). It has been hard to find the right man for the right job; overhead costs have been excessive for smaller projects, and political factors have been overly obtrusive, especially in bilateral technical assistance activities.

The remarks above are of a general nature and do not necessarily apply only to Southeast Asia. The following observations about the technical assistance work of two of the specialized agencies, on the contrary, have to be weighed against the background of the actual situation in the region. These observations concern the activities of the World Health Organization (WHO) and UNESCO.

There is a widespread feeling in Southeast Asia that medical experts of WHO do not fully realize the costs involved in their programs of medical and sanitary improvements. Developed countries have often been proud of their achievements in the field of medical assistance to developing countries. There is less reason for satisfaction, however, if one realizes how little it costs to prevent a human being from dying (a cost the developed countries are willing to bear) in comparison with the expenditure needed to keep him alive, and the even greater outlay needed to give him a productive job (an amount the developed countries are reluctant to provide).

UNESCO activities are criticized on two points in several countries. First, these activities are not sufficiently oriented toward the needs of the production process. Secondly, the way in which UNESCO plans to provide education (especially primary) is overambitious and too expensive; standards for school buildings, for instance, should be modest as

compared to those of developed countries. Southeast Asia is not in a position to permit itself luxuries in the field of education.

III.3 ECONOMIC CO-OPERATION IN SOUTHEAST ASIA

Many countries in Southeast Asia were born as independent nations only after World War II. The fact of newly gained political independence has had (and still is having) a great impact on the region's economic life. It has led many countries to orient their internal policies to the central issue of economic development. In the international setting, however, the results have been less favorable — at least initially. Just as more recently in Africa, the wave of independence broke several large economic and political units into a number of independent nations. Examples of this process of disintegration may be mentioned here.

After the war, the Indian subcontinent — from which Burma was already separated — was divided into India and Pakistan, and recently Nepal loosened the close economic ties which bound it to India. French Indo-China was split up into three nations — Cambodia, Laos, and Viet-Nam — and the last is at present divided into a northern and a southern part. Before the Second World War the economies of Taiwan and Korea formed part of the Japanese empire and were integrated with the Japanese economy; now they are independent units, and Korea itself consists of two separate entities.

Lately, serious thought has been given to the possibility of reversing this movement. The ECAFE Secretariat has played a part in this development. It should be noted, however, that the present tendency toward regional co-operation has to be seen, to a large extent at least, as a reaction to European integration moves and Latin American co-operation plans. Southeast Asia's interest in regional co-operation was born out of need rather than desire. This is not to deny that, once the process has been set in motion, several countries will probably find themselves greatly in favor of economic collaboration or even integration. These are, understandably, those countries that have most to gain by the establishment of a regional market.

The prospects for an Asian common market would seem to be bright considering that a substantial part — one-third — of the international trade of the Southeast Asian countries is intraregional trade. A ratio of 33 to 35 per cent compares very favorably with the corresponding ratios for Latin America (only 10 per cent) and Africa. Burma, Laos,

North Borneo, Sarawak, Southern Korea, Taiwan, and Thailand sell 60 per cent or more of their exports on the regional markets. Today the most important regional trade products are textiles, rice, petroleum, rubber, and machinery and equipment; these products account for 40 per cent of intraregional trade.

Even apart from the retaliation argument, there is a real need for regional co-operation in the economic field. Several factors may be distinguished here. Many Asian countries have perpetual balance of payments problems, and the only way out seems to be a contraction of imports. For example, it is for this reason that Ceylon's Ten-Year Plan calls for a great reduction in imports of agricultural products. Since the bulk of Ceylon's agricultural imports comes from Burma and India, these countries will experience a decline in their exports which they will try to compensate for by substituting home-produced goods for imports. Consumer manufactures, at present exported by countries like Japan, Hong Kong, and India, will also meet increasing sales resistance because of industrial expansion in other countries of the region (textiles are the chief products concerned). These and similar cases clearly call for a more co-ordinated approach to development problems, so that some sort of specialization and division of labor can be obtained on the basis of comparative advantages within the region.

There is also scope for co-ordinating complementary activities. The future cotton requirements of Japan and India could well serve as an important guidepost for the production plans of the region's major raw cotton exporter, Pakistan. Another case in point is that of iron ore; the region's importers — making their plans individually — are counting on a larger total supply from the region's exporters than the latter can possibly provide. The chances for a successful co-ordination of regional development activities are greater the earlier a start is made; later on, (newly) vested interests may be a serious hindrance to an optimum distribution of productive capacity.

Right now, the main obstacles to regional co-operation lie in the political sphere. This is, of course, most obvious with regard to the centrally planned economies of the region. Because of the great differences in economic organization and policy no close political co-operation is possible between the Communist and non-Communist countries, although inter-group trade might be expanded. But there are also political tensions and conflicting views among the non-Communist nations, particularly between the neutralist and the pro-Western countries. Po-

litical distrust is often based on differences in national size and strength.

Apart from political differences, many other factors make for heterogeneity within the Asian region. On the economic side, there are marked differences in the level of development, and — at least in the short run — in the balance of payments position of the countries. There are also important contrasts in the fields of linguistics, anthropology and religion.

Because of the above-mentioned obstacles and the short period of time which has elapsed since co-operation first came under study, no attempts have been made so far to achieve thoroughgoing regional economic co-operation, co-ordination, or integration. The few plans that have been formulated are only sub-regional in extent, and they aim, not at integration, but at the creation of a free-trade area, a commodity common market, or an even lesser objective. These plans will be reviewed briefly.

The most concrete possibilities for economic co-operation probably exist with regard to those countries that — in one way or another — form part of the Commonwealth of Nations, i.e., India, Pakistan, Ceylon, the Federation of Malaya, Singapore, North Borneo, Brunei, Sarawak, and Hong Kong. Products of these countries enjoy the Commonwealth preferential treatment in each other's markets. The former Commonwealth member Burma abolished these preferences in 1954. India is strongly in favor of increasing tariff preferences and of extending co-operation to other fields. Pakistan is opposed to this for both political and economic reasons; along with most of the other countries in the group, she is afraid of India's competitive power.

A group of smaller Commonwealth countries is aiming at co-operation within a geographically limited area. The plan extends to the so-called Greater Malaysia, comprising the Federation of Malaya, Singapore, North Borneo, Sarawak, and Brunei. Greater Malaysia is conceived of as basically a political association; economic co-ordination and integration would seem easier and more firmly based with such an arrangement than without it. The countries involved already have a common currency. The association should come into being during 1963, when the political status of Singapore (a Crown Colony with substantial self-government) is due to be reconsidered. In the meantime, Malaya and Singapore are discussing on what terms they might co-ordinate or integrate their economies.

The Federation of Malaya also participates in the Association of

Southeast Asia (ASA or ASAS), which was established in July 1961 and includes Thailand and the Philippines. The three governments have stressed that the organization is definitely nonpolitical. It aims at providing an exchange of data and other assistance in the field of economic development; activities are restricted to economic, cultural, technical, and administrative matters. Other Southeast Asian countries are welcome to join ASA. Indonesia, which has the most natural affinities for this group, is not likely to join because of the political orientation of the three present members.

Two more plans — if they deserve that name — may be mentioned. One is the Central Treaty Organization (CENTO), which includes the West Asian countries of Pakistan, Iran, and Turkey. The economic aspects of this co-operation are very limited in scope and subordinated to the military aspects. The other idea concerns the establishment of a Pacific Trade Area in which Australia and New Zealand would participate. This idea has been launched by Far Eastern exporters of manufactured products (Hong Kong and Japan) but it is unlikely to receive sympathetic consideration in Oceania's high-income countries.

In summary it may be said that the more developed a country is, the more it is likely to be in favor of close regional economic co-operation. Japan is, of course, the strongest nation in the area in many respects, and the less developed countries would like to keep her out of any regional arrangement. But if this were done, India would be economically the most powerful nation, a prospect which is generally regarded with disfavor. There are complaints in many parts of Southeast Asia about the high-handed attitude of Indian officials — a condition which is not conducive to better understanding and mutual co-operation. As, for obvious reasons, mainland China cannot be included in regional integration or co-ordination schemes, we are for the present left with the smaller countries of Southeast Asia as the ones most likely to engage in regional economic co-operation.

Achievements in the field of economic co-operation are still modest. On an incidental basis sub-regional co-operation has been realized in the Mekong River Project, in which Cambodia, Laos, Thailand, and Southern Viet-Nam are working in collaboration. More permanent and broader co-operation exists within the framework of ECAFE, especially the ECAFE Secretariat. Regional co-operation in the technical assistance field is welcomed by all countries; experts from Japan, Taiwan, India, and other nations are at work all over the region. Other in-

stances of regional co-operation are to be found in the study of planning methods and techniques, in a few activities in the transport sector, in regional geological studies, and in some other fields. These are only the first steps on the long road toward co-ordinated regional economic development. It is to be hoped that Asian political leaders and economists will have the wisdom and the courage to proceed farther along this road.

Economic Development and Co-operation in Latin America

by Henri Rijken van Olst

IV.1 CHARACTERISTICS OF THE REGION: SCOPE OF THE DEVELOPMENT PROBLEM

Latin America comprises, in this text, all the countries of the Western Hemisphere to the south of the United States. The great majority of these countries obtained political independence about a century and a half ago and, until the beginning of the twentieth century, went through a slow process of economic development. This process has accelerated during the last two decades, notably in Brazil, Mexico, and Argentina; Venezuela's industrial achievement has also been remarkable, but somewhat onesided. Nevertheless, the area as a whole — and at least parts of each country — may be regarded as still in the process of development. Some of the poorest countries in the world, in terms of per capita national income, are to be found in the Latin American area, namely Bolivia, Paraguay, and Ecuador.

Among the factors responsible for the slow rate of economic growth in Latin America, the following deserve mention:
(i) the low density of population and the consequent scarcity of manpower, together with a lack of educational facilities;
(ii) the lack of adequate communication between countries;
(iii) the conservatism of large parts of the population, which is reflected in, among other things, outmoded production methods.

These points will be discussed below, with special emphasis on aspects which are typically Latin American.

(i) The area has for a long time been relatively thinly settled, with a concentration of population in the coastal districts and cities. Only in recent times has a movement toward the interior started — a most re-

markable and symbolic example being the transfer of the Brazilian capital to the interior of the country.

The population of Latin America is ethnically the most heterogeneous in the world. Latin American Indians, Negroes, white people and the descendants of various Asian peoples are in the process of merging into what will one day be a new "race." The "white" republics — Argentina, Uruguay, and Chile — may be an exception to this rule.

Human scarcity and human heterogeneity have for many years barred the way to an economic and industrial development comparable to that of Europe and North America. Both factors, however, are likely to lose significance in the course of the next forty years or so. The rapid rate of population growth in many Latin American countries — more than 2.5 per cent per annum in various instances, a rate which is among the highest in the world — will provide more workers in the future, although there is a danger of increased unemployment. The growing awareness in the world that no race can validly claim to be superior, and the growing economic and spiritual unity among population groups, will undoubtedly give Latin Americans greater confidence in their own abilities and lead to greater Latin American solidarity. The feeling of solidarity has been greatly enhanced by the work of the Economic Commission for Latin America, which has repeatedly pointed out the advantages of co operation in the economic field.

These developments will, possibly with the help of experts from outside the region, lead to a higher standard of professional training for the working population, and to a greater degree of specialization in those activities which are best suited to the temperament of the people and the climate of the region.

(ii) Difficulties lie ahead because of certain geographic features of the continent. The Andes are a formidable barrier between the nations to the east and the west. There are practically no east-west roads or railways in Latin America. Moreover, part of the interior of the continent has not been explored and may even be impenetrable. Trade between the countries has always been very modest because of the lack of important buyer's markets, the lack of a variety of salable products, and the absence of adequate communications. The natural trade partners of Latin America have always been Europe and the United States. Until recently, trade has also been impeded by high protective tariffs on many

products in many countries and by the instability and heterogeneity of exchange rates.

The construction of new roads will have to be given a high priority in Latin America. Because roads are costly and not immediately remunerative, foreign investment aid on a large scale will be necessary and, as far as we can determine, very welcome.

(iii) In our opinion, the greatest obstacle to rapid economic development is the conservatism of parts of the population. This manifests itself in: outmoded inefficient production methods, especially in agriculture but also in manufacturing; the latifundium system of large land holdings in various areas, which leaves agricultural workers tied to the land with hardly sufficient means to subsist; and political systems which center around individual politicians, their families, and their interests rather than around well-organized political parties with clearly formulated programs. Stagnation in its various aspects decreases the incentive to work, at least in some of the countries in the area. There is sometimes more interest in acquiring political influence and getting rich quickly by playing the lottery than in undertaking entrepreneurial activities.

In this connection the efficiency of labor in the organs of the governments — ministries and state and municipal services — and in banks, commercial organizations, etc., should be considered. The degree of efficiency varies greatly from country to country and from service to service. On the whole, however, the level of labor productivity is unsatisfactory. This is partly a consequence of low wages, partly its cause. The government staff is often excessive and could easily be reduced to one-fifth or one-fourth, if the remaining force was adequately paid and actually present and working during office hours. One explanation for the large number of civil servants lies in the widespread custom of appointing to office the relatives of new presidents, ministers, and other officials, together with a prohibition on the discharge of officials appointed by prior administrations. This is one way of avoiding serious unemployment, but, as remarked before, it exacts a toll in the form of low labor productivity.

It is of course impossible to tell other peoples how they should organize their economic and political life. On the other hand, the governments of the less developed countries must realize that they will have to

take the initiative in doing away with certain undesirable practices. Otherwise part of the development assistance they require will go past their door to the more developed countries, where greater certainty exists that the funds made available will be used efficiently. In countries like Brazil and Mexico, which have already attained a relatively advanced stage of development, this is generally realized at the national level, though not always at the state or provincial level.

One way of helping the peoples concerned to break through the bonds of conservatism is to give them better information about what has been done in other countries — preferably not the most developed ones, but countries where similar difficulties have been conquered in the recent past (Italy, Mexico, Brazil, and India, for example). A liberal immigration policy is another way to bring in new ideas, as illustrated by the Brazilian experience.

IV.2 BRAZIL'S POSITION IN LATIN AMERICA

Brazil is unique among the countries in the area under consideration. Its size, its geographic location vis-à-vis Europe and Africa, its mentality, and its outlook are different from those of the other countries.

In the size of its population and in its natural resources, Brazil is the largest nation in Latin America. It lies nearest to the Old World, and has gone farthest in merging population elements of the Old World with those of the new. Consequently it has close cultural ties with both Europe and Africa, and economic ties with the United States. It is one of the most highly industrialized countries in the area; only Argentina and Mexico are on a par with it. Its population is sophisticated with a markedly more enterprising attitude toward economic affairs, and its government and business system works more efficiently than that of most of its neighbors. Furthermore, Brazil has demonstrated an ability to settle disputes without bloodshed, and to find in difficult situations solutions which are economically and politically optimum.

Brazil may be considered the leading nation of the Latin American world. Soon it will be able to play a part in assisting other less developed countries of the Western Hemisphere. Psychologically, it is better suited to this role than the European and North American nations, whose motives are sometimes questioned. Brazil is the natural link between Europe and the rest of Latin America and, according to some politicians, it may soon serve as an intermediary between Europe and

Africa, as it has no "colonial past." Brazil's actions are already watched closely and attentively all over Latin America, and their consequences are felt in many countries in this area. It is to be hoped that its present monetary difficulties will soon be overcome.

IV.3 THE STATE OF ECONOMIC PLANNING

National economic plans exist in many Latin American countries. Mexico and Colombia perhaps have the most elaborate plans. In some countries, however, the idea of planning has not yet taken root properly; only lip service is paid to it. Most plans are detailed plans drawn up by government services, aiming at either the development of certain regions or the development of certain economic activities. Balanced, internally consistent, national plans with priorities for detailed projects are being worked out, but often without adequate provision for their implementation. An example concerns plans for the redistribution of land, generally known as "agrarian reform." Although open opposition to such plans is not strong, leading government officials — often themselves the owners of huge tracts of land — do not always actually support them, and occasionally countermand them, even when they represent official policy.

There is a need for more and better houses and roads practically everywhere in the region. But there is opposition to allotting high priorities to housing and roadbuilding plans, since both will accentuate the pronounced movement of population from rural districts to the great cities. This movement has already led to a shortage of labor in agricultural districts and to unemployment in the cities. For the same reason, it is often urged that new industrial plants be erected in rural districts.

The main theme of all types of economic plans, whether scientific or purely political, is the need for more rapid industrialization. The consequent increase in national debt does not seem to worry many industrialists, who count on a continued inflationary movement to reduce the debt burden. The opinion is often expressed that rapid industrialization will be impossible without some measure of inflation.

Planning bureaus are poorly organized and their authority is in many cases weak. Thus they usually have a short life. One Latin American country already has its fourth planning bureau. The value of a well-organized planning bureau is seldom fully recognized.

In several countries, it is openly admitted that planning bureaus are simply a means to obtain foreign credits. On the other hand, one must appreciate the difficulty of economic planning in countries where an interest rate of 25 to 30 per cent is considered normal because of persistent inflationary trends, and where reliable economic statistics are largely lacking.

IV.4 REGIONAL CO-OPERATION

Latin America has surpassed all other areas except Europe in regional co-operation. Owing, among other things, to the great number of studies on the subject undertaken by the Economic Commission for Latin America, the idea of co-operation has taken firm root in the minds of economists and political leaders. There is some skepticism, however, about the practical outcome of the plans which have recently been formulated and about the length of time needed for their execution. The skeptics generally point out that Latin America has small buyer's markets and that internal land communications are inadequate; they also mention the old spirit of distrust among neighbors. We have the impression, nevertheless, that the positive aspects of economic co-operation are being recognized more and more, and that the optimistic view of the future economic possibilities of the region predominates. This is most true in the countries that have the greatest interest in the free-trade area recently set up. These are the more industrially developed countries: Mexico, Brazil, and Argentina.

Psychologically, Latin America is at present more ready and fit for economic co-operation than Africa or Asia. Because it has known political independence for a longer time than most African and Asian countries, sovereign rights are not so strongly insisted upon; this may materially facilitate the economic integration movement.

Another factor which makes for a more favorable climate for regional co-operation is the fact that only two languages are spoken in Latin America: Spanish and Portuguese.

Regional co-operation will provide a partial solution to the balance of payments difficulties of many Latin American countries. By establishing new industries, which will operate on a continental scale, import needs can certainly be decreased. The advantages of a further division of labor among countries and of a co-ordination of complementary activities are now clear to leading Latin Americans. This refers espe-

cially to machinery and other manufactured goods. It will be more difficult to bring about international agreements on specialization with regard to those lines of production where vested interests already exist. It seems advisable, therefore, to start the co-ordination movement in new lines of production. When the geographic location of new industries is determined, not only economic but also social factors, such as unemployment and low standards of living, should be taken into account.

The earliest steps toward integration took place during the fifties among the five Central American republics: Guatemala, San Salvador, Honduras, Nicaragua, and Costa Rica. This integration movement apparently has not been a complete success, although a number of agreements concerning a common trade policy have been arrived at. Its main importance, according to several specialists, lies in the fact that it brought the idea of economic integration to the attention of Latin Americans. In any event, the relatively small size of the five republics did not allow for an important integration movement. We will therefore concentrate our attention on the more recent and more significant form of co-operation prescribed in the so-called Montevideo Treaty.

On February 18, 1960 seven Latin American countries — Argentina, Brazil, Chile, Mexico, Paraguay, Peru, and Uruguay — signed a multilateral treaty, the Treaty of Montevideo, in order to establish a Free Trade Zone and to initiate the Latin American Free Trade Association (LAFTA). This treaty expresses[1] the belief that the widening of the markets resulting from the liberalization of trade between the member countries would stimulate a better utilization of the available factors of production and permit the initiation of new enterprises; increased returns on investments and the growth of employment opportunities are also expected to follow. However, taking into account the existing differences between the economies of the participating countries in structure and rate of development, the liberalization program of the Zone had to be elaborated on a flexible basis. During the preparation of the program it was emphasized that:

(i) the liberalization process should be gradual;
(ii) the concessions should be reciprocal;
(iii) relations between the countries should be based on the uncon-

1. Some of the remarks following have been taken from *La Asociación Latino-americana de Libre Comercio, Tratado de Montevideo,* Buenos Aires, 1961.

ditional and unlimited extension of the advantages accorded the most favored nation.

Other clauses have been added; some relate to the expansion and diversification of interchanges, while others grant preferences to countries with a relatively low degree of economic development.

Once the Zone is well established, an effort will be made to satisfy other basic objectives of the Treaty, namely to increase the area's trade with other Latin American countries and with the rest of the world, for example, by the elimination of tariff barriers. The Treaty aims to integrate the economies of the participating nations. It is possible that the remaining Latin American countries will someday be incorporated.[2]

The Treaty provides for the elimination of the obstacles to mutual trade by means of annual negotiations over the course of twelve years. As far as annual negotiations on the reduction of import duties are concerned, the rule is that, in order to obtain advantages for its exports in the other countries of the Zone, each country must grant equivalent tax exemptions to importers.

The most-favored-nation clause will simplify the annual negotiations within the Zone, because these can be carried on between pairs of countries — namely those most directly interested in the trade of each product — and the results will automatically apply to the other members of the Association.

The negotiators aim at setting up two lists of goods: a National List, which for every country contains the products on which it has granted import concessions to some members, and a Common List, naming the products which, according to an agreement among all contracting parties, will be totally free of trade restraints at the end of a period of twelve years.

IV.5 LATIN AMERICA'S INTERCONTINENTAL TRADE RELATIONS

Roughly 10 per cent of Latin America's trade is internal; the rest consists mainly of trade with the United States and Western Europe. However, Latin America's trade with Europe has decreased significantly since the Second World War.

2. Other Latin American nations have already joined the Association.

The main export products are coffee, bananas, cocoa, wool, meat, oil, sugar, and copper. As is well known, several countries in the region depend on the export of a very small number of primary products, in some instances only foodstuffs. Because supplies and prices of these export products fluctuate widely, while the prices of imported goods, e.g., manufactures and machinery, remain relatively stable, many Latin American countries periodically or even permanently find themselves in balance of payments difficulties. Trade barriers, especially in Western Europe, are also a cause for concern.

The situation in regard to many export products — not all — is as follows: the United States market is considered to be saturated (e.g., the coffee market); the Western European market, on the other hand, could — in the opinion of Latin American experts — be expanded considerably, were it not for high import duties, quantitative restrictions on imports, and internal taxes. The opening of the European market, that is, the removal of the trade barriers mentioned, is considered of paramount importance, especially because a decrease in export opportunities in Europe is envisaged in the immediate future. EEC's preferential treatment of associated territories (mainly the former French colonies in Africa), where dangerous competition with respect to coffee, cocoa, etc., could develop, and the possible entry of the United Kingdom into EEC, give rise to great concern. Argentine and Uruguayan meat exporters are especially fearful of competition if the continental European preferential system should be extended to Commonwealth countries, such as Australia and New Zealand.

Latin Americans generally feel that Western Europe discriminates against their exports. Also, the United States is accused of discriminating against Latin American exports of cotton, sugar, wool, meat, nonferrous metals, etc., in favor of home producers.

These attitudes contain an element of truth, although it should be pointed out that some Latin American countries that complain of discrimination levy export duties on the goods concerned. Even if more facilities for meat imports into Europe were granted, the complaining meat exporters would not in the short run be able to make more meat available, for a considerable part of the Latin American supply is consumed at home. Another example of Latin America's inconsistent trade policy is the fact that there are prohibitions on the export of certain products for which export markets were built up earlier, the reason be-

ing the fear that increased exports would lead to higher prices on the home market, with ensuing social unrest. Such fears are usually not justified by the importance of these products for the home market.

The predominating attitude toward European economic integration is one of fear and distrust; the unfairness of leaving Latin America "out in the cold" is repeatedly pointed out. This view is partly based on the fact that no European producer's interests, but only Treasury interests, are directly involved in high tariffs and taxes on tropical foodstuffs such as coffee, cocoa, and bananas. Latin Americans also resent the fact that some European countries lower import duties (by agreement, in the framework of GATT) while at the same time they increase internal taxes on the same product. The formation of the Latin American Free Trade Association must be regarded chiefly as a defensive measure against a future strong and protective European economic bloc. Europeans are often reproached for not realizing that Latin America can import more from Europe only if it is allowed to export more. It is of course true that Latin America's intricate system of import permits and its high import duties do not contribute to better trade relations, but if Europe, as the stronger trade partner, does not take the initiative in breaking this vicious circle, it will, in the opinion of many experts, never be broken. In general, little attention is paid by Latin Americans to the positive aspects of European integration, such as the increased demand for their products which may follow the raising of the European standard of living. There seems to be no definite and unanimous opinion as to the probable future effects of European and Latin American economic integration on the prices of imports and exports.

Bilateral trade agreements with European partners are preferred to multilateral ones at the moment, because they offer greater assurances of export advantages, assuming that import concessions are given in return.

Practically all the Latin American experts consulted insisted on the speedy lowering or removal of European trade barriers. They pointed out that if this were not done either their economies would stagnate or they would have to increase their trade with Communist countries. The latter are ready to export the needed capital goods and to import almost any surplus. A move to new lines of production, involving as it does the retraining of workers and the writing off of existing investments along with the making of new ones, is generally considered to be impossible in the short run, taking into account the conservative atmos-

phere mentioned earlier. In Brazil this possibility is regarded with more optimism, doubtless because Brazil has already achieved remarkable progress in its industrialization. However, retraining should be considered as a solution in other Latin American countries also; practically all countries have light consumer goods industries, which could easily be expanded.

In connection with the important place of certain primary products and tropical foodstuffs in Latin America's exports and their influence on the balance of payments position of many countries in the region, international agreements aimed at stabilizing the prices of these products are considered necessary and urgent. Such agreements should be effected between the main producing and consuming nations and should include, if possible, some regulation of production.

IV.6 FINANCIAL AND TECHNICAL ASSISTANCE

More financial assistance is unanimously regarded as essential to the steady and continued economic growth of the region. Capital is, in general, even scarcer than labor. Experience in the more industrialized countries of the region has shown that the training of workmen in the technical skills necessary to the development of new lines of production can easily be kept in step with any new investments which may be made. The labor shortage is not serious except in highly specialized technical jobs and in fields such as business economics, industrial efficiency and organization, and finance. The need of assistance in these specialized fields, especially the technical one, is recognized, and experts from more developed parts of the world are welcome.

Training programs in the Latin American countries should, of course, be continued and expanded in many fields. There is no reason to fear a lack of interest on the part of the Latin American trainees. On the contrary, it is well understood that the social unrest which exists in many areas can best be counteracted by providing work for everyone.

There are a number of factors in the Latin American region which might easily deter new foreign investments or foreign expert assistance. Foreign investors fear the possibility of nationalization and the losses connected with it. This fear is not always justified and it does not apply generally. But the recent Cuban and the earlier Mexican experience in this respect, the lack of information concerning future government policies, and the instability of certain Latin American regimes, together

with the availability of excellent investment opportunities in the more developed parts of the world, tend to direct investments away from Latin America. It should be noted that the probabilities of nationalization are greatly reduced if investments are made in "joint ventures," i.e., ventures in which local capital is also involved. Nationalization of such enterprises would injure a country's own investors.

Joint ventures are desirable psychologically, for they are looked upon as "national" enterprises. It is considered good policy to grant the inhabitants of the assisted countries the right to buy the shares in foreign hands at some future date. It is also deemed desirable to require foreign investors to reinvest their profits in the same or other enterprises of the assisted nation. In some countries this obligation exists.

Joint ventures are the best solution for enterprises which are of primary importance to the government (road, rail, and air communications, electricity, water, and telephone installations, certain types of heavy industry like armaments, etc.) but which are too expensive to be financed by purely local capital. It is often remarked that the less developed countries are not in a position to furnish part of the capital in joint ventures. It is just as often observed, however, that many Latin Americans who possess the necessary means prefer to invest in the United States or Europe instead of in their own country, because of fear of nationalization, lack of confidence in domestic economic policy, and political uncertainties.

The inefficiency of many public administrations, the corruption in some services, the network of regulations and red tape, the prohibitive import restrictions, the time and money involved in getting imports cleared by customs authorities, the low productivity of the protected industries, the persistent inflation, and until recently the multiple exchange rates, are factors which have discouraged foreign capitalists from investing in Latin America.

Partly because of the above considerations, more is expected in Latin America from private initiative in financial (investment) operations than from government initiative.

As regards foreign technical assistance, the instability of the local currencies and the comparatively low level of salaries have certainly made many experts refrain from offering their services. Payment in dollars or sterling also has its drawbacks. If the monetary unit of the country receiving assistance is decreasing in value — as is usually the case — paying outside experts in a key foreign currency will be in-

creasingly costly and will make for an increasing discrepancy in the receipts of nationals and foreigners who hold comparable positions. This is not the best kind of co-operation imaginable.

Many Latin Americans pointed out the desirability of having private European study groups travel in the area and report on the most desirable method of conducting practical trade policy. The work of such teams should be financed by foreign businesses. The same idea was put forward with regard to information concerning the practical execution of economic and social policy in Europe. In this way, the repercussions of each trade partner's decisions on the other partner's economy could be studied more fully and the European and Latin American nations would better understand each other's motives and needs. In Latin America almost the only knowledge concerning social policies and their practical application comes from Communist countries. Why, many Latin Americans ask, is it impossible for them to study economics, sociology, and political science at the university level in Europe? The number of Latin Americans studying at universities behind the iron curtain runs into the thousands or tens of thousands. Many Latin Americans now visit universities in the United States, but their number is still too small and there is a danger that their competence will decrease after their return to their own country because of a lack of informed compatriots.

The five desiderata regarding technical assistance mentioned in Appendix III on Southeast Asia (p. 236) apply equally well to Latin America.

It should perhaps be emphasized at this point that, although foreign capital and technical aid is welcome in Latin America, the preference is for more trade. Most Latin American countries feel that if greater trading opportunities were open to them, they could take care of most of their capital needs themselves. President Kennedy's Alliance for Progress program, submitted at a meeting at Punta del Este, Uruguay, in August 1961, should be judged in the light of this last remark. Hopeful as many Latin American countries may be concerning the assistance they will be given, they fully realize the importance of self-help and have expressed the wish that the avenues open to them could be broadened, especially by means of a more liberal trade policy on the part of the rest of the world.

Capital Invested by Mother Countries in Colonies, and Rates of Return on Capital

V.1 BRITISH INVESTMENT IN INDIA, 1900–1914

According to S. Y. Pandit the net capital flow from the London capital market to India amounted to 1,500 million rupees during the period 1900 to 1914. M. Mukherjee has estimated Indian per capita income at 203 rupees on the average for the period 1901–1909, and at 220 rupees for the years 1906–1914, both expressed in prices of 1948–49. We may therefore take 210 rupees (in 1948–49 prices) as the average per capita income for the period 1900–1914. Mukherjee also gives a price index on the basis of 1948–49, which stands at 22.5 for the period under consideration. Thus, annual per capita income for 1900 to 1914 can be put at 47 rupees in current prices. Using G. F. Shirras' population estimates (1901, 223.5 million; 1911, 242.7 million; 1921, 247.0 million), it is assumed that the Indian population during 1900–1914 numbered on the average 235 million. Average annual national income may then be computed at 11,000 million rupees. Comparing this figure with the annual net capital inflow from Britain (100 million rupees), we find that during the years 1900 to 1914 net capital inflow from Great Britain amounted to 0.9 per cent of Indian national income.

The above figure of S. Y. Pandit excludes reinvestments, about which no direct information is available. We will try to estimate the order of magnitude of this variable by two different methods. In both cases it is assumed that virtually all income from investments was reinvested in India.

According to C. K. Hobson, British income from foreign investments was £101 million in the fiscal year 1910–11. H. Feis estimated that of total British overseas investment at the end of 1913, 10 per cent was located in India (including Ceylon). If this ratio is applied to £101

million — even though the years of reference are different — we get £10 million as a rough estimate of British annual income from investment in India at that time.

As an alternative way of estimating income from investment, we may take the rate of return on capital as our starting point. According to estimates made by Sir George Paish (quoted by Sir Robert Kindersley in an article in the *Economic Journal*), in the year 1907–08 the return on securities issued by dominion and colonial governments was 3.6 per cent, and that on investments in Indian railways was 3.9 per cent. In the same year, British investments in dominion and colonial government securities amounted to £531.5 million. Of all investments in securities publicly issued in the British Empire, India (including Ceylon) accounted for 21.1 per cent. British income from investment in securities issued by the Indian government may therefore be estimated at $(0.211 \times £531.5 \times 0.036 =)$ £4 million. As to investments in Indian railways, Feis gave a figure of £140.8 million, referring to the end of 1913. Applying the rate of return of 3.9 per cent to this amount, we arrive at an annual income of £5.5 million. Total income from public securities and railways amounts thus to £9.5 million. As only minor amounts of capital were otherwise invested, this approach leads to about the same figure for annual income from investments in India as the first approach, i.e., about £10 million.

On the assumption that all income earned on investments was reinvested in India, we may conclude that annual reinvestments were of an order of magnitude of £10 million or 100 million rupees in the period 1900–1914. This amount is the same as that of new investments, and may again be put at about 1 per cent of Indian national income. It is obvious from the above calculation that this figure of 1 per cent is far from accurate. It indicates, nevertheless, the order of magnitude of the capital flow between Great Britain and India during the first decade or so of the present century.

SOURCES

H. Feis, *Europe, the World's Banker 1870–1914*, New Haven, 1930, pp. 23, 27.

C. K. Hobson, *The Export of Capital*, London, 1914, pp. 199–201.

Sir Robert Kindersley, "A New Study of British Foreign Investments," *Economic Journal*, March 1929, p. 20.

M. Mukherjee, "A Preliminary Study of the Growth of National Income in India 1857–1957," a paper presented to the Asian Conference of the

International Association for Research in Income and Wealth, August 21–28, 1960.

S. Y. Pandit, *India's Balance of Indebtedness,* London, 1937.

Royal Institute of International Affairs, *The Problem of International Investment,* Oxford, 1937, pp. 120–122, 149, 160.

G. F. Shirras, *Science of Public Finance,* London, 1924, pp. 138–145.

V.2 DUTCH CAPITAL INVESTED IN INDONESIA, 1938

The total stock of Dutch capital invested in Indonesia in 1938 has been estimated by J. B. D. Derksen at about 4 billion guilders. A crude estimate of total Dutch wealth in 1938 was made by the same author; he puts this figure at 20 to 25 billion guilders. Hence his statement that about one-sixth of the Dutch national wealth was invested in Indonesia immediately before the outbreak of World War II. At the same time one-sixth of the Dutch national income was earned from ties with Indonesia. The importance of Dutch capital in relation to Indonesia's total material wealth is even more difficult to estimate. Indonesian national income was calculated by J. J. Polak for the period 1921–1939; his 1938 estimate amounts to 2.8 billion guilders. National income figures for Indonesia show large fluctuations because of changes in the prices of the raw materials exported. Since 1938 prices were substantially below the average or normal level, valuing national income in current prices has a depressing effect on this variable. These considerations do not apply to the above-mentioned valuation of capital stock, which is based on the price of the level of the past. In order to make a comparison between national income and capital stock, we have to correct the national income figure for price differences.

As we said, Indonesian national income in 1938 valued in current prices totaled 2.8 billion guilders; valued in 1929 prices it totaled 5.6 billion guilders, or exactly twice as much. Obviously, 1929 prices were abnormally high and should not be considered as indicative of the "average price level of the past" on which the capital stock estimate is based. We will assume for our purposes that Indonesian national income in 1938, when valued at "average" or "normal" prices, was 4.0 to 4.5 billion guilders.

To obtain a very rough estimate of the total material wealth of Indonesia in 1938 we may convert the national income figure into a capital stock figure by multiplying it by an over-all capital-output ratio. Roughly again, this ratio may be put at 3 to 3.5 in view of the fact

that agriculture and basic facilities (infrastructure) were the most important sectors in the Indonesian economy in 1938. Multiplying the above national income estimates by 3 to 3.5, we arrive at a figure for total capital stock in 1938 of 12 to 16 billion guilders.

As the total value of Dutch investment in Indonesia was estimated at 4 billion guilders, we may conclude tentatively that in 1938 Dutch capital invested in Indonesia constituted one-third to one-fourth of Indonesia's total capital stock.

SOURCES

J. B. D. Derksen, "De economische betekenis van Nederlandsch-Indië voor Nederland met cijfers en statistieken toegelicht," *Hecht verbonden in lief en leed,* ed. by W. H. van Helsdingen and H. Hoogenberk, Elsevier, Amsterdam, 1946, pp. 360 ff.

J. J. Polak, *The National Income of the Netherlands Indies 1921–1939,* New York, 1943 (mimeographed).

J. J. Polak, "Het nationale inkomen van Nederlandsch-Indië, 1921–1939," *Statistische en Econometrische Onderzoekingen van het Centraal Bureau voor de Statistiek,* W. de Haan, Utrecht, September 1947, pp. 104 ff.

V.3 RATE OF RETURN ON INVESTMENT—
UNITED KINGDOM AND COLONIES COMPARED

In Chapter 2 the rate of return on "colonial" capital is compared with the rate of return on capital invested in the United Kingdom. The tabulation given in Chapter 2 is reproduced below.

Interest on Bonds

	United Kingdom	Colonies
1870–80		
Government	3.8	4.4
Railways	5.3	6.3
1900–09	3.4	3.6
1921–30	4.5	5.3

The figures are not comparable through time, as the type of investment is not exactly the same for all periods. A short description of the type of securities involved follows.

1870–1880. The figures for the colonies are calculated as the ratio between the total annual yield and the market value of investments in government bonds and in securities of Indian railways. The corres-

ponding figures for the United Kingdom represent the average yield on
Consols and on a representative holding of British railways debentures.

SOURCE: A. K. Cairncross, "Did Foreign Investment Pay?," *Review of Economic Studies,* October 1935.

1900–1909. The figures show the average return (including yield on
redemption) offered by certain groups of borrowers in the United Kingdom and in the colonies.

SOURCE: C. K. Hobson, *The Export of Capital,* London, 1914, p. 204.

1921–1930. These figures represent the average yield on UK Consols and the average price of new dominion and colonial public borrowing.

SOURCE: Royal Institute of International Affairs, *The Problem of International Investment,* Oxford, 1937, p. 135.

V.4   RATE OF RETURN ON INVESTMENT — THE
      NETHERLANDS AND THE NETHERLANDS EAST
      INDIES COMPARED

A comparison similar to that made between British colonial and
home investment returns can be made between the rate of return on
capital in the Netherlands East Indies and that in the Netherlands. In
Chapter 2 the following table is given:

Rate of Return on Shares

	Netherlands	*Netherlands East Indies*
1900–12	5.7	6.5
1922–29	4.0	7.5
1930–37	3.0	3.2

Again, the figures have to be used carefully. All rates of return have
been calculated as follows. The dividends per share paid out in a given
year by an enterprise were divided by the average value of the share
during that particular year and expressed in percentage form; the
average value of the share was computed as the arithmetic average of
the highest and the lowest value of the share during the year. These
rates of return were determined for a representative number of enterprises in the Netherlands and in the (former) Netherlands East Indies
and then an (unweighted) arithmetic average was computed for each

group. Finally, arithmetic averages of the yearly figures were calculated for the three separate periods indicated in the table.

Although the procedure just outlined is not the most precise and painstaking one imaginable, the figures have no systematic bias with respect to either of the two countries compared. They may safely be used to determine the order of magnitude of the difference in rates of return on capital in the metropolitan country and the colony.

SOURCE: J. Tinbergen and J. J. J. Dalmulder, "De factoren welke het koers-verloop van aandelen bepalen," *De Nederlandsche Conjunctuur*, August 1939, pp. 111 ff.

APPENDIX VI

An Analysis of World Trade Flows

VI.1 AIM AND NATURE OF THE ANALYSIS

The purpose of the present analysis is to determine the normal or standard pattern of international trade that would prevail in the absence of discriminating trade impediments. We assume that this pattern coincides with the "average" pattern actually prevailing; this means that we assume the impediments to be of a stochastic nature. We will statistically determine the basic factors governing the volume of trade between any pair of countries; with this information at hand we shall be able to determine what foreign trade volume may be expected for a great number of individual countries. A comparison of the actual trade volume with the volume expected on theoretical grounds may show discrepancies indicating that a country's exports are either receiving preferential treatment in importing countries (in case of a positive deviation) or being discriminated against (in case of a negative deviation). The significance of the deviation between actual and calculated trade depends on the accuracy and reliability of the theoretical values of the trade volume as estimated with the help of econometric methods. The better the standardized pattern of international trade describes reality, the more significant are the individual exceptions or deviations from the normalized empirical trade pattern. It is precisely these deviations that we are interested in. The purpose of this econometric exercise is to find out which countries show substantial negative deviations, for these would be indicative of the existence of special barriers and obstacles to the optimum flow of international trade.

An economic model describing international trade flows can be formulated in varying degrees of detail. The present model is a very simple one, having only that aspect which is relevant to the aim of this study, i.e., the deviations from the normalized trade pattern. It consists

262

of only one equation in which the value of total exports from one country to another is explained by a small number of variables. The explanatory variables that play a preponderant role are:

(i) the Gross National Product (GNP) of the exporting country;

(ii) the GNP of the importing country; and

(iii) the distance between the two countries.

In several calculations other explanatory variables were introduced; however, their contribution to an explanation of the value of exports was very limited as compared to that of the three main variables. Other important characteristics of the present analysis are that:

(i) no separate demand and supply functions for exports are introduced — meaning that the equation is a turnover relation in which prices are not specified; and

(ii) only a static analysis is made — no attention is paid to the development of exports over time.

It is obvious that the model could be elaborated considerably so as to give more attention to other aspects of world trade.[1] However, for the purpose of this book a simplified model will suffice.

VI.2 THE FLOW OF TRADE BETWEEN TWO COUNTRIES

The main factors that determine the size of the trade flow between any pair of countries have been mentioned above. Their relevance is as follows:

(i) the amount of exports a country is able to supply depends on its economic size (i.e., its GNP);

(ii) the amount that can be sold to a particular country will vary with the size of that country's market (i.e., the GNP of the importing country); and

(iii) the volume of trade will depend on transportation costs (these are assumed to correspond roughly with the geographic distance between the two countries).

The factor of distance may also stand for an index of information about export markets. It will be clear that distance — in contrast to the other two factors — has a negative influence on trade flows.

1. The analysis described in this appendix forms part of a larger study of world trade flows which is presently being undertaken at the Netherlands Economic Institute. A report on this study is to be published later.

The trade flow equation can be written, in its simplest form, as follows:

$$E_{ij} = a_0 \, Y_i^{a_1} \, Y_j^{a_2} \, D_{ij}^{a_3} \tag{1}$$

The meaning of the symbols used is:

E_{ij} = exports of country i to country j

Y_i = GNP of country i

Y_j = GNP of country j

D_{ij} = distance between country i and country j

The exponents a_1, a_2, and a_3 indicate that there is not necessarily direct proportionality between the explanatory variables (Y_i, Y_j, and D_{ij}) and the variable to be explained (E_{ij}). Such proportionality would exist only if the a's are all equal to 1. The factor a_0 is a constant; the numerical value of the constant depends on the units in which the variables are measured.

The equation implies that exports have a constant elasticity with respect to each of the three explanatory variables; this means that a 1 per cent increase in the GNP of country j always results in an increase of a_2 per cent in the exports of the supplying country i.

Equation 1 was used to calculate the "normal" or "standardized" flow of trade between countries. Before normal trade flows could be calculated, the numerical values of the four a's had to be estimated. This was done on the basis of actual trade flows, the underlying assumption being that the actual trade of most countries does not substantially diverge from the normal or standard pattern and volume of trade. Of course, a number of important divergencies can be expected in reality, but it is the aim of this study to trace these divergencies. It is assumed that the individual deviations from the normal pattern are relatively few in number, so that the actual trade flows follow the usual or standard pattern closely. As national trade statistics do not disclose the export and import of services on a country-by-country basis, the analysis had to be confined to commodity trade flows. In section VI.5 the total inflow or outflow of services will be introduced in the interpretation of the results.

The hypothesis that the three explanatory variables are the most relevant ones was tested first for a limited number of countries of similar economic structure. From data on the 1958 exports of 18 countries — mainly the more developed ones (see Table VI–2) — the unknown

values of the a's were estimated by least squares regression analysis. Equation (1) was rewritten for this purpose as:

$$\log E_{ij} = a_1 \log Y_i + a_2 \log Y_j + a_3 \log D_{ij} + a'_o \qquad (1')$$

in which

$$a'_o = \log a_o \quad \text{or} \quad a_o = 10^{a'_o}$$

Exports were expressed in $100 million, GNP in $10 billion, and distance (measured between the commercial centers of the countries involved) in 1,000 nautical miles.[2] The values of the a coefficients were fitted to 306 (18 x 17) sets of observations by the method of least squares. The results of the calculation (calculation A–1) are given in Table VI–1; the correlation coefficient was 0.82 — a figure high enough to encourage further research along these lines. The deviations of actual trade from the calculated trade volume (the "residuals," in technical terminology) are given in Table VI–2.

The figures for the export values used in calculation A–1 were taken from the export statistics of the country of origin. An alternative (and sometimes more reliable) source of information about international trade flows is the import statistics of the country of destination. In calculation A–2 export figures derived from import statistics were taken as the variable to be explained; the other variables had the same values as in the first calculation. The results of calculation A–2 turned out to be not much different from those of A–1, although the correlation coefficient was slightly lower (see Table VI–1). In all subsequent calculations trade figures were taken from export statistics.

A final exercise undertaken with the data from 18 countries was the introduction of additional explanatory variables. Apart from purely economic variables it is likely that political or semi-economic factors play a part in determining the volume of trade between countries. We considered the existence of special trade agreements as the most outstanding of these additional factors. The importance of such special ties was estimated by the introduction of a so-called dummy variable for the British Commonwealth preference. Where the trade flow analyzed concerned two members of the Commonwealth, a certain positive value was given to the dummy variable to indicate that the goods traded received preferential treatment in the importing country; where the two countries were not members of the Commonwealth, the variable had a

2. 1 nautical mile = 1,852.27 meters or 1.15 land miles.

zero value — no preferential treatment. The Benelux preference was represented by another dummy variable; this variable was given a zero value in all cases except for trade flows between Belgium (actually the Belgium-Luxembourg Economic Union) and the Netherlands.

A third variable was introduced for adjacent or neighboring countries. The results of calculations A–1 and A–2 seemed to indicate that adjacent countries have more intense trade contacts than can be explained by (short) distance alone. Again, the variable was given a positive value in the case of neighboring countries and a zero value in all other cases.[3]

With the three additional variables introduced, the trade flow equation reads:

$$E_{ij} = a_0 \, Y_i{}^{a_1} Y_j{}^{a_2} D_{ij}{}^{a_3} N^{a_4} P_C{}^{a_5} P_B{}^{a_6} \qquad (2)$$

or

$$\log E_{ij} = a_1 \log Y_i + a_2 \log Y_j + a_3 \log D_{ij} + a_4 \log N + $$
$$a_5 \log P_C + a_6 \log P_B + a_0' \qquad (2')$$

in which:

N = dummy variable for neighboring countries

P_C = dummy variable for Commonwealth preference

P_B = dummy variable for Benelux preference

The calculation of the multiple correlation between the export values and the six explanatory variables led to the results shown in Table VI–1 (calculation A–3). Surprisingly enough, the introduction of three additional variables increased the correlation coefficient to 0.84 only. Although the algebraic signs of the regression coefficients of the three variables were all positive, as they should be, two of the three coefficients did not differ significantly from zero at the 99.7 per cent probability level. Only the dummy variable representing the Commonwealth preference made a statistically significant contribution to the explanation of the export flow. This illustrates again the dominant role played by the first three variables, exporters' and importers' GNP and distance. The coefficients of these variables were almost the same in calculations A–1 and A–3. Table VI–3 gives the deviations between actual and theoretically expected trade volume.

3. It is, in principle, irrelevant what value (other than zero) is given to a dummy variable to express the fact that a special tie or situation exists, as the choice of this value influences only the size of the coefficient (a), but not the correlation coefficient or the residuals. In all cases where the dummy variables mentioned in the text had to differ from zero, the value 1 (in logs) or 10 (in antilogs) was assigned to them.

VI.3 ANALYSIS OF INTERNATIONAL TRADE FLOWS FOR 42 COUNTRIES

The results obtained from the study of data from 18 countries encouraged further research. The number of countries included in the analysis was enlarged to 42. The mutual export trade of these 42 countries amounted to about 70 per cent of total world trade in 1959, the year to which the following calculations refer.

After the discussion in the preceding section, a brief description will be sufficient to explain the procedure followed in the 42-country analysis. First of all, the coefficients of equation (1′) were estimated from 1,722 (42 x 41) sets of observations (calculation B–1; see Table VI–4). In calculation B–2 a fourth explanatory variable was introduced, namely a dummy variable for neighboring countries (with the value, in logarithms, of either 1 or 0). In this case the trade flow equation is:

$$E_{ij} = a_0 \, Y_i{}^{a_1} \, Y_j{}^{a_2} \, D_{ij}{}^{a_3} \, N^{a_4} \tag{3}$$

and the corresponding equation in logarithms is:

$$\log E_{ij} = a_1 \log Y_i + a_2 \log Y_j + a_3 \log D_{ij} + a_4 \log N + a'_0 \tag{3′}$$

The correlation coefficient was only slightly higher than in calculation A–1.

Thus far all computations were made on the basis of GNP figures converted into US dollars but calculated in national prices. As the dollar exchange rates of most countries do not adequately reflect the differences in domestic buying power between the dollar and the national currency, these GNP figures may not be the best yardstick of a country's export potential, or its import market. On the other hand, they may well be a prime indicator of a country's buying power on international markets. Although it is hard to arrive at firm conclusions as to the merits and demerits of GNP figures based on domestic prices, it seemed worth while to experiment with GNP figures corrected for differences in price level. Thus calculation B–3 was performed; this was completely similar to B–2 except that GNP figures based on US prices were used instead of nominal GNP data. Judged by the correlation coefficient that was found, B–3 was not an improvement over previous computations (see Table VI–4).

In a fourth calculation using the 42-country data another explanatory variable was added to the ones already mentioned. This fifth variable was a dummy variable, standing for all preferential trade relations. It was given a value of 2 in logarithms (or 100 in antilogarithms) for the

trade flows between the United Kingdom and a Commonwealth partner, and for trade flows between a metropolitan country and its (former)
colony or colonies. It was given a value of zero for all trade flows without preferential treatment. In a number of cases the value 1 was given
to the dummy variable, expressing the existence of a semi-preferential
trade relation. This applied – in 1959 – to the trade of the United
States with Cuba, the Philippines, or Venezuela; it also applied to trade
among the EEC countries. The results of calculation B–4 are given in
Table VI–4.

The same table also includes the estimates obtained in a fifth calculation, (B–5). Here GNP was measured in US prices rather than domestic
prices. Also, the value given to the dummy variable representing preferential treatment of imports was different in the case of the so-called
semi-preferential trade relations (the EEC countries; the US and Cuba,
the Philippines, or Venezuela); in calculation B–5 the value 1.53 in
logs (which corresponds to 34 in antilogs) was used. The two extreme
values of the dummy variable, 2 and 0 (both in logs), were not changed.

Altogether five calculations (B–1 to B–5, inclusive) were made using
the data from 42 countries; the coefficients resulting from the calculations are given in Table VI–4. For each calculation the dollar difference
between the actual trade flow and the standardized trade flow – as
estimated with the help of the regression equation – was computed
separately for each country included in the analysis. These deviations –
which may, of course, be either positive or negative – were then expressed as a percentage of the actual (1959) foreign trade figures. The
absolute and the relative deviations of the export values and of the import values are shown in Tables VI–5 to VI–9. Table VI–10 compares
the deviations resulting from calculation B–1 with figures on the service trade of the countries concerned. The conclusions to be drawn from
Tables VI–5 to VI–10 will be discussed in section VI.5.

As a final exercise we introduced still another explanatory variable.
It was thought that the trade flows of a country that specialized in exporting a small number of products might well differ in size from those
of a country with a more diversified export structure. The degree of
commodity concentration in exports can be measured in various ways;
here the so-called Gini coefficient of concentration was used.[4] If a country exports only one commodity, the value of the Gini index is 100; the

4. See M. Michaely, "Concentration of Exports and Imports: An International
Comparison," *Economic Journal*, December 1958, pp. 722 ff.

more diversified the export package is, the lower is the value of this index. Because of the requirement of comparability, the Gini coefficient could be computed only for those countries that base their export statistics on the three-digit SITC code. This procedure was possible for only 28 of the 42 countries.

From the trade data of these 28 countries — listed in Table VI–12 — the coefficients of the trade flow equation were estimated, first (calculation C–1) for the equation in its simplest form (equation 1′), and then (calculation C–2) for the equation enlarged by a fourth explanatory variable. In this case the trade flow equation is:

$$E_{ij} = a_0\, Y_i{}^{a_1} Y_j{}^{a_2} D_{ij}{}^{a_3} G_i{}^{a_8} \tag{4}$$

or

$$\log E_{ij} = a_1 \log Y_i + a_2 \log Y_j + a_3 \log D_{ij} + a_8 \log G_i + a'_0 \tag{4'}$$

In these equations, G = the Gini coefficient of export commodity concentration.

The results of the estimation procedure — again the least squares method — are given in Table VI–11. Table VI–12 reveals the absolute and relative deviations of actual from calculated trade figures.

VI.4 A DISCUSSION OF THE RESULTS: THE COEFFICIENTS

In the present section we will discuss the statistically derived trade flow coefficients which are reproduced in Tables VI–1 (calculations A), VI–4 (calculations B), and VI–11 (calculations C). The three sets of calculations differ mainly in the number and type of countries from which the basic data were taken, that is, in the sample from which the coefficients were estimated. The same three explanatory variables — actually the most important ones — were used in all cases; for this reason it is perhaps not surprising that the correlation coefficient varied little from calculation to calculation. The average value of the correlation coefficient was not very high — around 0.81 — but certainly not unsatisfactory if we keep in mind that the actual pattern of trade is almost certain to deviate substantially from the normal (or "ideal," or "theoretical") pattern. As was pointed out earlier, it is precisely these deviations which we hope to identify in this analysis. In the next section we will discuss the pattern of deviations which emerged from the study, but first the coefficients of the export equation will be examined in some detail.

Table VI-1

FACTORS DETERMINING THE SIZE OF INTERNATIONAL TRADE FLOWS

Results of Calculations A (18 countries)

$$\log E_{ij} = a_1 \log Y_1 + a_2 \log Y_j + c_3 \log D_{ij} + a_4 \log N + a_5 \log P_C + a_6 \log P_B + a'_0$$

Calculation No.	ESTIMATED VALUE OF THE COEFFICIENTS							Correlation Coefficient
	a_1	a_2	a_3	a_4	a_5	a_6	a'_0	
A-1	0.7338 (0.0438)	0.6238 (0.0438)	−0.5981 (0.0405)	—	—	—	−0.3783	0.8248
A-2	0.7907 (0.0497)	0.6766 (0.0496)	−0.6252 (0.0460)	—	—	—	−0.4013	0.8084
A-3	0.7357 (0.0421)	0.6183 (0.0422)	−0.5570 (0.0473)	0.0191 (0.0082)	0.0496 (0.0111)	0.0406 (0.0272)	−0.4451	0.8437

E_{ij}　Exports from country i to country j
Y_i　GNP of exporting country
Y_j　GNP of importing country
D_{ij}　Distance between countries i and j
N　Dummy variable for neighbor countries
P_C　Dummy variable for Commonwealth preference
P_B　Dummy variable for Benelux preference

In A-2 the trade amount is measured in the importing country.
Figures in brackets are standard deviations.

Table VI–2

RESULTS OF CALCULATION A-1
Total Actual Trade (1959) minus Total Calculated Trade

	EXPORT DEVIATION		IMPORT DEVIATION	
	$100 million	as per cent of actual value	$100 million	as per cent of actual value
2. Brazil	−3.9557	−41.7	−5.1039	−45.9
8. Venezuela	6.2016	42.7	0.6412	4.8
14. S. Africa	−4.2625	−73.0	−1.0445	−8.6
21. Japan	−17.5284	−143.6	−17.9657	−127.6
29. Canada	13.3283	28.6	7.4520	17.2
30. USA	−62.2634	−64.1	−35.6173	−42.8
31. Austria	−2.2080	−35.4	−3.2195	−41.0
32. BLEU	6.8092	30.2	4.4003	18.7
33. Denmark	2.0741	19.5	4.8586	48.3
34. France	−24.5112	−107.6	−23.3826	−94.5
35. Germ. (F. R.)	20.6698	34.0	−1.7209	−3.8
36. Italy	−12.5307	−79.3	−10.5317	−50.5
37. Netherlands	10.7927	44.0	9.8278	36.6
38. Norway	−1.3860	−23.7	0.9802	9.1
39. Sweden	1.5372	9.4	0.2750	1.6
40. Switzerland	−0.2352	−2.1	−0.2583	−1.8
41. UK	−4.5593	−9.7	−1.9270	−3.9
42. Australia	−4.9965	−43.6	−8.2613	−68.0

Table VI–3

RESULTS OF CALCULATION A-3
Total Actual Trade (1959) minus Total Calculated Trade

	EXPORT DEVIATION		IMPORT DEVIATION	
	$100 million	as per cent of actual value	$100 million	as per cent of actual value
2. Brazil	5.0224	53.0	5.6738	51.0
8. Venezuela	10.8338	74.5	7.8142	58.1
14. S. Africa	1.5811	27.1	6.6088	54.6
21. Japan	4.9034	40.2	6.1048	43.4
29. Canada	16.1715	34.7	7.0446	16.2
30. USA	18.4515	19.0	26.7411	32.1
31. Austria	−0.3717	−6.0	−0.6402	−8.2
32. BLEU	−2.1779	−9.6	−4.8247	−20.5
33. Denmark	3.8964	36.7	1.4313	14.2
34. France	−25.7047	−113.9	−21.5758	−87.2
35. Germ. (F. R.)	8.1052	13.3	−2.7045	−6.0
36. Italy	−3.2974	−21.0	0.5861	2.8
37. Netherlands	4.6582	19.0	3.6813	13.7
38. Norway	0.9463	16.2	4.3637	40.5
39. Sweden	7.2137	44.3	11.1680	63.8
40. Switzerland	−0.3338	−3.0	−0.0915	−0.6
41. UK	4.5122	9.6	9.4642	19.1
42. Australia	5.8824	51.3	5.3055	44.7

Table VI-4

FACTORS DETERMINING THE SIZE OF INTERNATIONAL TRADE FLOWS

Results of Calculations B (42 countries)

$$\log E_{ij} = a_1 \log Y_i + a_2 \log Y_j + a_3 \log D_{ij} + a_4 \log N + a_7 \log P + a'_0$$

Calculation No.	ESTIMATED VALUE OF THE COEFFICIENTS						Correlation Coefficient
	a_1	a_2	a_3	a_4	a_7	a'_0	
B-1	1.0240 (0.0270)	0.9395 (0.0269)	-0.8919 (0.0455)	—	—	-0.6627 (0.6802)	0.8094
B-2	1.0250 (0.0269)	0.9403 (0.0269)	-0.8225 (0.0517)	0.2581 (0.0920)	—	-0.7188 (0.6789)	0.8104
B-3	1.1832 (0.0323)	1.0752 (0.0323)	-0.9325 (0.0584)	0.2217 (0.1037)	—	-1.0296 (0.7645)	0.7987
B-4	0.9965 (0.0267)	0.9116 (0.0267)	-0.7803 (0.0511)	0.2484 (0.0903)	0.4703 (0.0588)	-0.7798 (0.6668)	0.8180
B-5	1.1567 (0.0319)	1.0486 (0.0319)	-0.9165 (0.0574)	0.2367 (0.1018)	0.8926 (0.1100)	-1.0641 (0.7505)	0.8070

E_{ij} Exports from country i to country j

Y_i GNP of exporting country ⎫

Y_j GNP of importing country ⎬ Nominal in B-1, B-2 and B-4; real in B-3 and B-5.

D_{ij} Distance between countries i and j

N   Dummy variable for neighboring countries

P   Dummy variable for preference

Because of difference in treatment of preferential relations, the coefficients are not comparable between B-4 and B-5.

Figures in brackets are standard deviations.

Table VI–5

RESULTS OF CALCULATION B-1
Total Actual Trade (1959) minus Total Calculated Trade

	EXPORT DEVIATION		IMPORT DEVIATION	
	$100 million	as per cent of actual value	$100 million	as per cent of actual value
1. Argentina	5.0964	55.7	4.7385	49.5
2. Brazil	3.3425	29.0	1.2239	11.5
3. Chile	3.9033	80.6	2.0000	60.7
4. Cuba	3.1881	53.8	2.6871	40.4
5. Mexico	2.2217	38.0	5.6074	55.3
6. Peru	2.0595	71.9	1.4236	55.2
7. Uruguay	−0.0654	−11.1	0.5141	36.3
8. Venezuela	12.6139	80.7	9.0302	68.5
9. Belg. Congo	3.9269	87.9	1.6360	68.0
10. Ethiopia	0.0448	8.5	−0.0591	−9.5
11. Ghana	2.7051	87.1	1.8204	75.4
12. Morocco	1.5026	55.3	1.4155	45.2
13. Nigeria	3.1806	78.0	2.2665	58.1
14. S. Africa	5.3207	68.6	9.0982	74.9
15. Sudan	1.2605	79.7	0.8445	64.3
16. Fr. W. Africa	1.0269	44.8	1.1348	39.2
17. Afghanistan	0.3812	62.5	−0.0157	−4.9
18. Ceylon	2.2433	83.5	2.2386	78.4
19. India	−0.3248	−3.9	3.9851	26.1
20. Indonesia	2.1414	38.0	−1.0253	−32.9
21. Japan	9.8839	42.1	8.2853	35.2

Table VI–5 (continued)

	EXPORT DEVIATION		IMPORT DEVIATION	
	$100 million	as per cent of actual value	$100 million	as per cent of actual value
22. Malaya	4.1737	81.5	1.6654	57.0
23. Pakistan	−0.0642	−2.5	0.8008	20.0
24. Philippines	3.0292	59.6	2.6830	50.6
25. Thailand	1.6002	67.4	2.0352	66.6
26. UAR (Egypt)	−0.4674	−28.9	1.0550	28.2
27. Iran	6.8885	89.9	3.3109	62.1
28. Turkey	−0.7195	−27.2	0.1299	29.9
29. Canada	4.2285	8.2	−6.2503	−12.5
30. USA	−52.3708	−39.5	−16.2260	−12.6
31. Austria	2.3735	32.2	0.9483	10.6
32. BLEU	−0.0218	−0.8	−2.9781	−9.9
33. Denmark	6.1899	51.0	5.2071	41.6
34. France	−36.8338	−102.4	−41.1475	−128.5
35. Germ. (F. R.)	−8.6616	−10.6	−26.7576	−43.6
36. Italy	−8.3864	−36.6	−6.3180	−23.4
37. Netherlands	9.2862	30.0	12.0314	30.8
38. Norway	2.7429	39.2	4.6363	46.4
39. Sweden	9.5557	51.8	8.9136	46.4
40. Switzerland	0.6489	4.6	1.6872	9.6
41. UK	−17.1995	−24.5	−13.5735	−18.7
42. Australia	11.0060	70.1	9.1865	62.2

Table VI–6

RESULTS OF CALCULATION B-2
Total Actual Trade (1959) minus Total Calculated Trade

	EXPORT DEVIATION		IMPORT DEVIATION	
	$100 million	as per cent of actual value	$100 million	as per cent of actual value
1. Argentina	4.7849	52.3	4.4288	46.2
2. Brazil	3.1119	27.0	1.0369	9.7
3. Chile	3.8871	80.3	1.9837	60.2
4. Cuba	3.4298	57.8	3.0453	45.8
5. Mexico	0.8985	15.4	3.7375	36.9
6. Peru	2.0569	71.8	1.4255	55.3
7. Uruguay	−0.1599	−27.9	0.3231	22.8
8. Venezuela	12.7595	81.5	9.2475	70.2
9. Belg. Congo	3.9352	88.1	1.6533	68.7
10. Ethiopia	0.0542	10.3	−0.0474	−7.6
11. Ghana	2.7166	87.2	1.8363	76.1
12. Morocco	1.5942	58.6	1.5383	49.2
13. Nigeria	3.2057	73.6	2.2982	58.9
14. S. Africa	5.3324	68.5	5.1007	42.0
15. Sudan	1.2569	79.5	0.8509	64.8
16. Fr. W. Africa	1.0895	47.5	1.2159	42.0
17. Afghanistan	0.3754	61.5	−0.0247	−7.7
18. Ceylon	2.2016	82.0	2.1179	74.2
19. India	−0.7913	−7.7	3.7119	24.3
20. Indonesia	2.0931	37.2	−1.0506	−33.7
21. Japan	10.0539	42.8	8.1123	34.5

Table VI–6 (continued)

	EXPORT DEVIATION		IMPORT DEVIATION	
	$100 million	as per cent of actual value	$100 million	as per cent of actual value
22. Malaya	4.1292	80.6	1.6822	57.6
23. Pakistan	−0.4499	−17.8	0.3945	9.9
24. Philippines	3.0501	59.9	2.7119	51.2
25. Thailand	1.6161	68.1	2.0430	66.8
26. UAR (Egypt)	−0.3745	−23.1	1.1668	31.2
27. Iran	6.8572	89.5	4.2748	80.2
28. Turkey	−0.6015	−22.7	0.3020	7.0
29. Canada	−17.1569	−33.2	−32.5137	−64.9
30. USA	−77.2627	−54.5	−36.0097	−28.0
31. Austria	0.1372	18.6	1.0980	12.3
32. BLEU	−3.1011	−10.7	−6.7707	−22.5
33. Denmark	5.8836	48.4	4.8331	38.6
34. France	−47.3966	−135.5	−51.2126	−159.9
35. Germ. (F. R.)	−21.8076	−26.8	−38.3570	−62.4
36. Italy	−11.2287	−49.0	−9.1054	−33.7
37. Netherlands	6.2773	20.3	7.8825	20.2
38. Norway	3.0422	43.5	6.1717	61.8
39. Sweden	9.9411	53.9	9.3473	48.6
40. Switzerland	−2.4002	−13.1	−1.8655	−10.6
41. UK	−5.5993	−8.0	−2.5886	−3.6
42. Australia	10.9715	69.9	9.1442	61.9

Table VI–7

RESULTS OF CALCULATION B-3
Total Actual Trade (1959) minus Total Calculated Trade

	EXPORT DEVIATION		IMPORT DEVIATION	
	$100 million	as per cent of actual value	$100 million	as per cent of actual value
1. Argentina	4.3607	47.6	3.6394	38.0
2. Brazil	3.4364	29.9	0.9850	9.2
3. Chile	4.1491	185.7	2.2588	68.6
4. Cuba	4.0737	68.7	3.6697	55.2
5. Mexico	0.8602	14.7	3.4205	33.7
6. Peru	2.2182	77.4	1.5728	61.0
7. Uruguay	0.0836	14.6	0.6781	47.9
8. Venezuela	13.8315	88.5	10.4295	79.2
9. Belg. Congo	3.8902	87.1	1.5449	64.2
10. Ethiopia	0.1208	22.9	0.0099	1.6
11. Ghana	2.7872	89.4	1.9087	78.9
12. Morocco	1.7904	65.8	1.7138	54.8
13. Nigeria	3.2366	73.7	2.2533	57.7
14. S. Africa	5.5264	71.0	9.2029	75.7
15. Sudan	1.2674	80.2	0.8401	63.9
16. Fr. W. Africa	1.2441	54.3	1.3409	46.3
17. Afghanistan	0.3444	56.5	−0.0841	−25.3
18. Ceylon	2.1512	80.1	2.0778	72.8
19. India	−8.3539	−81.0	−3.6134	−23.7
20. Indonesia	2.2224	39.5	−1.0716	−34.3
21. Japan	4.6310	19.7	1.8296	7.8

Table VI–7 (continued)

	EXPORT DEVIATION		IMPORT DEVIATION	
	$100 million	as per cent of actual value	$100 million	as per cent of actual value
22. Malaya	4.1933	81.8	1.7674	60.5
23. Pakistan	1.9757	78.3	−1.5756	−39.4
24. Philippines	3.4523	67.8	3.0796	58.1
25. Thailand	1.4414	60.7	1.7655	57.8
26. UAR (Egypt)	−0.3373	−20.8	1.0880	29.1
27. Iran	6.8734	89.7	4.2387	79.5
28. Turkey	−0.5597	−21.1	0.1724	4.0
29. Canada	−11.9796	−23.2	−31.2743	−62.4
30. USA	−107.3510	−80.9	−53.3661	−41.5
31. Austria	−1.0587	−14.4	−1.8453	−20.6
32. BLEU	−12.0177	−41.6	−18.7425	−62.2
33. Denmark	5.6492	46.4	4.1175	32.9
34. France	−40.7830	−118.7	−48.8181	−152.4
35. Germ. (F. R.)	−75.0172	−92.2	−85.6230	−139.4
36. Italy	−22.0290	−96.0	−90.3563	−75.4
37. Netherlands	−8.0587	−26.0	−9.8826	−36.6
38. Norway	3.5756	51.1	6.5380	65.5
39. Sweden	11.4527	62.1	10.5792	55.0
40. Switzerland	0.2828	1.5	0.1486	0.8
41. UK	−45.2828	−64.5	−76.1651	−104.9
42. Australia	10.9524	69.8	8.8808	122.3

Table VI–8

RESULTS OF CALCULATION B-4
Total Actual Trade (1959) minus Total Calculated Trade

	EXPORT DEVIATION		IMPORT DEVIATION	
	$100 million	as per cent of actual value	$100 million	as per cent of actual value
1. Argentina	5.3632	58.6	5.1265	53.5
2. Brazil	4.3373	37.7	2.4947	23.4
3. Chile	3.9733	82.1	2.1106	64.1
4. Cuba	−7.3330	−123.6	−13.5711	−204.2
5. Mexico	1.6515	28.2	4.7439	46.8
6. Peru	2.1319	74.4	1.5396	59.7
7. Uruguay	−0.0743	−13.0	0.5102	36.1
8. Venezuela	1.7217	11.0	−7.8795	−59.8
9. Belg. Congo	3.9135	87.6	1.6106	66.9
10. Ethiopia	0.0852	16.2	0.0143	2.3
11. Ghana	2.5381	81.4	1.5200	63.0
12. Morocco	0.7391	27.2	0.3989	12.7
13. Nigeria	2.6674	60.7	1.6335	41.9
14. S. Africa	4.3987	56.5	7.9967	65.8
15. Sudan	1.2783	80.9	0.8736	66.5
16. Fr. W. Africa	0.4470	19.5	0.5367	18.5
17. Afghanistan	0.3861	63.3	−0.0066	−2.0
18. Ceylon	2.0454	76.2	1.7938	62.8
19. India	−4.2768	−41.5	0.0386	0.3
20. Indonesia	2.5019	44.4	−0.5485	−17.6
21. Japan	12.3115	52.5	10.7090	45.5

Table VI–8 (continued)

	EXPORT DEVIATION		IMPORT DEVIATION	
	$100 million	as per cent of actual value	$100 million	as per cent of actual value
22. Malaya	3.8835	75.6	1.4188	48.6
23. Pakistan	−1.0878	−43.1	−0.3819	−9.6
24. Philippines	−2.5083	−49.3	−5.4494	−102.9
25. Thailand	1.6747	70.5	2.2265	72.9
26. UAR (Egypt)	−0.1497	−9.2	1.3154	35.2
27. Iran	6.9233	90.4	4.3613	81.8
28. Turkey	−0.0264	−1.0	1.7279	39.8
29. Canada	−9.1852	−17.8	−22.0186	−43.9
30. USA	−72.8100	−54.9	−26.3946	−20.5
31. Austria	1.4094	19.1	1.6623	18.6
32. BLEU	−24.6476	−85.2	−30.6452	−101.7
33. Denmark	6.9251	56.9	5.9395	47.4
34. France	−93.2285	−266.5	−94.7244	−295.8
35. Germ. (F. R.)	−75.5436	−92.8	−90.3075	−147.0
36. Italy	−25.8298	−112.6	−28.5444	−105.8
37. Netherlands	−10.1536	−32.8	−10.7905	−27.6
38. Norway	3.6184	51.7	6.8922	69.0
39. Sweden	11.2796	61.1	10.9252	56.8
40. Switzerland	0.0973	0.5	2.6579	15.2
41. UK	−12.2561	−17.5	−6.9914	−9.6
42. Australia	9.9304	63.3	7.8489	53.2

Table VI-9

RESULTS OF CALCULATION B-5

Total Actual Trade (1959) minus Total Calculated Trade

	EXPORT DEVIATION		IMPORT DEVIATION	
	$100 million	as per cent of actual value	$100 million	as per cent of actual value
1. Argentina	4.8111	52.6	4.3485	45.4
2. Brazil	4.4793	38.9	2.2988	21.5
3. Chile	4.2067	86.9	2.3520	71.4
4. Cuba	−3.9057	−65.9	−9.9832	−150.2
5. Mexico	1.4034	24.0	4.1646	41.1
6. Peru	2.2734	79.4	1.6643	64.6
7. Uruguay	0.1089	19.0	0.7185	50.8
8. Venezuela	6.9547	44.5	−1.0628	−8.1
9. Belg. Congo	3.8396	86.0	1.5019	62.4
10. Ethiopia	0.1462	27.7	0.0519	8.3
11. Ghana	2.4838	79.7	1.4338	59.4
12. Morocco	0.7727	28.4	0.3202	10.2
13. Nigeria	2.0685	47.1	0.6443	16.5
14. S. Africa	3.6182	46.5	6.7849	55.8
15. Sudan	1.2842	81.2	0.8673	66.0
16. Fr. W. Africa	0.6352	27.7	0.2331	8.0
17. Afghanistan	0.3575	58.6	−0.0618	−19.2
18. Ceylon	1.8312	68.2	1.5990	56.0
19. India	−22.3940	−217.1	−18.3810	−120.5
20. Indonesia	2.5937	46.0	−0.5896	−18.9
21. Japan	7.5894	32.3	5.2963	22.5

Table VI–9 (continued)

	EXPORT DEVIATION		IMPORT DEVIATION	
	$100 million	as per cent of actual value	$100 million	as per cent of actual value
22. Malaya	3.7044	72.3	1.0821	37.1
23. Pakistan	−4.0108	−158.9	−4.1363	−103.5
24. Philippines	−0.4353	−8.6	−3.1177	−58.8
25. Thailand	1.5194	64.0	1.8815	61.6
26. UAR (Egypt)	−0.1475	−9.1	1.3567	36.3
27. Iran	6.8000	88.8	4.3254	81.1
28. Turkey	−0.2155	−8.1	0.6391	14.7
29. Canada	−20.7608	−40.2	−39.1819	−78.2
30. USA	−96.1700	−72.5	−40.8139	−31.7
31. Austria	−0.1662	−2.3	−0.6762	−7.5
32. BLEU	−28.0265	−96.9	−33.7112	−111.9
33. Denmark	6.3465	52.2	6.1837	49.4
34. France	−27.9418	−79.9	−38.4934	−120.2
35. Germ. (F. R.)	−50.5130	−62.1	−62.0982	−101.1
36. Italy	−15.5433	−67.8	−13.3369	−49.4
37. Netherlands	−24.1979	−78.2	−24.8702	−63.6
38. Norway	3.9350	56.3	7.3327	73.5
39. Sweden	12.2893	66.6	11.6533	60.6
40. Switzerland	1.7841	9.7	2.0509	11.7
41. UK	−76.5683	−109.1	−65.7695	−90.6
42. Australia	8.5513	54.5	6.1230	41.5

Table VI–10

RESULTS OF CALCULATION B-1
"Unexplained" Balance of Trade Compared with International Service Transactions
(in $100 million)

	Actual Balance of Trade minus Calculated Balance of Trade (1)	Balance in Service Transactions (2)	Positive (+) or Negative (−) Sum of (1) + (2) (3)
1. Argentina	0.3579	−0.023	+
2. Brazil	2.1186	−4.090	−
3. Chile	1.9033	−0.493	-|
4. Cuba	0.5010	−0.780	−
5. Mexico	−3.3857	2.379	−
6. Peru	0.6357	−0.880	−
7. Uruguay	−0.5795	−0.184	−
8. Venezuela	3.5836	−8.330	−
9. Belg. Congo	2.2909	n.a.	n.a.
10. Ethiopia	0.1039	−0.153	−
11. Ghana	0.8847	−0.454	+
12. Morocco	0.0871	n.a.	n.a.
13. Nigeria	0.9141	n.a.	n.a.
14. S. Africa	−3.7780	−2.968	−
15. Sudan	0.4160	−0.115	+
16. Fr. W. Africa	−0.1079	n.a.	n.a.
17. Afghanistan	0.3969	n.a.	n.a.
18. Ceylon	0.0047	−0.023	−
19. India	−4.3099	1.199	−
20. Indonesia	3.1667	−2.100	+
21. Japan	1.5986	0.231	+

Table VI–10 (continued)

	Actual Balance of Trade minus Calculated Balance of Trade (1)	Balance in Service Transactions (2)	Positive (+) or Negative (−) Sum of (1) + (2) (3)
22. Malaya	2.5083	1.137	+
23. Pakistan	−0.8650	−2.876	−
24. Philippines	0.3462	−0.305	+
25. Thailand	−0.4350	−0.001	−
26. UAR (Egypt)	−1.5224	0.985	−
27. Iran	3.5776	−2.950	+
28. Turkey	−0.8494	−0.549	−
29. Canada	2.0218	−9.920	−
30. USA	−36.1448	−8.160	−
31. Austria	1.4252	1.866	+
32. BLEU	2.9563	1.020	+
33. Denmark	0.9828	1.222	+
34. France	4.3137	2.062	+
35. Germ. (F. R.)	18.0960	5.457	+
36. Italy	−2.0684	6.896	+
37. Netherlands	−2.7452	4.435	+
38. Norway	−1.8934	3.731	+
39. Sweden	0.6421	2.026	+
40. Switzerland	−1.0383	4.161	+
41. UK	−3.6260	3.360	−
42. Australia	1.8195	−5.286	−

n.a.: not available.

Table VI-11

FACTORS DETERMINING THE SIZE OF INTERNATIONAL TRADE FLOWS

Results of Calculations C (28 Countries)

$$\log E_{ij} = a_1 \log Y_i + a_2 \log Y_j + a_3 \log D_{ij} + a_8 \log G_i + a_o'$$

Calculation No.	ESTIMATED VALUE OF THE COEFFICIENTS					Correlation Coefficient
	a_1	a_2	a_3	a_8	a_o'	
C-1	1.0318 (0.0428)	0.9647 (0.0428)	-0.9228 (0.0657)	—	-0.6555	0.8089
C-2	0.8569 (0.0593)	0.9682 (0.0424)	-0.8633 (0.0664)	-0.7779 (0.1843)	+0.4927	0.8090

E_{ij} Exports from country i to country j
Y_i GNP of exporting country
Y_j GNP of importing country
D_{ij} Distance between countries i and j
G Degree of onesidedness (lack of diversification) of export products (as measured by the Gini coefficient).

Figures in brackets are standard deviations.

Table VI–12

RESULTS OF CALCULATION C-2
Total Actual Trade (1959) minus Total Calculated Trade

	EXPORT DEVIATION		IMPORT DEVIATION	
	$100 million	as per cent of actual value	$100 million	as per cent of actual value
1. Argentina	4.2879	49.0	3.8440	47.4
2. Brazil	6.9218	62.3	1.8474	19.5
5. Mexico	2.2504	39.5	5.6106	56.8
11. Ghana	2.7809	90.3	1.8790	80.5
13. Nigeria	3.2969	75.2	2.4498	63.8
14. S. Africa	4.5324	59.7	8.5226	76.4
17. Afghanistan	0.1929	38.3	0.0125	4.5
18. Ceylon	2.2721	85.8	2.0681	80.3
19. India	−0.5551	−5.8	4.9675	35.7
20. Indonesia	2.8110	51.9	0.5105	16.7
21. Japan	6.6403	32.5	7.3546	35.2
22. Malaya	4.2290	83.4	1.4607	51.2
25. Thailand	1.8075	76.8	2.1612	72.3
26. UAR (Egypt)	0.1843	13.8	1.0902	31.4
28. Turkey	−0.5692	−22.3	0.4003	9.5
29. Canada	−28.6987	−57.3	−31.7429	−65.1
30. USA	−60.2068	−54.6	−79.8669	−76.0
31. Austria	−1.2126	−18.2	1.5182	18.1
32. BLEU	−6.0168	−23.1	−7.0561	−27.1
33. Denmark	4.6445	40.0	3.3137	27.5
34. France	−53.4680	−193.5	−38.6289	−149.5
35. Germ. (F. R.)	−7.5066	−11.0	−36.9269	−67.4
36. Italy	−15.5108	−81.7	−5.7025	−24.0
37. Netherlands	−7.9116	−27.4	7.0206	19.5
38. Norway	0.9220	13.8	3.0467	31.9
39. Sweden	8.1125	46.0	9.0841	50.4
41. UK	−28.2981	−44.5	−23.6279	−36.2
42. Australia	12.2809	79.5	8.3953	59.8

A comparison of the results of series A calculations with those of series B and C shows that the absolute value of all coefficients is lower in A than in B and C. The three coefficients a_1, a_2, and a_3 all are about 0.3 greater (in absolute value) in B and C. The standard deviations of these coefficients are small, particularly in the series B calculations. The coefficients a_4 and a_5 show much greater deviations in the various calculations; and the standard errors are high. The trade-increasing effect of adjacency according to calculation A–3 is about 5 per cent of the normal trade volume; according to calculations B–2 to B–5 it is something like 75 per cent. Similarly, the trade-stimulating effect of preferential treatment is estimated to be 10 to 12 per cent of the standardized trade flow in calculation A–3, whereas in B–4 and B–5 full preferences appear to give rise to no less than 10 times the usual trade volume, while semi-preferential trade relations bring about a fivefold increase. However high a "colonial or ex-colonial trade multiplier" of 10 may seem to be, a verification ex-post from trade statistics confirms this order of magnitude.

The difference between the coefficients derived from the calculations of series A and those derived from series B and C is due to the different coverage of the samples. The list of countries included in series B (42 in number), and also, but to a lesser extent, in series C (28 countries), differs from that in series A in three respects:

(i) whereas series A consists predominantly of developed countries, series B and C include a number of developing nations, which means that GNP indicates mainly geographic size in series A and both geographic and economic size in series B and C;

(ii) the countries added in series B and C generally have a low GNP in comparison to those included in series A, so that the range of values that the first two explanatory variables may take is enlarged (in one direction) in B and C;

(iii) the countries added in series B and C are in general the more remote countries, and so the role of the distance factor can be estimated more accurately here than in the geographically less balanced sample used in A.

As these three changes occurred simultaneously when the data were enlarged, their individual consequences cannot be estimated from the change in the coefficients. It is obvious, however, that in the present context the calculations with the broader coverages — i.e., those of series B and C — are more meaningful than the ones based on the trade pattern of industrialized countries only.

Confining ourselves to the results of calculations B and C, we find that the values of a_1 and a_2 are always close to 1. This means that the export flow is almost proportional to the GNP of the exporting and the importing country. It also implies that the analysis could have been based on an *a priori* value of 1 for both a_1 and a_2 without much loss of information. Still, the values of a_1 and a_2 deviate from 1 in most calculations, even though the difference often is barely significant statistically. This is especially true of a_2, which tends to be smaller than 1; this may indicate that with increasing GNP, imports decline relatively because of more varied domestic production.

An interesting aspect of the results obtained for a_1 and a_2 is that in all calculations — except in C–3, which will be discussed below — the value of a_1 was about 0.1 higher than the value of a_2. This means that export volume depends somewhat more on the GNP of the exporting country than on the GNP of the importing country; it also implies that there is no equilibrium in the balance of trade between two countries with different levels of GNP. From the difference between the two coefficients a_1 and a_2 it follows that large countries (in terms of GNP) always export more to small countries than they import from them; this leads to a positive balance of trade for the bigger countries and a negative trade balance for the smaller ones. According to the present estimates, the United States should have a surplus on its trade accounts of something like 25 per cent; countries with an "average" GNP (the larger industrialized countries, mostly) should find that their trade flows were in approximate equilibrium; and countries at the lower end of the GNP scale (most underdeveloped countries and the smallest industrial countries) should experience a deficit amounting to some 30 per cent of their imports.

The coefficients a_1 and a_2 of the trade flow equation as fitted to the various sets of data can hardly be considered indicative of the desired pattern of trade; they merely describe reality. It will be necessary, in interpreting the deviations between actual and calculated trade, to keep in mind the preceding considerations. If we assume that, by and large, trade balances should be in equilibrium, it may be stated that the trade flow equation resulting from our calculations overestimates the normal exports of the bigger countries (in terms of GNP) and underestimates the exports of the smaller countries (i.e., underestimates the imports of bigger countries). A deviation of about 25 per cent between actual and calculated exports (in the sense that the latter exceed the former) for the United States could be due to this effect. Similarly, a positive devia-

tion of up to about 30 per cent in the export volume of countries with a low GNP (most developing countries and the small industrial nations) could well be caused by this factor alone. The figures for the larger industrialized countries like the United Kingdom, France, and Germany will not be much influenced by this consideration; the deviations recorded will not be appreciably biased in either direction.

Finally, a word may be said about the coefficients found in calculation C–2. This is the only case in which the value of a_1 is lower than that of a_2. The value of a_1 is not too reliable, however, because of intercorrelation between the GNP of the exporting country and the fourth explanatory variable, the concentration coefficient of exports. The intercorrelation was not very high (–0.54), but it was sufficiently significant to cast doubt upon the estimates of a_1 and a_8.[5] It should be noted that the foregoing discussion of the consequences of the difference between a_1 and a_2 applies to the results obtained in calculation C–2 as well, but in exactly the opposite sense. In spite of the fact that the value of a_1 in calculation C–2 is itself somewhat unreliable, it provides a useful check on our analysis of the impact of the values of a_1 and a_2 on the deviations between actual and calculated trade.

As to the effect of specialization in the export sector, it follows from the negative sign of a_8 that an increase in commodity concentration leads to a smaller flow of exports. In other words, the more diversified the export package, the greater the export volume. This tendency is counteracted by the fact that in this calculation the export-increasing effect of a higher GNP is less strong than in other calculations (a higher GNP generally means a more diversified export line). More research will be needed before a clear economic interpretation can be made of the effects of the degree of commodity concentration on the size of a country's export flow.

VI.5 A DISCUSSION OF THE RESULTS: THE DEVIATIONS

For most of the calculations, the deviations of actual trade from standardized or theoretical trade were computed. This was done first for

---

5. There was only one other case of a significant intercorrelation between explanatory variables, and that occurred in calculation A-3. In the latter calculation the variable distance and the dummy variable for neighboring countries showed an intercorrelation of –0.54 also. All other coefficients of intercorrelation were, in absolute value, less than 0.5.

each trade flow individually; subsequently these deviations were totaled for each exporting country and each importing country. Along these lines figures for total export deviations and total import deviations were derived. They are given in Tables VI–2, VI–3, VI–5 to VI–9, and VI–12. In these tables the sum total of the deviations is also expressed as a percentage of the actual value of the economic magnitude concerned.

The relative deviations are quite considerable. This is not surprising in view of the correlation coefficient of 0.8, which leaves 36 per cent of the variance of the variable concerned "unexplained." Substantial deviations were to be expected because of the existence of many types of trade impediments (or occasionally trade stimuli) with varying degrees of effectiveness. It is also true that the present analysis is a fairly crude one which clearly needs to be supplemented by further research. The results reported here must be used with a good deal of care; only provisional and qualified conclusions are possible.

As the purpose of the investigation was to find out which countries are hurt most by discriminatory trade restrictions, we are particularly interested in the negative deviations; a negative deviation implies that actual trade — export or import, or both — is lower than what could be expected based on the experience of other countries. Since the ultimate target of all foreign trade is to make available necessary capital and consumption goods with the least possible sacrifice, the level of imports would seem to have the greatest claim to our attention. In this context exports are important only as a means of paying for imports. Thus we will analyze the import deviations first.

Deviations of actual from calculated imports may be due to several causes:

   (i) a positive deviation may be due to a positive deviation on the export side (e.g., preferential treatment of the exports of the country concerned), to the running down of previously accumulated stocks of foreign exchange, to a positive service balance, or to a net inflow of new capital, or amortizations;

  (ii) a negative deviation may be due to a negative deviation on the export side (most likely to be caused by discriminatory treatment of the exports of the country concerned), to import restrictions imposed by the importing country itself (e.g., in order to build up foreign exchange reserves, or to obtain foreign exchange for debt repayment), to a negative service balance, or to a net outflow of new capital or amortizations.

Confining ourselves to negative import deviations — which are sum-

marized also in Table 3–2 of Chapter 3 — we may note first that these deviations cannot be explained by service balances. The latter are given in Table VI–10; it appears that, in general, neither their magnitude nor their algebraic sign is sufficiently correlated with the import deviations to contribute much to an explanation of them.

The role of capital flows is of greater importance than that of service exchanges. In the year under consideration, there was a substantial flow of capital from the developed countries to the newly developing parts of the world. This apparently enabled the developing countries to import more than they could have imported on the basis of export proceeds alone. Positive deviations could be expected, therefore, in the developing countries on the import side and in the developed countries on the export side. To be sure, the deviations caused by this factor might be compensated for or reinforced by other factors.

It is difficult to quantify the effects of service balances and capital flows on the volume of imports without going into a large amount of detailed work. The implications partly offset each other as these factors work in opposite directions in most cases. For all developing countries together, the net effect seems to be such as to allow a deficit on the commodity trade balance, i.e., a higher level of imports than would follow from the export level. Insofar as this is true for all developing countries, it would not invalidate the present analysis of the import deviations as possible indicators of discriminatory trade impediments, because the coefficients of the trade flow equation essentially describe the "average" or "normal" trade flows for developed as well as developing countries. As the newly developing countries (i.e., the countries having higher imports than exports) are all among the countries with low GNP, the fact of an import surplus in developing countries would probably be brought out by the GNP coefficients resulting from the correlation. In this way systematic divergencies are incorporated in the standard pattern of trade, so that random deviations will be indicative of discriminatory or preferential treatment of trade flows. The discussion in the preceding section regarding the values of the coefficients points in this direction, and seems to confirm the hypothesis that the net effect of service balances and the capital flows is incorporated in the standardized trade pattern as described by the trade flow equation.

Thus, in spite of some ambiguities and uncertainties, the negative deviations of actual from calculated imports can be considered as indicative of the existence of discriminatory trade impediments. Cases of subnormal imports fall into two distinct categories. In the first instance

an importing country has deliberately and voluntarily erected import barriers. In the second instance an importing country has been forced to reduce its purchases from abroad because its exports have suffered from discriminatory treatment. It is obvious that in the latter case not only imports but also exports will be lower than the normal values as calculated from the trade flow equation.

In Chapter 3 the negative deviations, on both sides of the trade flow, are summarized in one table (Table 3–2) and discussed along the lines of the above distinction. For the main conclusions, the reader is referred to that chapter. Only one technical remark need be inserted here. The results of the calculation show that, with respect to the special trade relations of the United States with Cuba, the Philippines, and Venezuela, the preferential treatment is less important than it was assumed to be (in relation to the Commonwealth imperial preference and the preference within the French Community). Particularly in the cases of Cuba and the Philippines, the trade flow equation overestimates the trade-increasing effect of the special economic links so that these countries show substantial negative deviations both for exports and imports. This being so, these negative deviations (or at least their magnitude) cannot serve as the basis for further analysis.

Finally, it must be stressed once more that the present analysis is only a first step in what the authors consider to be an interesting and promising approach to the study of world trade flows. As was pointed out earlier, the analysis is so crude that only tentative conclusions are possible. Further research is being undertaken which might lead to a more accurate model of world trade flows and to firmer conclusions about the "location" and impact of trade impediments.

SOURCES

Direction of International Trade, Annual Issue 1959, Statistical Papers Series T, Vol. XI, No. 9, United Nations, IMF, IBRD, New York, 1960.

M. Gilbert and associates, *Comparative National Products and Price Levels,* OEEC, Paris, 1958.

S. Luensee, *Entfernungstabellen — Die Entfernung zwischen den Haupthaefen der Erde,* 3 vols., Eckhardt und Messtorff, Hamburg, 1958–1960.

M. Michaely, "Concentration of Exports and Imports: An International Comparison," *Economic Journal,* December 1958, p. 725.

P. N. Rosenstein-Rodan, "International Aid for Underdeveloped Countries," *Review of Economics and Statistics,* May 1961, pp. 107–138.

Yearbook of National Accounts Statistics 1959, United Nations, New York, 1960, Sales No. 60.XVII.3.

Tariff Reductions and Their Consequences

VII.1 THE PROPOSED REDUCTIONS AND THEIR TIMING

In Chapter 8 suggestions are made for reducing the EEC outer tariff. Specific proposals for a number of commodities are given in Table 8–1 and in section 8.7. The percentage reductions advocated for these particular products are as follows:

	Per Cent
Coffee	80
Bananas	80
Sugar	70
Tea	70
Cocoa beans	60
Dried fruits	60
Cotton fabrics	50

These reductions should be made gradually; in the section referred to above we propose that they should be fully in force by the end of 1967. In the accompanying graphs (Figs. VII–1 to VII–7) are plotted the possible time paths of the movements to a common outer tariff for the EEC countries and the United Kingdom on the basis of the new outer tariff implied by the proposed reductions of the actual outer tariff.

The main purpose of the graphs is to illustrate the changes in customs tariffs necessitated by the specific proposals made in section 8.7 of Chapter 8. The number of steps in which the new outer tariff is to be reached and the time interval of two years between each successive step represent a somewhat arbitrary choice out of an unlimited number of possibilities. Nevertheless, they are considered to be sufficiently realistic to serve as a starting point for discussions.

As it is difficult to obtain reliable and current information about im-

FIG. VII–1 *Proposed Lowering of EEC Outer Tariff on Coffee*

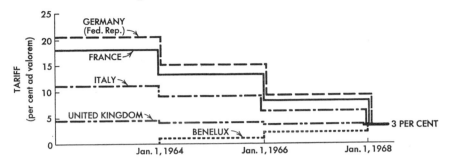

port duties (both specific and ad valorem) and internal fiscal charges — and more particularly about their incidence on import prices — all figures given here should be considered estimates rather than hard facts. For this reason, the incidence of the charges (expressed as a percentage of the import price) is always mentioned explicitly in the calculations of this appendix, so as to show clearly on what figures the proposals or computations are based.

FIG. VII–2 *Proposed Lowering of EEC Outer Tariff on Bananas*

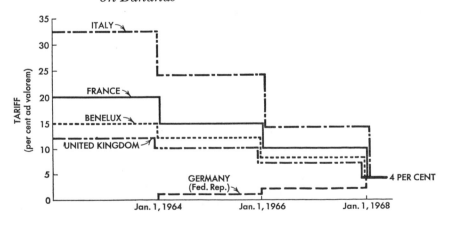

FIG. VII-3   *Proposed Lowering of EEC Outer Tariff on Sugar*

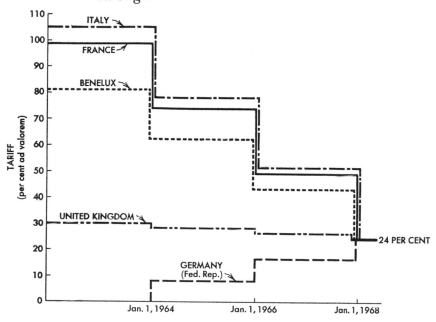

VII.2 CONSEQUENCES OF TARIFF REDUCTION OR ABOLITION

To gain some insight into the sacrifices which a reduction or abolition of tariffs and internal duties would require on the part of the developed countries, an attempt was made to calculate — for a few products and for a varying list of developed countries — the impact of a complete removal of trade barriers on the balance of payments, the employment situation, and government revenue. The results are presented and discussed in Chapter 8; they are reproduced in the tables of this appendix. The findings suggest the order of magnitude of the effects; they do not pretend to be refined estimates of great reliability. Also, it must be clear from the outset that the effects as indicated in these tables are much greater than those which would result if our proposals concerning the tariff of the EEC countries and the United Kingdom were accepted (they related to a reduction rather than an abolition of duties and do not apply to internal taxes). As linear rela-

FIG. VII–4   *Proposed Lowering of EEC Outer Tariff on Tea*

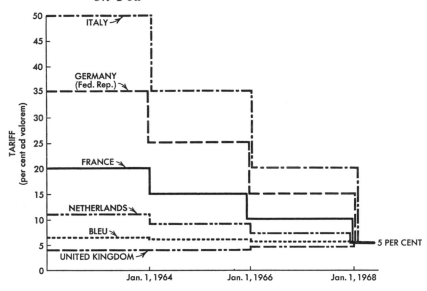

tionships between the economic variables concerned were assumed, the effect of a tariff reduction can be calculated as a simple fraction — equal to that part of the tariff which is to be abolished — of the maximum impact as shown.

It was assumed in the calculations of this appendix that import duties and consumption taxes are the only impediments to imports of the

FIG. VII–5   *Proposed Lowering of EEC Outer Tariff on Cocoa Beans*

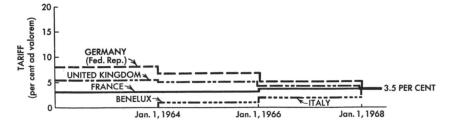

FIG. VII-6   *Proposed Lowering of EEC Outer Tariff*
              on Raisins

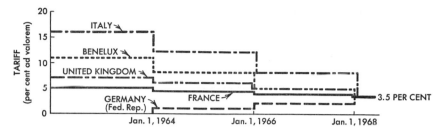

particular commodity; in other words, that quantitative import restrictions are either absent or not active because of a low level of imports.
In cases where this assumption would not be justified by the facts, the
results of the calculations have to be interpreted in a somewhat different way. If a certain country uses quantitative restrictions to hold down
imports of a commodity, the abolition of import duties and internal
charges will have the consequences discussed in this appendix only if it
is accompanied by a corresponding (partial) "liberalization" of the
quantitative restrictions. The increase in imports calculated below
should in such a case be regarded as the result of a sufficient relaxation
of the quantitative restrictions rather than as the result of the operation
of the market mechanism. Apparently, if the quantitative restrictions
were reduced still further (so as to make them ineffective), the effects
would be larger than those estimated in this appendix. As information

FIG. VII-7   *Proposed Lowering of EEC Outer Tariff*
              on Cotton Grey Goods

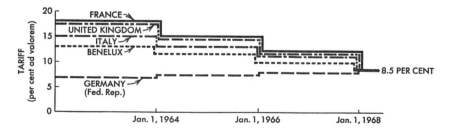

on the existence and effectiveness of quantitative restrictions is hard to obtain, the analysis could not be pursued further. It is clear that this adds another element of uncertainty to the interpretation of our results.

VII.3 THE RESULTS OF FREE IMPORTING: NONCOMPETING AGRICULTURAL PRODUCTS

The effect on imports of an abolition of all duties and taxes was estimated first for three agricultural commodities not produced in the importing (temperate) countries: bananas, coffee, and tea. The results are given in Table VII–1. The consequences for government revenue of the abolition of charges on these same products are shown in Table VII–2.

The estimates were arrived at in the following way. The basic data all refer to the year 1959, and comprise:

   (i) actual imports (preferential and nonpreferential);

  (ii) import duties;

 (iii) internal charges;

 (iv) retail prices (in relation to import prices); and

  (v) price elasticities of demand.

It was assumed that retail prices would be lowered by an absolute amount equal to the sum of the abolished import duties and internal charges. With the help of price elasticities, this decrease in consumer price is translated into an increase in quantity demanded, and hence into additional imports. In order to judge its relative importance, the import increase was related to the actual volume of these commodities imported and to the total imports of the country concerned.

The impact on the government budget was found very simply by multiplying the value of actual imports by the rate of total charges. The resulting loss in revenue was compared with total government income from indirect taxes. As the products concerned are not produced in temperate climates, there is no direct effect on domestic production and employment.

The results of the calculations are necessarily subject to some uncertainty since insufficient information was available about some of the variables involved. Imports were known, of course, for all countries. The relation between retail prices and import prices had to be estimated for some countries; this was done on the basis of the ratio observed in other countries. Elasticities of demand were also unknown for many

Table VII–1

ESTIMATED EFFECT ON IMPORTS OF THE ABOLITION OF
TOTAL CHARGES ON COFFEE, TEA, AND BANANAS (1959 data)

	Increase in Imports in Millions of Dollars				Increase in Imports as Per Cent of Total Imports of the Three Commod- ities	Increase in Imports as Per Cent of Total Imports
	Coffee	Tea	Bananas	Total Three Commod- ities		
Total 17 countries	54.3	1.5	8.2	64.0	2.3	0.08
BLEU	—	—	0.3	0.3	0.5	0.01
France	8.3	—	2.4	10.7	4.2	0.21
Germany (F. R.)	20.7	0.7	0.6	22.0	8.5	0.26
Italy	13.2	0.1	0.9	14.2	15.3	0.43
Netherlands	—	0.3	0.4	0.7	1.2	0.02
Austria	0.4	—	0.1	0.5	4.4	0.04
Denmark	1.3	—	—	1.3	3.5	0.08
Finland	6.7	0.1	—	6.8	23.9	0.08
Norway	—	—	0.1	0.1	0.4	0.01
Sweden	1.8	—	0.3	2.1	2.8	0.09
Switzerland	0.7	—	0.4	1.1	3.4	0.06
UK	0.1	0.1	1.5	1.7	0.4	0.02
Canada	0.4	—	0.9	1.3	1.2	0.02
USA	—	—	—	—	—	—
Australia	0.1	0.1	—	0.2	0.5	0.01
New Zealand	—	—	—	—	—	—
Japan	0.6	0.1	0.3	1.0	6.6	0.03

— negligible or nil.

Sources: See end of appendix for sources used in constructing this and all other tables.

Table VII–2

ESTIMATED EFFECT ON GOVERNMENT REVENUE OF THE ABOLITION
OF TOTAL CHARGES ON COFFEE, TEA, AND BANANAS (1959 Data)

	Loss of Government Revenue in Millions of Dollars				Loss of Govt. Revenue as Per Cent of Total Indirect Taxes
	Coffee	Tea	Bananas	Total Three Commodities	
Total 17 countries	392.1	19.3	32.0	443.4	0.5
BLEU	—	0.1	1.6	1.7	0.2
France	55.5	0.6	9.2	65.3	0.7
Germany (F. R.)	183.8	10.8	2.1	196.7	2.5
Italy	78.8	1.2	4.7	84.7	2.1
Netherlands	—	1.2	1.4	2.6	0.3
Austria	2.5	0.3	0.3	3.1	0.4
Denmark	9.3	0.5	—	9.8	1.5
Finland	41.9	0.6	—	42.5	7.3
Norway	—	0.1	0.7	0.8	0.1
Sweden	9.0	0.2	1.5	10.7	0.9
Switzerland	3.4	0.2	1.7	5.3	1.4
UK	1.5	0.7	5.9	8.1	0.9
Canada	2.5	0.1	1.7	4.3	0.1
USA	—	—	—	—	—
Australia	0.6	1.8	—	2.4	0.1
New Zealand	—	—	0.1	0.1	0.3
Japan	3.3	0.9	1.1	5.3	1.6

— negligible or nil.

Table VII–3

ASSUMED PRICE ELASTICITIES OF DEMAND FOR COFFEE, TEA,
AND BANANAS

	Coffee	Tea	Bananas
BLEU	—0.4	—0.2	—0.7
France	—0.4	—0.2	—0.7
Germany (F. R.)	—0.4	—0.3	—0.7
Italy	—0.6	—0.3	—0.7
Netherlands	—0.4	—0.4	—0.7
Austria	—0.5	—0.3	—0.7
Denmark	—0.4	—0.3	—0.7
Finland	—0.6	—0.3	—0.7
Norway	—0.4	—0.3	—0.7
Sweden	—0.4	—0.3	—0.7
Switzerland	—0.4	—0.3	—0.7
UK	—0.3	—0.2	—0.7
Canada	—0.3	—0.2	—0.7
USA	—0.3	—0.2	—0.7
Australia	—0.3	—0.2	—0.7
New Zealand	—0.3	—0.2	- 0.7
Japan	—0.5	—0.2	—0.7

countries, and the same estimating procedure was followed. The assumed values of the elasticities are given in Table VII–3. Table VII–4 gives the figures for total charges on which our estimates were based.

VII.4 THE RESULTS OF FREE IMPORTING: COMPETING AGRICULTURAL PRODUCTS—SUGAR

The consequences of a tariff abolition are less easy to estimate in the case of imports which compete with domestic production than in the case of noncompeting imports. It is not difficult to calculate the loss of government revenue, but the increase in imports will depend upon two factors:

(i) the increase in total consumption; and
(ii) the changes in domestic production and supply.

Table VII–4

TOTAL CHARGES ON COFFEE, TEA, AND BANANAS
AS PER CENT OF IMPORT PRICE

	COFFEE		TEA		BANANAS	
	Non-prefer-ential	Prefer-ential	Non-pref-erential	Prefer-ential	Non-prefer-ential	Prefer-ential
BLEU	—	—	19	17	27	12
France	51	33	20–30	16–24	20	15
Germany (F. R.)	94		105		4	
Italy	101		62	52	39	36
Netherlands	—		11	9	20	5
Austria	26		39		36	
Denmark	30		24		1	
Finland	160		80		1	
Norway	—		11		18	
Sweden	15		7		19	
Switzerland	14		13		27	
UK	5	2	4	—	12	—
Canada	4	—	14	—	7	
USA	—		—		—	
Australia	8	8	6	6	21	5
New Zealand	3	—	2	—	12	3
Japan	43		48		20	

— negligible or nil.

The employment effect also has to be considered. The most important agricultural commodity which is both imported and produced locally in the developed countries is sugar. The results of our calculations with regard to this product are shown in Table VII–5.

The basic information required is the same as that described in the preceding section under items (i) to (v); in addition it is necessary to ascertain (vi) domestic production, (vii) employment per unit of production, (viii) exports, and (ix) price elasticities of domestic supply. It is obvious that the last mentioned item in particular presents a serious problem for statistical investigation. Unpublished studies by one

Table VII-5

ESTIMATED EFFECT ON GOVERNMENT REVENUE, ON IMPORTS, AND ON EMPLOYMENT OF THE ABOLITION OF TOTAL CHARGES ON SUGAR (1959 data)

	Loss of Govt. Revenue as Per Cent of Total Indirect Taxes	Increase in Demand in 1,000 Tons	Decrease in Domestic Supply in 1,000 Tons		Increase in Imports in Millions of Dollars		Average Increase in Imports as Per Cent of Total Imports	Percentage Decrease in Production and Employment		Average Decrease in Employment in Sugar Refining in Thousands
			Ass. 1	Ass. 2	Ass. 1	Ass. 2		Ass. 1	Ass. 2	
BLEU	1.2	13	167	231	11.3	15.4	0.4	72	100	n.a.
France	0.9	132	692	870	105.5	121.5	2.3	80	100	28.3
Germ. (F. R.)	0.5	40	n.a.	n.a.	n.a.	n.a.	n.a.	n.a.	n.a.	n.a.
Italy	3.5	114	1,021	1,247	96.5	115.7	3.2	82	100	18.3
Neth.	6.4	47	365	503	26.0	34.7	0.8	72	100	9.2
Austria	1.8	24	189	282	23.0	33.0	2.5	66	100	n.a.
Denmark	—	7	117	176	8.2	12.1	0.6	40	60	1.4
Finland	3.8	19	41	43	5.9	6.1	0.1	96	100	n.a.
Norway	0.3	2	no production		0.2	0.2	—	—	—	—
Sweden	1.5	12	n.a.	n.a.	n.a.	n.a.	n.a.	n.a.	n.a.	n.a.
Switz.	2.3	10	13	22	2.3	3.2	0.1	47	70	0.3
UK	2.3	147	n.a.	n.a.	n.a.	n.a.	n.a.	n.a.	n.a.	n.a.
Canada	0.5	19	55	83	6.3	8.7	0.1	37	55	1.4
USA	0.3	162	380	566	64.5	86.6	0.5	15	22	5.6
N. Zeal.	1.0	3	no production		0.2	0.2	—	—	—	—
Japan	5.4	98	102	146	17.0	20.7	0.5	70	100	n.a.

— negligible or nil.
n.a.: not available, or impossible to estimate.
Assumption 1: Price elasticity of domestic supply 1.6.
Assumption 2: Price elasticity of domestic supply 2.4.

of the authors, J. Tinbergen, reveal the existence of great regularity in the shape of the frequency distribution of production costs of industries in the agricultural sector and in the manufacturing sector.[1] Assuming that the market price is equal to the cost of producing the last unit of output, the price elasticity of supply would tend to be around 2 in many branches of production. In the case of the production of sugar from sugar beet, the price elasticity of supply was assumed to be 1.6, and, alternatively, 2.4.

With the help of these supply elasticities, the impact of an abolition of import duties on domestic production was calculated; it was assumed that the price received by domestic producers would fall by the same amount as the import duties. Several countries in our group relied predominantly or exclusively on import quotas as a means of protecting their domestic sugar industry. Obviously, the above procedure, which postulates a tariff reduction, could not be followed for these countries. For this reason the effect on domestic production of an abolition of import duties could not be estimated for Germany and Sweden. The United Kingdom was excluded because of her particular position in world sugar trade and in the Commonwealth Sugar Agreement. The estimates of the impact on production in the remaining countries are liable to substantial errors. They suggest, nevertheless, that an abolition of import duties would mean the end of most, if not all, sugar production in Europe and Japan. Complete abolition might therefore be considered too drastic a measure; it should be remembered that in Chapter 8 only a reduction of import duties is proposed.

The effect on employment was supposed to be proportional to the impact on production. It should be noted that the employment effect could be calculated in absolute terms for sugar refineries only. An element of uncertainty in this respect is introduced by the fact that sugar can be imported either raw or refined. Here the maximum impact was estimated, i.e., we assumed that only refined sugar would be imported in the future. It is not accurately known how many people in the agricultural sector are dependent on beet sugar production; however,

---

1. This regularity can be indicated by stating that the cost of production at the ninth decile of the cumulative frequency distribution of production costs (i.e., the cost of producing the 90th unit out of total production of 100) is 50 to 100 per cent higher than the cost of production at the first decile (i.e., the cost of producing the 10th unit). The empirical evidence comes from industries with relatively many independent production units.

Table VII–6

IMPORT DUTIES, INTERNAL TAXES, AND ASSUMED PRICE ELASTICITIES
OF DEMAND FOR SUGAR (duties and taxes as per cent of import price)

	IMPORT DUTIES[a]		INTERNAL TAXES	PRICE ELASTICITY OF DEMAND
	Non-preferential	Preferential		
BLEU	81	67	31	0.3
France	99	88	12	0.4
Germany (Fed. Rep.)	0		36	0.4
Italy	105	88	122	0.6
Netherlands	81		107	0.4
Austria	71		2	0.4
Denmark	33		0	0.2
Finland	151		0	0.5
Norway	0		11	0.3
Sweden	0		60	0.3
Switzerland	41		0	0.3
United Kingdom	30		55	0.3
Canada	30	17	11	0.3
United States	10		11	0.3
New Zealand	41		0	0.3
Japan	78		86	0.6

a. Weighted averages for raw and refined sugar.

as sugar production is usually not the sole activity of farmers in the developed countries, it may be supposed that the agricultural population — even in the case of a complete elimination of beet sugar production — could shift gradually to the cultivation of other products, albeit with some difficulty.

The import duties, internal charges, and price elasticities of demand which underlie the present estimates are given in Table VII–6.

VII.5 THE RESULTS OF FREE IMPORTING: COMPETING MANUFACTURED PRODUCTS— COTTON GREY GOODS

The estimation of the effects of a tariff and revenue abolition in the case of a manufactured item proceeds in principle along the same lines

as in the case of an agricultural commodity. The procedure described earlier was applied to one of the typical products of the manufacturing industry of several developing countries, i.e., to cotton grey goods. However, there were a number of complications, mainly stemming from the fact that cotton grey goods are an intermediate product rather than a good for final consumption.

The direct impact (through substitution) on imports and on domestic production — of the improved competitive position (lower price) of imported cotton grey goods — is fairly easy to estimate; there is a complete identity with the case of the preceding section. Only the indirect effect of the greater consumption of the commodity cannot be measured directly. It was assumed that the price of cotton grey goods (as an intermediate product) was equal to 0.3 of the price of the final product (cotton fabrics), so that lowering the price of cotton grey goods by a certain percentage would mean lowering the price of cotton fabrics by only 0.3 of that percentage (the reference is to prices at the wholesale level). Price elasticity of demand for cotton fabrics was put at −0.8 (again wholesale prices); this corresponds with an empirically derived elasticity of about −1.0 at the retail level.

Another problem was the fact that few if any figures were available for production and employment in the cotton grey goods industry. It is known, however, that there is very little weight loss in processing. Therefore the production of cotton grey goods (measured in tons) was assumed to be equal to the domestic production of cotton fabrics, taking into account the import and export of the former but neglecting inventories. Production was valued, where necessary, at an average (import) price of cotton grey goods of $1.5 per kilogram. In calculating the employment effect, it was assumed that labor inputs are the same per dollar of production value in the cotton grey goods industry as in the cotton industry as a whole.

As in the case of sugar, alternative assumptions were introduced with respect to the price elasticity of supply. Calculations were carried through based on an elasticity of 1.5, and, again, based on an elasticity of 2.0. The results of both computations are given in Table VII–7 (import effect) and Table VII–8 (employment effect). Because of insufficient information, some countries had to be dropped from the list.

As Table VII–7 shows, the import-increasing effect of an abolition of the duties on cotton grey goods is rather substantial, although the percentage increase in imports would not be greater than 1 per cent, except

Table VII-7

ESTIMATED EFFECT ON IMPORTS OF THE ABOLITION OF TOTAL CHARGES ON COTTON GREY GOODS (1959 data)

	Production of Cotton Grey in 1,000 Tons	Import Duty as Per Cent of Import Price	Decrease in Production in 1,000 Tons		Total Charges on Cotton Grey in Per Cent Ad Valorem	Increase in Consumption in 1,000 Tons	Increase in Imports in 1,000 Tons		Increase in Imports in Millions of Dollars		Average Increase as Per Cent of Total Imports
			Ass. 1	Ass. 2			Ass. 1	Ass. 2	Ass. 1	Ass. 2	
BLEU	64	13	11.0	14.7	13	1.3	12.3	16.0	18.5	24.0	0.6
France	183	18	41.9	55.9	51	11.1	53.0	67.0	79.5	100.5	1.8
Germ. (F.R.)	270	7	26.4	35.3	13	7.4	33.8	42.7	50.7	64.1	0.7
Italy	n.a.	15	n.a.	n.a.	15	3.6	n.a.	n.a.	n.a.	n.a.	n.a.
Neth.	54	13	9.3	12.4	13	1.5	10.8	13.9	16.2	20.9	0.5
Austria	14	26	4.7	6.3	28	1.0	5.7	7.3	8.6	11.0	0.9
Denmark	3	10	0.4	0.5	24	0.7	1.1	1.2	1.7	1.8	0.1
Norway	3	15	0.6	0.8	15	0.3	0.9	1.1	1.4	1.7	0.1
Sweden	18	13	3.1	4.0	13	0.9	4.0	4.9	6.0	7.4	0.3
Switz.	18	11	2.6	3.5	18	n.a.	n.a.	n.a.	n.a.	n.a.	n.a.
UK	143	18	32.7	43.6	18	8.6	41.3	52.2	62.0	78.3	0.6

n.a.: not available, or impossible to estimate.
Assumption 1: Price elasticity of domestic supply 1.5.
Assumption 2: Price elasticity of domestic supply 2.0.

Table VII–8

ESTIMATED EFFECT ON EMPLOYMENT OF THE ABOLITION OF TOTAL CHARGES ON COTTON GREY GOODS (1959 data)

	Est. Value of Production in Cotton Textile Industry in Millions of Dollars	Decrease in Cotton Grey Production in Millions of Dollars		Percentage Decrease in Prod. and Employ. in Cotton Textile Industry		Employees in Cotton Textile Industry in Thousands	Decrease in Employment in Thousands	
		Ass. 1	Ass. 2	Ass. 1	Ass. 2		Ass. 1	Ass. 2
BLEU	204	16.5	22.1	8.1	10.8	17[a]	1.3[a]	1.8[a]
France	580	62.9	83.9	10.8	14.5	118	12.7	17.1
Germ. (F. R.)	900	39.6	53.0	4.4	5.9	185	7.9	10.9
Italy	400	n.a.	n.a.	n.a.	n.a.	166	n.a.	n.a.
Neth.	212	14.0	18.6	6.6	8.8	50	3.3	4.4
Austria	55	7.1	9.5	12.9	17.3	24	3.0	4.1
Denmark	17	0.6	0.8	3.5	4.7	n.a.	n.a.	n.a.
Norway	15	0.9	1.2	6.0	8.0	4	0.2	0.3
Sweden	75	4.6	6.0	6.1	8.0	n.a.	n.a.	n.a.
Switz.	60	3.9	5.3	6.5	8.8	22	1.4	1.9
UK	670	49.1	65.4	7.3	9.8	210	15.4	20.6

a. Unreliable.   n.a.: not available, or impossible to estimate.
Assumption 1: Price elasticity of domestic supply 1.5.
Assumption 2: Price elasticity of domestic supply 2.0.

for France. The figures of Table VII–8 are more interesting. They reveal that, on the average, employment in the cotton textile industry would go down by some 10 per cent; for some countries (France, Austria) the percentage is around 15. It goes without saying that these figures are not more than tentative estimates.

VII.6 SOME CONCLUDING REMARKS

The estimates presented here regarding the impact of a complete abolition of tariffs and duties on imports, government revenue, and employment must be considered very rough and tentative. A more refined analysis would certainly be worth while, particularly with respect to the employment effect. This would require, however, the full support and collaboration of the industries involved — in the present case, the sugar industry and the cotton textile industry — in both the importing and the exporting countries. A major ground for uncertainty is the limited information available about quantitative restrictions and their trade-reducing effect. It is believed, nevertheless, that the significance of the estimates surpasses that of simple illustration; the figures — however approximate they may be — give an impression of the order of magnitude of the various consequences of a removal of trade impediments.

As was noted in section VII–2, the present estimates indicate the maximum impact of free-market forces in that they are based on the most ambitious of targets: the complete removal of tariffs and internal duties. In a sense this aim is overambitious, as there is no need to abolish a general turnover tax which does not discriminate against the products of developing countries. Actually, the abolition of import duties and discriminating internal taxes will take place only very gradually, so that the impact on the economy will manifest itself in a piecemeal way over a number of years.

Studying the results of our calculations with these considerations in mind, it is apparent that the effects of a very substantial lowering or even a full abolition of import duties and discriminating internal taxes are not of such a magnitude as to present a serious problem to the developed countries of the West. On the contrary, under the present conditions of full employment and rapid economic expansion, it would not be difficult for the developed countries to adapt their economies to the changes that would occur in the event of a major move in the direction of trade liberalization. In the case of the sugar industry, and also,

but to a lesser extent, the cotton textile industry, some factors of production would have to adapt to the change by moving to other occupations or other specialties within the same branch. However, the small losses and inconveniences which would be involved are far outweighed by the gain to the nation as a whole (particularly to the consumers).

The analysis of this appendix has deliberately been confined to an evaluation of the sacrifices to be made or the changes to be effected in the developed economies. It should be kept in mind that the benefits of less restricted trade accrue not only to the developing countries but to the developed countries as well. These benefits take the form of lower consumer prices and, ultimately, an improved allocation of productive forces.

SOURCES

Commodity Trade Statistics 1959, Statistical Papers Series D, Vol. IX, No. 4, United Nations, New York, 1960.

J. B. D. Derksen, *The Demand for Coffee in the United States 1920–1941*, 1957 (unpublished).

Yearbook of International Trade Statistics 1959, Vol. I, United Nations, New York, 1960, Sales No. 60.XVII.2.

Economische Voorlichtingsdienst (Economic Information Service), of the Ministry of Economic Affairs, The Hague.

H. Linnemann, *An Analysis and Projection of the Exports of Ecuador*, Junta Nacional de Planificación y Coordinación Económica, Quito, 1960.

Monthly Bulletin of Agricultural Economics and Statistics, FAO, Rome, March 1960 and September 1960.

Production Yearbook 1960, FAO, Rome, 1961.

Statistical Yearbooks of the countries concerned.

The Textile Industry in Europe — Statistical Study 1959; Trend in 1960, OEEC, Paris, 1960.

The World Sugar Economy in Figures 1880–1959, Commodity Reference Series No. 1, FAO, Rome, 1961.

Zahlen zur Industriewirtschaft 1959, Statistisches Amt der Europäischen Gemeinschaften, Brussels, 1961.

Trade by Commodities, Vol. II: Imports 1959, OEEC, Statistical Bulletins, Foreign Trade, Series C; OEEC, Paris, 1960.

INDEX